TELETHEORY

TELETHEORY

GRAMMATOLOGY IN THE AGE OF VIDEO

GREGORY ULMER

ROUTLEDGE · NEW YORK & LONDON

for
TYSON
and
LELAND

Published in 1989 by

Routledge
an imprint of
Routledge, Chapman & Hall, Inc.
29 West 35 Street
New York, NY 10001

Published in Great Britain by

Routledge
11 New Fetter Lane
London EC4P 4EE

Visual Studies Workshop
Research Center
Rochester, N.Y.
1991
Gift of Publisher

© 1989 by Routledge, Chapman & Hall, Inc.

Printed in the United States of America

Library of Congress Cataloging in Publication Data

Ulmer, Gregory L., 1944–
   Teletheory :
Gregory L. Ulmer.
     p. cm.
   Bibliography: p.
   Includes index.
   ISBN 0-415-90120-0; ISBN 0-415-90121-9 (pbk.)
    1. Television broadcasting—Social aspects. 2. Popular culture.
3. Derrida, Jacques. I. Title.
PN1992.6.U46   1989
302.23'45—dc20   89-33157
                                                CIP

British Library Cataloguing in Publication Data
Ulmer, Gregory L., 1944–
   Teletheory :

   1. Learning by man. Role of television
   I. Title
   153.1'5

   ISBN 0-415-90120-0
      0-415-90121-9

Contents

Preface   vii

Introduction: Academic Discourse in the Age of Television
   The Apparatus of Literacy   1
   Sampling   9

Part One: Theory

Chapter One: Experiment
  1. Historiography   18
  2. Freud: The New Instauration   21
  3. After Method   26
  4. The Life Story   33

Chapter Two: Conduction
  1. The Voice of the Code   44
  2. The Joke   50
  3. VITA—TV/AI   61
  4. Text   73

Chapter Three: Mystory
  1. Mystoriography   82
  2. Allegory as Post-Meaning   94
  3. Theory Diegesis   101

Part Two: Models and Relays

Introduction: Figures of Thought
   Fragments   115
   Documents   128

Chapter Four: Memory I: Place/Roots
  1. Mnemonic Autoportrait   133
  2. Rhizomes and Mushrooms   139
  3. Pre/Signature   152
  4. Otobiography   159

Chapter Five: Memory II: Tour/Routes
1. A Nomadic Relay   166
2. Monu/Mentality   175
3. Catastropical Tourists   184
4. Breaking Rout/ines   194

Part Three: Practice

Introduction   209

Chapter Six: "Derrida at the Little Bighorn": A Fragment
1. Vita Minor   212
2. TV/AI   225

Works Cited   244

Index   252

Preface

Teletheory is the application of grammatology to television in the context of schooling, not as a way to interpret or criticize television, or rather, video, but to learn from it a new pedagogy. This application or consultation assumes first that the theories of Derrida and the other French poststructuralists (supported by certain art practices) offer the best hope for understanding an era in which the technology of culture is shifting from print to video; and second that this understanding includes not only a pedagogy, but a program for popularization capable of reuniting the advanced research in the humanities disciplines with the conduct of everyday life.

Teletheory (the book) offers a rationale and guidelines for a specific genre—mystory—designed to do the work of schooling and popularization in a way that takes into account the new discursive and conceptual ecology interrelating orality, literacy, and videocy. The genre of mystory elaborates at the level of discourse the hieroglyphic/alphabetic translation made possible by the Rosetta Stone, whose contemporary equivalent may be found in the multi-track capabilities of video. As such, it brings into relationship the three levels of sense—common, explanatory, and expert—operating in the circulation of culture from "low" to "high" and back again (plus the register of "bliss-sense," which provides the unconscious dynamics driving the exchanges across registers). Teletheory offers mystory, that is, as a translation (or transduction) process researching the equivalencies among the discourses of science, popular culture, everyday life, and private experience.

A mystory is always specific to its composer, constituting a kind of personal periodic table of cognitive elements, representing one individual's intensive reserve. The best response to reading a mystory would be a desire to compose another one, for myself. This book concludes with a sample of the genre, my own, entitled "Derrida at the Little Bighorn." It is based on the specifics of my life experience, my socialization as a white, male, middle-class, American academic. Whatever the value might be of the stereotypes associated with this ideological interpellation, a mystory assumes that one's thinking begins not from the generalized classifications of subject formation, but from the specific experiences historically situated, and that one always thinks by means of and through these specifics, even if that thinking is directed against the institutions of one's own formation. The advantage of a pedagogy based on such assumptions is that a student is not expected to reject his/her culture before starting to think.

"Derrida at the Little Bighorn" draws upon three stories for its inventio: a "private" biography, about my employment as a truck driver at my father's Sand, Gravel, and Concrete Products Plant in Miles City, Custer County, Montana, during the summers from 1960–1965; a public story (shared by a community), Custer's Last Stand, and one of its direct consequences—the founding of Miles City (next to Fort Keogh); a discipline story, of the development of Derrida's grammatology and the colonization of American universities by deconstruction.

My account is not meant to be definitive or final, but is offered as a contribution to the larger program of renewal underway in the language and literature disciplines. I am narrating an account of trying to understand how to do something in education, how to make a certain kind of text, in response to the problem stated, for example, by Wayne Booth in his Presidential Address to the Modern Language Association.

> When we fail to test our scholarship by making its most important results accessible to non-specialists, we also lose our capacity to address and thus recreate in each generation, the literate public who can understand its stake in what we do. . . . Our critical and scholarly jargons grow more recondite by the day. While there's nothing inherently wrong in specialized vocabulary for special subjects, there is something inherently pathetic in a profession that cannot explain its work to the public at least as well as the more articulate sciences manage to explain theirs (*PMLA*, 98, 1983).

Booth identifies what I take to be one of the major contemporary social and cultural issues challenging our profession. The failure of the Humanities disciplines to communicate with the public may be due in part to the fact that what separates specialized humanists from laymen is not only our conceptual apparatus and the discourses of the academy, but the very medium in which we work—the printed word. It is time for the humanities disciplines to establish our cognitive jurisdiction over the communications revolution.

During the Renaissance, humanists led the educational reforms associated with the rise of literacy and the new technology of the press. Humanists today are no less responsible for developing the educational potential of the new technologies of memory and communication. Following the lessons of our Renaissance counterparts, this responsibility is two-fold: first, to translate into the "vulgate" (audio-visual writing in the formats of film and video,

rather than the national languages) the principal works of the discip
knowledge; and second, to develop new genres that will serve educators in
the electronic era as well as did the literary essay in the Gutenburg era. These
genres will provide the "software" allowing the classroom to harness the
cognitive potential forming within the new apparatus.

This motivation for my study includes a desire to offer an alternative to the
negative view that characterizes so many discussions of television in the
context of education and politics. Neil Postman's view of television and
its "communication environment" (the interaction among all the means of
representation available to a culture), developed in such works as *Teaching
as a Conserving Activity* and *Amusing Ourselves to Death,* is typical of the
kind of thinking that prohibits the invention of a productive role for video in
schooling. My approach to the problem is not to refute Postman through a
critique of his arguments, but to propose an alternative practice and its
theoretical rationale that finds a place for electronic cognition. To refute
Postman's representative position would involve a demonstration of his projection of the qualities of literacy as universal, absolute values. At the same
time, his reduction of video to the image would have to be criticized. Video
images are always framed in verbal discourse and mediated through cultural
interpretations available in everyday language (part of the comprehension of
images includes paraphrasing). Television organizes information narratively,
ordering the complex interaction of sound and image through time by means
of a combination of oral and pop culture forms, extending the simple forms
of anecdote, joke, proverb, riddle, legend, and the like to new functions of
classification and evaluation.

Postman's refusal to consider the cognitive capacities of video reflects his
failure to acknowledge the changed status of the image and story in the field
of cognitive science over the past fifteen years or so. While the tradition of
science derived from literacy devalued image and story cognitively, the new
communications ecology has forced a reassessment of this devaluation.
Current work in Artificial Intelligence promotes the "scripts" and "schemas"
of a narrative organization of memory. Similarly the long tradition of excluding images from the cognitive processes of abstraction, generalization, concept formation, is no longer accepted by cognitive psychology. The development of prototype theory demonstrates that people reason and classify as
much by means of images and stories as by logic and argument. Postman's
advice to limit schools to criticism of TV is shortsighted. There is no technological determinism that dictates what will become of video in our culture,
even if that technology is now institutionalized in television. Television is
indeed a rival didactic institution, promoting an alternative mode of thought,
just as the critics warn. But what should the response of the schools be? I
would like us to participate in the invention of a style of thought as powerful
and productive as was the invention of conceptual thinking that grew out of

the alphabetic apparatus. I want to learn how to write and think electronically—in a way that supplements without replacing analytical reason.

"Television," then, is best understood as the name for the institution that has arisen to manage and distribute the medium of video (just as cinema is said to be the institutionalization of film). The institutionalization of video within the entertainment industry has created a didactic enterprise that rivals the schools in terms of total budget and hours attended (statistically). By the time the average American reaches eighteen years of age, he or she will have spent more time watching television than attending school. Our institutions, meanwhile, are beginning to assimilate video—business, government, military, religion. Within the university, the humanities alone seem to be committed irrevocably to the book. We study the media on the margins of our curriculum, but we are not learning how to use them. We stick with the treatise and the essay, and to a segregation of oral, literate, and video cultures. Our concern, however, should be not only with the relation of our students to television, but also to video.

What is the most important effect of television on our students? Here we have a question that has generated much debate but very little insight or agreement. A great quantity of research has been devoted to the effect of television on the behavior and motivation—the conduct—of Americans. The only agreement so far to come out of this research is the conviction that the effect of TV on our culture is massive and profound. In this context at least one effect has been overlooked. Three years ago at the University of Florida the students, entirely on their own, organized a film and video society, petitioned for and received from student government funding for the purchase of video production and post-production equipment, and began making video texts. The organizers explained that it made no sense to study the audio-visual media without ever using them, nor that the only access to this practice (at our institution) was vocational training rather than liberal arts exploration. In short, the effect of television (and cinema) on these students was to raise their desire to make texts in video, and this is the most significant effect, the most positive and encouraging effect, I could imagine of the new conditions of culture.

Teletheory is a response to this "effects research," investigating the possibility of an electronic thinking that is not dependent upon video equipment, that is not medium specific. The organization of my argument reflects the problematic of the apparatus—technology is only one element in a complex cultural ecology that includes ideology and institutional practices as well. Part One is an attempt to explain in detail the theoretical rationale that persuaded me that something like mystory was not only reasonable but practical. In Part Two I bring together a set of texts from several different arts and media to serve as examples for a discourse. My assumption is that oral, literate, and video representation and communication should not be kept apart in schooling any more than they are in everyday experience. Academic discourse, in any case, is not medium specific, and the genre of mystory is designed to be a vehicle for learning across the several media in which education operates (including video). In Part Three I offer an example of one version of a mystory that might be assigned to the students as an alternative way to represent research, involving a kind of thinking that is more "euretic" (concerned with invention and making) than hermeneutic.

I introduce a number of neologisms in my commentary, in order to specify the new order of learning in question. The principal ones include "tele-theory," "mystory," "euretics," and "oralysis," all of which are defined as they occur. I want to call attention, however, to "oralysis" referring to the way in which oral forms, derived from everyday life, are, with the recording powers of video, applied to the analytical tasks associated with literate forms. This hybrid of speaking-writing created by video reflects the general interaction and interdependence of oral, literate, and video conduct in our society. One of the primary tasks of grammatology as a disciplinary field is not only to study, but to practice, a cognitive style articulating these three orders of discourse.

"Derrida at the Little Bighorn" is not the only way to do a mystory, although it is a way that is readily accessible to a student discourse. The purpose of couching my account of teletheory as an attempt to invent a genre is to appeal to my colleagues to help design the forms for an educational apparatus that *includes* video and television. The best way to test my claim that a theory may be told like a story is to try the genre oneself. Or to invent a different one, since the first point to realize in the imaginative confrontation with electronic technology is that we do not yet have ready to hand the forms that will be to video what the essay and the novel are to print. Meanwhile, it is possible to expand the reach of the traditional academic forms—the lecture, the research paper, the discussion—by imitating in writing the features of videocy.

Some of the peculiarities of my approach to this topic may derive from my agreement with Fredric Jameson's argument that video has not yet been theorized, a project that is all the more urgent given the hegemonic status of video in our culture. Nor is film theory the best source for a theory of video, according to Jameson.

The very richness of film theory today makes this decision and this warning unavoidable. If the experience of the movie screen and its mesmerizing images is distinct, and fundamentally different, from the experience of the television monitor—something that might be scientifically inferred by technical differences in their respective modes of encoding visual information, but which could also be phenomenologically argued—then the very maturity and sophistication of film conceptualities will necessarily obscure the originality of its cousin, whose specific features demand to be reconstructed afresh and empty-handed, without imported and extrapolated categories." (Jameson, 1987: 201)

Jameson's suggestion is supported by the contributors to *Channels of Discourse,* who collectively register their suspicions that film theory, especially with respect to the question of subject positioning, to the way the subject is formed ideologically in the cinema, does not account for the spectator's relation with television (Allen).

My project, however, does not take video as its object, but as its cause. My assumption is that the apparatus of culture is changing, which includes change not only in technology but in institutional practices and the ideology of the subject as well. My goal within this process is not to explain video, but to think with it. As Jameson suggests, the blockage of a theorization of video may not be overcome simply by deciding to do so. Hence my approach, which is to assume that video is not something in need of explanation, but something whose operations have changed the conditions of explanation itself. Video may not be readily represented in the academic discourse that has so successfully appropriated the discipline of film studies. The problem of the theorization of video is not so much one of "ideas" as of "forms." We need a new genre that will give us better access to the thought that video has already given us to think, if not to represent in alphabetic writing. The scope of the problem may be assessed in Jameson's observation that, in a television culture, "what used to be called critical distance seems to have become obsolete" (202). My study diverges from Jameson's important "ground-clearing" essay, however, when he adds that "memory seems to play no role in television, commercial or otherwise." In the oblique teletheorizing of video that follows, memory provides the theory and practice for a new intervention in the discussion of how to go on from here.

In the preparation of an academic book, of course, there are always many debts that never receive proper acknowledgment. There are two groups, however, without whom this experiment could not have been completed. First I should thank the students in my seminars, who have shown me that teletheory is possible and practical. Second there are my colleagues whose encouragement and criticism are one of the great resources of the University of Florida. Thanks especially to the InvestiGATORS: Alistair Duckworth, Robert D'Amico, Robert B. Ray, and Jack Zipes. To this I want to add thanks to Kathy Ulmer, without whom none of this would have been thinkable.

In preparing this book I have remotivated a number of previously published articles, including parts of the following pieces: "Mystory: The Law of Idiom in Applied Grammatology," in Ralph Cohen, Ed., *The Future of Literary Theory,* Routledge, 1988. "Teletheory: A Mystory," in Clayton Koelb and Virgil Lokke, Eds., *The Current in Criticism: Essays on the Present and Future of Literary Theory,* Purdue, 1988. "'A Night at the Text': Roland Barthes's Marx Brothers," in *Yale French Studies,* 73 (1987). "The Object of Post-Criticism," in Hal Foster, Ed., *The Anti-Aesthetic; Essays on Postmodern Culture,* Bay Press, 1983. "The Discourse of the Imaginary," in *Diacritics,* 10 (1980).

Part 1
Theory

Introduction:
Academic Discourse in
the Age of Television

The Apparatus of Literacy

This may have been a book after all, although it is too soon to tell. There is a book I have been looking for whenever I go into a bookstore, that I have never found, and now I understand that I never will find it. I keep looking for it, finding many others that interest me almost as much, whose worth I measure against this prototype. These others will be the reserve upon which I draw to define the features of the text I want to make, whose title is "Derrida at the Little Bighorn." Nor is it this text, but its making, and the desire to make it, that concern me the most.

"Derrida at the Little Bighorn" is not in fact a book. It is a video. Its existence as a tape, however, is immaterial to the present project, the goal of which is to invent or discover a genre for academic discourse that could function across all our media—voice, print, and video. That is one reason why I came away dissatisfied from Goerings Bookstore. (It is owned by my friend, Tom Rider, but it still bears the name, and what a name, of his predecessors.)

I leave each time with a sack of books, but with the desire unsated. That is what makes it a desire. If I say that what I desire is a tape rather than a book, will that change my experience of making a text? No, because the desire, the love of knowledge that drives academic discourse, is not medium specific. The drives of intellectual curiosity do not depend on the object or text, and can function as well with electronics as with print. This desire to speak, write, and perform in the context of knowledge will be treated now as an explicit feature of academic discourse, expressed in teletheory as the work of mourning (achieving detachment from the lost object) that remains to be undertaken collectively.

Besides the regular visits to Goerings, I asked the students in my graduate seminar to write versions of this genre. I had intuited, and found in their experiments the outlines of the pedagogy I am calling "teletheory." The

1

question guiding those assignments for a time was the one posed by Jonathan Culler, having to do with the "force" of theory. Culler suggested that "theory" is or has become a new, hybrid genre, recognizable by its peculiar effect and function.

> These works exceed the disciplinary framework within which they would nor-mally be evaluated and which would help to identify their solid contributions to knowledge. To put it another way, what distinguishes the members of this genre is their ability to function not as demonstrations within the parameters of a discipline but as redescriptions that challenge disciplinary boundaries. The works we allude to as "theory" are those that have had the power to make strange the familiar and to make readers conceive of their own thinking, behavior, and institutions in new ways. Though they may rely on familiar techniques of demon-stration and argument, their force comes—and this is what places them in the genre I am identifying—not from the accepted procedures of a particular disci-pline but from the persuasive novelty of their redescriptions. (Culler, 1982: 9)

In the seminar we asked ourselves: what is the "force" of theory? How might we construct a practice, a spoken and written performance, that could tap this force? We wanted to think about this practice theoretically, rather than to have information about theory only from the side of scholarship. Could theory be learned theoretically? We did identify some of the features of such an approach which seemed distinctive enough to deserve a different name: "teletheory." This book is an account of this pedagogy, in at least one of its possible genres, identified provisionally by means of another neologism—"mystory." "Derrida at the Little Bighorn" is a mystory. My belief is that in the age of television, academic discourse in the humanities will function mystorically.

The "tele" is there to indicate that my concern is with how our discourse might be affected by electronic technology, not only in the sense that it might be important to learn how to use video for educational purposes, but also to account for the possibility that cognition itself might be changing in a civiliza-tion switching to electronics. People will not stop using print any more than they stopped talking when they became literate. But they will use it differently—will speak and write differently within the frame of electronics. Teletheory attempts to describe the nature of that difference.

Jack Goody's *Domestication of the Savage Mind* is a useful point of depar-ture for my project, since he argues for a direct correlation between the properties of alphabetic writing and critical, analytical thinking. At the begin-ning of a chapter entitled "Literacy, Criticism, and the Growth of Knowl-edge," Goody states his point clearly. The growth of knowledge, he says, is not only a matter of content, but "presupposes certain processes which are related to the modes of communication by which man interacts with man

and, more especially, transmits his culture, his learned behavior, from generation to generation" (Goody, 37). In short, pedagogy and the institutionalization of literacy in school are among the areas most sensitive to shifts in the
technology of communication.

Alphabetic literacy, he suggests, "made it possible to scrutinize discourse
in a different kind of way by giving oral communication a semi-permanent
form: . . . It increased the potentialities of criticism because writing laid out
discourse before one's eyes in a different kind of way; at the same time it
increased the potentiality for cumulative knowledge." Goody's argument
provides one of the claims that will inform our research: criticism, critical
thinking as we know it, is a function of alphabetic literacy. People reasoned
before the invention of the alphabet (whose very invention is proof enough
of the fact), and they will reason in a post-alphabetic culture. But this
reasoning will not be exclusively "critical." It is a mistake to hypostatize
"critical thinking" as an absolute value, transcending specific historical and
social conditions. Academic discourse will continue to be "critical" to the
extent that it continues—as it will—to exercise the forms of literacy. But that
is not all it will be. Against the "critics" of the new technology who charge
it with being "uncritical" or incapable of representing critical cognition,
teletheory offers this proposition: video can do the work of literacy, but no
better than literacy can do the work of speech. It has its own features and
capacities that are fully cognitive, whether or not they are "critical." The
interest of teletheory is in defining these areas, and integrating them with the
critical and rhetorical dimensions of academic discourse.

School is the institutionalization of literacy, writing as an "on-going activity," which does not mean that speech and video are to be excluded. Similarly
television is the institutionalization of video in our civilization, which does
not mean that the technology is limited to the purposes of entertainment or
information. School has experienced previously some profound changes in
adapting to changes in technology, as Goody notes. One of the most important such events had to do with the change of memory, with the storage and
retrieval of information, in schooled thinking following the appropriation of
print. The techniques of mnemonics or artificial memory, that is, were
replaced gradually with new ones "based upon 'dialectical order,'" as
worked out by Peter Ramus. "This order was set out in schematic form in
which the 'general' or inclusive aspects of the subject came first, descending
thence through a series of dichotomised classifications to the 'specials' or
individual aspects. Once a subject was set out in its dialectical order it was
memorized in this order from the schematic presentation" (Goody, 71).
Instead of the association of information with vivid images, the technique
of the classic rhetoricians, the students in the age of print organized and
memorized information with the aid of tree diagrams, which is to say they
brought the particular and the general together in an entirely different way.

Walter Ong noted in his book on Ramus that the shift to print included a new attitude to logic that may well have been suggested by the primers of young students preparing to enter the advanced and prestigious courses in scholastic logic. In the humanistic paradigm the simplified logic of the primers proved to be more powerful than the elaborations of scholasticism. Goody makes a similar observation about the contribution of pedagogical practices to the episteme of a period, this time having to do with grammar. The listing of basic phrases in grammars lent to speech a high degree of formalization. "The decontextualized form of the question ["what are we? what are you? what are they?"] appears to raise issues of greater generality than would occur in most oral contexts where the phrase "what are we?" has a more concrete significance" (127). Goody puts the point cautiously, suggesting the possibility negatively that school practices inform epistemo- logical principles, "that statements of the order, I am what I am, *Cogito ergo sum,* and similar phrases that have resounded down the centuries of written culture were generated as responses to the existential questions posed in a formal manner by academic grammarians instructing their pupils." Extrava- gant or not, such questions have to be taken seriously in teletheory, working without the advantages of hindsight, without knowing in advance exactly the phrase or its source that will express our *cogito.*

Goody's account, as sensitive as it is to the institutional practices that accompany literacy, needs to be supplemented with fuller attention to the concept of the "apparatus" (Rosen, 1986). Avoiding the technological deter- mination of an earlier generation of grammatologists, such as Marshall McLu- han, theorists of the apparatus approach our question in terms of the relation- ship among technology, ideology, and institutional practices. In terms of the academic apparatus, we would relate the technology of print and alphabetic literacy with the ideology of the individual, autonomous subject of knowl- edge, self-conscious, capable of rational decisions free from the influences of prejudice and emotion; and to the practice of criticism, manifested in the treatise, and even the essay, assuming the articulation of subject/object, objective distance, seriousness and rigor, and a clear and simple style. The "originality" that we require from the students engaged in making such works as well as the copyright with which we protect intellectual property are features of this apparatus.

Part of the project of teletheory is to imagine a different apparatus, begin- ning with a different technology. My assumption is that to inquire into the future of academic discourse in the age of a new technology we must include the possibility of a change not only in technology, but also in the ideology of the subject and the forms of institutional practice. Psychoanalysis provides us with a useful version of the change in the subject, and the experimental arts (literature as well as film and video) provide an extensive reserve of models for new practices. Poststructuralist theory, especially the texts of

Roland Barthes and Jacques Derrida, among others, provide the insights into the paradigm shift that motivated my concern for the academic apparatus in the first place.

The analogy between the shift from an oral to an alphabetic culture and the shift from the present book culture to an electronic one is part of this motivation as well—alphabetic literacy : criticism :: videocy : ? The modification of Goody's direct correlation between the features of writing and of critical analysis in the context of "apparatus," however, helps clarify the interdependence of oral, literate, and now electronic forms. As Derrida has pointed out, schools will accept almost any topic or material as objects of study, but they tend to represent this study only in the form of conventional academic writing, a situation that teletheory hopes to alter. My project is assisted by research in discourse analysis, which now assumes not only the commonality of orality and literacy, but that the privileging of the essay/treatise in school is ideological.

Brian Street's critique of Jack Goody, for example, places Goody's "formalist" association of critical thinking with alphabetic writing in the context of a "contingent" register of social convention. He rejects the view of technology as neutral and autonomous, productive in its use of predictable effects. Rather, claims made on behalf of literacy "derive from the writers' own work practice and belief system and serve to reinforce it in relation to other groups and cultures" (Street, 39), which is to say that such arguments have "the qualities of myth in validating shared benefits and providing a charter for social action"; "the particular forms adopted by Greenfield, Hildyard, and Olson can be related to the social formations and institutions that generated them, in this case specific academic institutions, just as in oral societies statements about truth are expressed and validated in terms of such complex forms and institutions as witchcraft, religion, cosmology and ritual."

Enforcement of the standards of the treatise and even of the essay in academic discourse as the best and highest expression of reason may no longer be taken seriously as "objective" fact, according to the argument of the apparatus, but as the projection of these forms onto writing itself, extending the conventions developed for the specialized needs of schooling to function as the norms of thought itself (76). Street contrasts the peculiarity of the standards of the essay tradition with the multitude of alternative reading practices cultivated in everyday life and popular culture. "Academic tutors not surprisingly experience considerable difficulty in attempting to teach their particular forms of reading and writing to students acculturated in the conventions of these popular uses of literacy. The use of tape recordings and videos adds further elaborations of form and function which are just being recognized and incorporated into this traditional complex of language use."

Street's goal is not to undercut the value of reason, but to suggest that the aims of critical thinking may be achieved in a variety of media and styles.

Teletheory is an investigation into this possibility, keeping in mind that the future of video is not determined in advance, is not identical with television (its most visible institutionalization to date). I like to think that there is more at stake than the survival of our own institution through the involvement of academics with electronic cognition. Nor should our interest in video constitute that "law of the suppression of radical results" noted in the history of invention (Winston). The point is not to harness video to writing, the way writing was harnessed to voice at the beginnings of the era of logocentrism, but to intervene in the apparatus of literacy on behalf of video.

The rational use of technology is contingent upon the context in which it is made available. Given my interest in video it is important to pursue the question of the relationship between graphic visualization and knowledge noted by Goody as instrumental to the power of writing. Heidegger's critique of science in "The Age of the World Picture" helps to identify the issue. The essence of science, Heidegger noted, is research, including: 1) a procedure projecting within the realm of nature or history "a fixed ground plan of events" (an object of study); 2) a methodology "through which a sphere of objects comes into representation," clarified by explanation. Explanation, bringing the known and the unknown into relation, takes place by means of investigation and experiment, controlled in advance by a program of calculation which guides the researcher; 3) ongoing activity, which is the process by which the methodology adapts to its own results over time, which is to say that to be a science a procedure must be capable of being institutionalized (Heidegger, 1977: 118–124). The primary examples noted were physics and historiography, the latter's demand for rigor bringing it closer to physics than to the humanities, which were still clinging, Heidegger said, to mere erudition and the empty Romanticism of scholarship. To think about academic discourse, then, requires a consideration of its institutionalization.

One of the interesting implications of "ongoing activity" is that the scientific way of knowing and the institution of the university are interdependent, if not synonymous, in Heidegger's account. The university as we know it is the institutionalized manifestation of science as ongoing activity, passed from one generation to the next by means of curriculum, pedagogy, and evaluation. A review of what the scientific way of knowing entails helps explain why there is so much controversy about whether or not poststructuralist or postmodernist procedures should or even can be institutionalized.

Knowing, as research, calls whatever is to account with regard to the way in which and the extent to which it lets itself be put at the disposal of representation. Research has disposal over anything that is when it can either calculate it in its future course in advance or verify a calculation about it as past. Nature, in being calculated in advance, and history, in being historiographically verified as past, become, as it were, "set in place" [*gestellt*]. . . . Only that which becomes object in this way *is*—is considered to be in being. (126–127)

The object of knowledge implies a subject, Heidegger's point being that in the modern age the essence of man changed, becoming *subjectum:* "Man becomes that being upon which all that is, is grounded as regards the manner of its Being and its Truth. Man becomes the relational center of that which is as such" (128)—an event made possible by the reframing of what is in terms of a "picture." In the age of the world picture (so named because only the modern age grasps the real as picture) thought is organized by the subject/ object relation, a relation know as Cartesian dualism, a characterization first formulated in Plato's *eidos* ("idea" as the aspect or view of a form, shape). Modern representing, Heidegger says, "means to bring what is present at hand before oneself as something standing over against, to relate it to oneself, to the one representing it, and to force it back into this relationship to oneself as the normative realm. Wherever this happens, man 'gets into the picture' in precedence over whatever is" (131).

The relation of subject/object to picturing is a crucial issue for academic discourse in the age of a technology capable of literally picturing the whole world. "Now for the first time is there any such thing as a 'position' of man," Heidegger noted. "There begins that way of being human which mans the realm of human capability as a domain given over to measuring and execut-ing, for the purpose of gaining mastery over that which is as a whole" (132).

Heidegger's discussion of science as the essence of the modern age places in a useful perspective all the critiques of modern culture from the situationist complaint about "spectacle" to the feminist analysis of narrative as structured for the masculine voyeur. In short, knowing in the modern paradigm is scopophilic. Regardless of the gender, sex, class, race, or nationality of the knower, the one who knows, the subject of knowledge in the mode of science, is in the position of voyeur. Such is the impasse of film theory with respect to the apparatus, due to the increasing difficulty in distinguishing the knowledge effect of a text (due to the display of its own production), and the ideological effect (the pleasure of recognition, by which a text reproduces in the spectator the dominant ideology of the society).

The ideology of the visible, related to the problematic of presence, is a major issue in the discussion of cinema as apparatus (a discussion whose very terms are being subverted by television). In teletheory the problematic of the apparatus is applied to academic discourse, to suggest that leverage for change may be found not only in the order of technology, but also in the order of institutional practices (such as the genres of student writing) as well as in the concept of the subject. This context makes it clear that electronic cognition will not come about automatically through a simple change in the technology of inscription.

The cinema machine, which is not essentially the camera, the film the projector, which is not merely a combination of instruments, apparatuses, techniques. Which is a machine: a *dispositif* articulating between one another different sets—technology certainly, but also economic and ideological. A *dispositif* was required which implicates in its motivations the arrangements of demands, desires, fantasies, speculations (in the two senses of commerce and the imaginary): an arrangement which give apparatus and techniques a social status and function. (Comolli, 1985: 122)

The ideology of the visible, the same desire that produced the telescope—the constituting metaphor of analytico-referential discourse—deriving theoretically from the privileging of sight in Plato's forms as idea, is the drive that produced the camera. To the extent that the camera becomes the image for cinema as a whole, as the means to think about filmic or video writing, it is serving this ideology, obscuring the invisible, the unconscious dimension of cinema as institution, which includes the whole technology of production, everything from photochemistry to box office receipts. "Thus is constituted this situation of theoretical paradox: that it is by identifying the domination of the camera (of the visible) over the whole of the technology of cinema which it is supposed to represent, inform and program (its function as model) that the attempt is made to denounce the submission of that camera, in its conception and its construction, to the dominant ideology of the visible" (125).

The result of this role of ideology within the apparatus is that the bias of analytico-referential cognition is imposed on the invention of cinema in the form of machines and genres favoring the codes of realism. A similar process takes places in the academic apparatus. Jean-Louis Comolli's key point is that the camera is an effect, not the cause, of the "depth of field" point of view that dominates Western thought from the Greeks through Freud. In short, all the developments of style and technology in the evolution of cinema up to now have been motivated by what Comolli calls the "ideology of resemblance."

It is possible to counter this ideological presupposition, however, although only a few filmmakers have managed to do so, according to Comolli. The camera may seem to be condemned to repeating the deceptions of the ideology that created it, but it may also do the work of disillusionment, Comolli argues, "to produce in our sight the very blindness which is at the heart of this visible" (141). Sight and the visible, in other words, may be used to think beyond the ideology that controlled thought in the age of the world picture. The use of pictures, images, indeed the entire figurative program, in teletheory is devoted to this project in the academic apparatus, to use the machine of realism operating in our discourse to say something else, something more and other.

Sampling

The problematic of the apparatus makes explicit the contaminated quality of the very terms of my project. As Eric Leed demonstrated, the distinction between "voice" and "print," between orality and literacy in general, is an explanatory myth (a "theory"). This myth was devised by bourgeois intellectuals, themselves products of literate culture, to define everything they were not—their other. Another case of the analytico-referential discourse constructing a primal order. Oral culture and its opposition to literate culture, then, is a "concept." The concept originated, Leed says, at the time of the French Revolution, generated by temporalizing the logic of a contemporary situation, "articulating modern divisions of communicative labor as periods in time. Just as Freud analyzed the conflicts and identifications inherent in the bourgeois family, defining the logic of that situation and deploying it in time as the history of civilization, we deploy those alternative forms of communication available to us—whether oral, literate, or electronic—as periods in history and a sequence of cultural norms" (44).

Leed is not contesting the obvious sequence of events in the evolution of technology. Rather, using the logic of the apparatus, he suggests that the qualities associated with orality and literacy are not so much effects as causes—capabilities turned into values. In the myth, then, orality represents the values of social integration into the folk community, while print represents the values of individualism and critical autonomy. The effects of mass media, in a postindustrial culture, are associated with oral culture—as secondary orality—and one's attitude to the electronic paradigm will tend to be determined by the attitude to these values. One's assumptions about the human subject direct this evaluation. Humanists such as Jerry Mander or Neil Postman condemn electronic orality because they assume that a free society depends on the subject of individualism as it is defined in the Enlightenment tradition. In this model, the subject produces identity out of the self, and does not derive it through formal relations to an external order. "The emergence of a self-defining subject was early associated with literacy," not only because it was through books on manners and the like that this model was disseminated, but by setting the situation of learning from books as the model of critical reason. Print is experienced as being neutral, impersonal, which meant that "the press, speech, and academic discourse should be free from domination by any specific cluster of social interests. Only then could these institutions function as a true 'marker' of opinion, becoming the structure through which individuals weave their private attitudes into a public opinion, a democratic version of the truth" (50). The symbiosis between individualism and literacy culminates, Leed says, in the "transmission view of communication: the belief that communication consists of channels for the transmission of information across space" (55). The "distance" afforded by alphabetic script suggests the model of the autonomous individuals "able to hold at a distance their community, tradition, and personalized forms of authority" (49).

In this context the name "teletheory" may seem ironic, since it refers to an academic discourse in which "criticism" must work without this distance, fully immersed in and integrated with community, tradition, and personalized forms of authority. Leed argues that the development of an electronic technology must be conceived in terms of the apparatus—it does not leave everything else in place, but produces what philosophers of science might describe as an incommensurate paradigm in which the issues of identity, freedom, and the like must be completely recast. Leed asks us to think about this situation in a way that draws not only upon criticism but upon invention. "Almost no one whom I know claims that the 'mass media' will create forms of autonomy, individuals who are adept at crafting the materials of popular culture, turning them into 'art.' But this possibility must be taken seriously, if only because of what we know about communications revolutions in the past. . . . With writing, the Greeks, and with print, the Humanists were able to become conscious of the logic and the illogicalities of the inherited culture and to draw up the rules for thinking, speaking, sculpting, building, and healing" (60). Leed goes further in stating his hopes for the future based on the historical analogy with previous communications revolutions—the analogy guiding teletheory. "Past communications revolutions have often presaged 'classical' periods of cultural development, periods of intense creativity. These periods were predicated upon the existence of new means for the consolidation and organization of the 'old.' New media always created conditions in which men could address their culture as conscious, rational individuals engaged in the recombination, the reintegration of its elements" (61). In the apparatus of print the Greco-Roman and Judeo-Christian traditions were integrated, an achievement maintained and defended by the contemporary heirs of Humanism. Their heirs do not recognize the opportunity afforded by electronics to include now in this synthesis what might be called the mythico-primitive tradition of oral civilization.

I want to linger over the attitude toward technological change suggested by Leed, since it is the one upon which everything that follows is based. In teletheory, postprint academic discourse is seen as a primary vehicle for still another renaissance. It is this attitude that informs postmodernism as a remotivating of all the styles of the past, as well as the transgression of the classification system of the modern order. The postmodernist style in architecture is perhaps the most discussed example of this tendency which Fredric Jameson, also viewing it through an Enlightenment defense, describes pejoratively as "the random cannibalization of all the styles of the past, the play of random stylistic allusion, and in general what Henri Lefebvre has called the increasing primacy of the 'neo' " (Jameson, 1984: 66). In this new culture of the "simulacrum" the past is itself modified, Jameson argues, becoming "a vast collection of images, a multitudinous photographic simulacrum," whose practice is informed by the emotion of nostalgia.

Jameson, with his typical astuteness, picks out two crucial points for bringing academic discourse into the age of television. First there is the phenomenon of intermedia influence, through which the fundamental and pervasive feature of the audio-visual media—mechanical reproduction of the sights and sounds of the lifeworld—begins to influence representation in print. Everything now, in its own way, wants to be television. Second there is the emotion experienced with this shift, with the turn away from one pattern of organization in which our cognition is invested to a different pattern. Is Jameson right? Is nostalgia the emotion that informs the representational practices to which he refers? One of my concerns will be to identify the predominant emotion associated with academic writing in this period of transition, while the liberal arts are still resisting the possibility of making films and tapes in addition to books and papers, even though all around us, in many of the other colleges of our universities, video production as well as consumption is a regular part of curriculum and research. Robert Burton, in *The Anatomy of Melancholy*, devotes a section to "Love of Learning, or overmuch Study, With a Digression of the Misery of Scholars, and why the Muses are Melancholy." Melancholy is an emotion much associated with nostalgia (as in the film *Nostalghia* [1983], by Andrei Tarkovsky). One of the best examples of educational television yet produced, Godard's *France/tour/ detour/deux/enfants* (1978), ends with a sentimental song, stating in its lyrics, "People. It would be advisable to recognize them as available. At certain pale hours of the night. Near a slot machine. With men's problems. Simply. Problems of melancholy." Walter Benjamin, whose "Theses on the Philosophy of History" provides the theory of historical time for mystory (to be discussed later), is characterized by Susan Sontag as "born under the sign of Saturn," possessing himself the melancholic sensibility he describes in his study of the *Trauerspiel* (Sontag).

Teletheory relates to the nostalgia and melancholy informing contemporary culture in two ways: first, it uses this emotion as a guide to the location of the myths (ideologies) informing the cultural reserve of an individual (using the *punctum* of recognition outlined by Roland Barthes); second, with respect to the arrested mourning, whose symptom is pathological melancholy, of the academic institution, it counters sadness with humor, with the surprise of the joke, again mounted in terms of a methodology, as an emotional guide to the location of significance. The desire to know, the love of learning, in any case is experienced emotionally, carried not in arguments but in images and stories, at the level of memory. The blockage in the theorization of video is most likely to be found at this level.

In contrast to Jameson, John Berger takes a more positive attitude to the effacement of the referent in postmodern culture, in a way that supports the idea (implied by Brian Street) that the new circumstances call for a violation of the boundaries separating academic from popular relations with the arts.

> What the modern means of reproduction have done is to destroy the authority of art and to remove it—or rather to remove its images which they reproduce— from any preserve. For the first time ever, images of art have become ephemeral, ubiquitous, insubstantial, available, valueless, free. They surround us in the same way as a language surrounds us. They have entered the mainstream of life over which they no longer, in themselves, have power.
>
> Yet very few people are aware of what has happened because the means of reproduction are used nearly all the time to promote the illusion that nothing has changed except that the masses, thanks to reproductions, can now begin to appreciate art as the cultured minority once did.
>
> If the new language of images were used differently, it would, through its use, confer a new kind of power. Within it we could begin to define our experience more precisely in areas where words are inadequate. . . . Not only personal experience, but also the essential historical experience of our relation to the past. (Berger, 32–33)

Berger thus identifies the nostalgia from which Jameson believes we cannot free ourselves as the attitude to the arts as holy relics, even in their incarnation as simulacra. That nostalgia would be what informs the melancholy of the specialist against the popular *use* of the information in the arts as a language by means of which to comprehend and intervene in history. The melancholy of the specialist is understandable as a response to the loss of property rights over the collection of representations supporting him. What has been lost in postmodernism, of which experimental video is one of the best example, is the very "object of study" defining the humanities as traditionally conceived:

> It is no accident that today, in full postmodernism, the older language of the "work"—the work of art, the masterwork—has everywhere largely been dis- placed by the rather different language of the "text," of texts and textuality— a language from which the achievement of organic or monumental forms is strategically excluded. (Jameson, 1987: 208)

The melancholy of mourning arises precisely in relation to this violation of the monumental, the monuments whose function it is to hold together the nation of scholars.

It may turn out, however, that academics are more open to the kind of discourse Berger suggests (he is extremely contemptuous of the academic art historian who treated Frans Hals's portraits of the Governors and Governesses of an Alms House for paupers in terms of their formal features) than either he or Jameson suppose. It may be that as researchers committed to realism of the book apparatus academics are unreceptive to the cognition of mechanical reproduction. As teachers, however, we are in a different relation to knowledge, and this is the relation that will come to predominate in a video age in which teaching as well as research is publishable. Hasn't pedagogy always positioned itself in this "postmodern" way in relation to the past as information? Haven't teachers always ransacked the past in order to perform the simulacrum of history, in period courses for which there is no original, whose authorship we deny? Haven't we always lived by the quotation in our scholarship and lectures? Postmodernism no longer produces monumental works, Jameson notes, "but ceaselessly reshuffles the fragments of preexistent texts, the building blocks of older cultural and social production, in some new and heightened bricolage: metabooks which cannibalise other books, metatexts which collate bits of other texts" (223). The description could be applied equally well to academic discourse, such that this temporary overlapping of scholarly and artistic styles could serve as the means of transduction of academic discourse into the age of television.

Schooling then is a place not at all inimical institutionally to the reinvention of reason and the subject of knowledge, even if this invention does require a transformation of practices and a different technology. We can undertake this invention by dropping the pretense of reference (of realism) and admitting that pedagogy is a discourse. The controversial Springhill (Minnesota) conference on graduate education in English (Spring, 1987) declared that "coverage" is no longer an appropriate goal for our curriculum. Released from coverage, a new curriculum, however, entails an opportunity to adopt alternative pedagogies not constrained exclusively by the poetics of realism. Teletheory, with its invention of mystory, is one response to this opportunity.

Leed provides a clue for how to think about the status of texts in teletheory when he notes that inevitably, within the problematic of the apparatus, not only is technology an effect of ideology, but vice-versa (dialectically). Once available, the technology becomes a metaphor used to think about the psyche (and all mechanisms of social control):

> Once we recognize that traditionally the machine has been an objectification of the self-regulating psyche, we can also understand the ambivalence which industrialized man feels toward "technology." Through the metaphor of technology in general, we address questions about our inner state to the outer world. In our images of the machine, we project our attitudes toward those internalized structures of repression which both confine and focus our energies. (Leed, 42)

The machine that perhaps best emblematizes the operations of the academic apparatus in the age of television is the synthesizer, especially in its capacity for "sampling." In sampling a sound is digitally encoded in the memory of the instrument and this data is manipulated so as to provide the sound at different pitches across the span of the keyboard or controller (Crombie, 111). Once recorded in memory, any sound may be imitated and manipulated, leading not only to the possibility of a single player simulating the performance of a symphony orchestra, but to the invention of a new world of sounds and the musicalization of new areas of experience through abstract/imaginative synthesis. Sine waves are the fundamental sound element and the workhouse in many contemporary synthesizers and computer music facilities (15). In teletheory pedagogy is thought of as a sampling of cultural history, which may also suggest a difference between this approach to meaning and the approach formulated by semiotics: the Sine as an alternative to the sign.

Another way to characterize the status of texts in teletheory is to compare it to a photographic archive, as defined by Alan Sekula.

> Archives constitute a *territory of images;* the unity of an archive is first and foremost that imposed by ownership. Whether or not the photographs in a particular archive are offered for sale, the general condition of archives involves the subordination of use to the logic of exchange. Thus, not only are the pictures in archives often *literally* for sale, but their meanings are up for grabs. New owners are invited, new interpretations are promised. The purchase of reproduction rights under copyright law is also the purchase of a certain semantic license. (Sekula, in Wallis, 1987: 116)

The notion of the archive, then, clarifies the condition of representations as property, commensurate with the position of the university in a capitalist society. The ownership of representations and intellectual property rights is an invention associated with print technology, and is one of the arrangements threatened by and constraining the deployment of the new technology of communication. Teletheory carries into academic discourse the lessons not so much of the deconstructive critics as of the deconstructive artists, who appropriate the stereotypes and conventions of available genres as well as the materials of particular works as part of a didactic inventio. What remains to be developed—the project motivating teletheory—is a genre capable of sampling at once the archives of the family, the school, and popular culture. This genre, in other words, is designed to facilitate the postmodernist process of "crossover," joining areas of culture that until now have been held apart as if autonomous (Wallis, 1984: xi–xviii).

What does it mean to compose out of an archive? It is not a question of medium, for this project is concerned with the writing of books and conducting of classes as much as it is with the making of tapes. Teletheory is only partially explicable, intelligible in the theories and examples described in the following sections. What remains must be shown, or practiced, with the explanatory exhibits being put to the extra work of allegory, saying something more and other than they mean literally. In teletheory academic discourse becomes figurative, allegorical. How to represent this new genre other than by practicing it? Thus this book could not have been a treatise. Perhaps the one rhetorical innovation in this choice is a greater emphasis on the poetic or associational mode of composition in relation to the narrative and expository modes more typically exercised in academic writing.

I should stress at the beginning, finally, the single most important distinction between teletheory and the current notion of critical thinking directing academic discourse. This distinction was clarified for me by one of William Safire's columns ("On Language," in the *Gainesville Sun* [September 20, 1987]) entitled "Herman Eutic's Original Intent."

> Hermes, the Greek god of speech and travel, commerce and thievery, who also answers to the Roman name of Mercury, zipped into my office the other day, wings flapping on his feet, with a message: he's back in the news.
>
> The chief of the manuscript division of the Library of Congress, James H. Hutson, helped resuscitate him, making headlines in July. . . . He is the author of a Texas Law Review article that challenges what some scholars call "the jurisprudence of original intention" from an original angle. He informs me "that the documentation of the Constitution is so corrupt that we cannot certainly know what the framers said; and if we cannot know what they said, how can we know what they intended?"
>
> The historian does not flinch from controversy. Attorney General Edwin L. Meese III, he told reporters peering at the Bill of Rights draft, "has expressed the notion that judges, in interpreting the Constitution, should be close to the original intent of those who wrote it." Then he called in Hermes: "But to try to recover original intent from records that are non-existent or not faithful to actual proceedings may be an impossible hermeneutic assignment.
>
> *Hermeneutic* is a word that calls for interpretation as well as definition. The word came into English more than three centuries ago as a kind of antonym for *euretic,* which meant "inventive." (Eureka! I found it!) Wrote Richard Burthogge, a 17th-century theological author, "Ratiocination Speculative, is either Euretick or Hermeneutick, Inventive or Interpretive."

Safire goes on in the article to contrast the "neocons" (Meese and other neoconservatives) with the "decons" (Jacques Derrida's crowd, for whom "this 'original intent' business is a lot of hooey"). It seemed fortuitous that this clarification should come in the popular press, since teletheory works to cross the division of knowledge into popular and specialized versions.

Is there something transgressive in teletheory, related to its shift from hermeneutics to euretics? Let me keep that spelling, to distinguish invention in teletheory from the strategies of heuresis common in learning theory, without excluding the insights of the latter from our practice. There is no need to be against hermeneutics in order to be for euretics, only that euretics provides an alternative to interpretation that has been lacking in most of the discussions of the problem. Hermeneutics, in any case, comes after euretics, applied to the invention as if it came from another, as the discourse of the other, to see what has been made; to note its meaning, value, or beauty. There is as of yet no interpretation of "Derrida at the Little Bighorn."

As Karen LeFevre noted, the contemporary trend in the approach to "invention," supported by the 1971 Report of the Speech Communication Association's Committee on the Nature of Rhetorical Invention, has been to broaden, "the territory to which the term 'rhetorical invention' might apply":

> [The report] advocates research to develop 'a theory of the structures of inquiry, deciding, and choosing' and research 'to examine the relationship between rhetorical invention and creativity.' This expanded treatment of rhetorical invention moves it away from its traditionally close association with persuasive discourse dealing with probable matters in a given situation, guiding it toward a more general view. 'It is important,' the report concludes, 'in an age in which fixed forms—whether in metaphysics, art, poetics, cultural patterns, and so forth—are under attack, to look at the world from the perspective of invention, taken as the generation of something new. . . . Invention (used now as the generic term) becomes in this context a productive human thrust into the unknown.'" (LeFevre, 3)

Euretics takes up this convergence of rhetorical *inventio* with innovation, of "rhetorical and aesthetic invention with modes of discovery in all areas," in the specific domain of academic discourse. My assumption is that it is not at all obvious how to enact such a program; that the means for such a convergence may itself have to be "invented," and invented more than once.

Why euretics now? On the same page in the morning newspaper in which I read Safire's column there was an article by Barbara Vobejda (*The Washington Post*), with the headline "College Presidents want to enhance status of teaching." Thirty-seven college presidents, the article says, addressed an open letter to 3,300 other leaders in higher education asking them "to act together as persistent and passionate advocates for reform," in response to a "national emergency" in education. The presidents suggest that what is needed is to enhance the status of teaching, increase the number of minority teachers, and work closely with elementary and secondary schools. "To maintain and enhance our quality of life, we must develop a leading-edge economy based on workers who can think for a living."

Reading this article I was reminded again of the question of the apparatus. Academic discourse does not occur in isolation from the other discourses in which we conduct our lives. Perhaps it was necessary to keep specialized discourse separate and distinct when it was a matter of orality and literacy. But now that the situation has been complicated by the addition of videocy, this segregation of discourses has become counter-productive. I have my own view of the crisis in education, which is that the time has come to think in positive terms about how to bring academic discourse into the age of television. This may be one way to act upon the appeal from the presidents, even if we were not among those who received the letter.

Chapter 1

Experiment

I. Historiography

Heidegger's discussion of historiography points to a dissatisfaction with both the scientific and humanistic models for the representation of history. What is less clear is the specific practice that might be an alternative to these models. The clearest statement of how to find this alternative is in Hayden White's "The Burden of History." This chapter in *Tropics of Discourse* outlines the project assigned to the seminar in teletheory. Challenging the absolute distinction separating literally truthful (scientific) explanations from purely imaginary (artistic) ones, White proposes an experimental approach to the representation of history. Texts composed in this spirit would not be expected to correspond to some preexistent body of raw facts, "for we should recognize that *what constitutes the facts themselves* is the problem that the historian, like the artist, has tried to solve in the choice of metaphor by which he orders his world, past, present, future" (White, 1978: 47). What are the practical implications of such an attitude toward historical (or theoretical) inquiry?

> It would permit the plunder of psychoanalysis, cybernetics, game theory, and the rest without forcing the historian to treat the metaphors thus confiscated from them as inherent in the data under analysis, as he is forced to do when he works under the demand for an impossibly comprehensive objectivity. And it would permit historians to conceive of the possibility of using impressionistic, expressionistic, surrealist, and (perhaps) even actionist modes of representation for dramatizing the significance of data which they have uncovered but which all too frequently they are prohibited from seriously contemplating as evidence. (47–48)

This prospect has held my interest for a decade. I cited it in "The Object of Post-Criticism" (Foster) as the context that best explained the innovations of critical theory in the postmodernist era. Why this "perhaps" qualifying the list of possible models for historical writing? White himself, reflecting a certain inconsistency in taste, keeps his distance from the possibilities his experiment inspires. In *Metahistory* White exploits fully the organizational capacities of alphabetic writing (manifested most purely, according to Jack Goody, in the list, the table, and the formula) by building a kind of periodic table of method. The four basic tropes provide the vertical axis, and the horizontal axis compiles and collates the following systems: aesthetics— Northrop Frye's archetypal plot structures; epistemology—Stephen Pepper's world hypotheses (four different theories of truth); ethics—Karl Mannheim's ideological categories (White, 1973: 426).

As in the periodic table, arranging the chemical elements into rows and columns, there is a natural affinity among certain of the items in each of the systems, and an incompatibility among certain others. There also appears to be something like the possibility of generating unstable, even dangerous combinations, as happened with the production of the artificial elements (those numbered higher than 92, Uranium). The trope creating this unstable row is the pun, emplotted as "absurdist," whose mode of truth is "aleatory," informed by the Nietzschean ethic of the eternal return—or so I would speculate. White's view of the theorists who embody the absurdist tropics— Bataille, Derrida, Foucault—is unambiguous. At the extreme limits of thought (even artificially generated in an unnatural state) such critics reduce literature to writing, "writing to language, and language, in a final paroxysm of frustration, to chatter about silence. This apotheosis of 'silence' is the inevitable destiny of a field of study which has slipped its cultural moorings" (White, 1978: 262). In short, we could say that the absurdist critics are to the historiographical table what Plutonium is to the table of chemical elements. This analogy between the Atomic bomb and poststructuralist composition will be important for teletheory, representing the peculiar temporality of euretic or inventive thinking. Such thinking is goal-directed without knowing exactly where it is going (it is tele-illogical), for which the already-not-yet temporality of the Bomb serves as an image. The Atomic catastrophe comes to us from a long way off, as Heidegger noted; it has already happened, even if it has not taken place. The Atomic and Hydrogen bombs are not phenomena to be explained, but serve now themselves as images of wide scope promoting further thought in the nuclear age. Walter Benjamin used the image of atomic energy, before the bomb existed, to express the way his dialectical images represented history ("an image is that in which the past and the present moment flash into a constellation"): "It was in the context of a conversation in which I set forth how this project [the arcades]— as in the splitting of the atom—releases the enormous energy of history that lies bonded in the 'Once upon a time' of classical historical narrative" (Benjamin, 1983: 8–9).

It could be, however, that "silence" includes more resources than White allows. André Jolles, for example, in his discussion of the "simple forms," organizes both oral and literate realization of these forms into five moods: interrogative, indicative, imperative, optative, and silence. The forms that function in the mood of silence are the riddle and the joke (Jolles, 8). Thus later in this study the account of the logic of teletheory in terms of the logic of the joke is an attempt to show that the exploration of silence by the absurdist critics is an experiment specifically grounded in the linguistics of mood and not a nihilistic gesture.

White's concern that the absurdist theory might blow up criticism needs to be answered, nonetheless, in order to show the positive potential of this destabilizing force, which does indeed shift our attention away from criticism, but not in order to abandon critical thinking. My book returns again to White's experiment, no longer to talk about it, as I did in *The Anti-Aesthetic*, but to do it while explaining how it can be done. The most important part of White's proposal for me is his suggestion that the vanguard arts should be used as sources of method, rather than as objects of interpretation. Teletheory approaches artistic texts as models for representational practice adaptable to education. Such is the lesson to be learned from the controversial "aporia" of deconstruction, that stops and derails the hermeneutic referential program. The lesson is not to reduce literature to silence, as White and others fear, but to let it speak in its own voice. What has critical science been in academic practice but the translation of artistic texts into the languages of the human sciences (allegoresis, the hermeneutics of suspicion)? The alternative proposed by the absurdists is to stop interpreting literature and start using literary devices as an original, native language, fully capable of doing the work of academic discourse as research and teaching. Far from being reductive with respect to literature, such an approach gives it full credit for being a cognitive mode in its own right, irreducible to but equatable with the other discourses mounted by the specialized disciplines. This is not to say that the distinction between literature and its study disappears, only that the study includes an immanent practice, sampling, as we noted, its own reserve in a new activity of production. Euretics, in short, does not interpret art; it uses art for the making of theory.

This possibility is the one White himself suggests by calling for contemporary historians to make as good a use of current models as the nineteenth-century historians made of the likes of Scott and Thackeray. In later sections I will suggest a number of examples, including texts by John Cage, Mary Kelly, and Ross McElwee, among others, that together contribute to the formation of a new genre called "mystory." First, however, I need to take up the other dimension of the proposal, suggesting that any such experiment in historiography also derives its protocols from contemporary science, in the same way that the founders of History drew upon the science of their day.

Although White deliberately chooses to exclude a consideration of personality types from his table, psychoanalysis is one of those "sciences" that provides an important part of the rationale for teletheory.

2. Freud: The New Instauration

To undertake White's experiment, then, requires a review of the history of method (remarking first of all that it *has* a history). First formulated in the *Phaedrus*, it is applied subsequently to religion, producing theology in the Middle Ages; to nature, producing science in the Renaissance and Enlightenment; to society, producing history in the nineteenth century. Finally, method is applied to the human subject as such, producing psychoanalysis at the turn of the century, at which point method turns itself inside out. Applied to the thinking subject, method reveals its own limits, and something more: its own alternative.

Timothy Reiss (1982) offers an excellent account of the history of method, focusing on the period from Galileo to Freud, during which time methodological discourse achieved dominance in Western culture. He shows the process in which an "analytico-referential" class of discourse becomes the single dominant structure and the necessary form taken by thought, knowledge, and cultural and social practices of all kinds (23). This history is framed by an argument suggesting that the dominance of the analytico-referential discourse is now being challenged and overcome.

Several aspects of Reiss's study are important for teletheory: that the rise to dominance of this discourse included certain occultations and repressions of the prior mode of discourse from which it emerged; that a similar crisis of emergence is underway in our own time, producing a similarly massive conceptual change. The analytico-referential discourse emerged, that is, from a discourse of "resemblance" or "patterning," manifested in the works of such figures as Paracelsus, Rabelais, or Bruno. It is a question of relations: "I am thinking of a relation of narration, assuming some commented exterior whose existence as a knowable reality is taken as prior to that of discourse (the discourse of analysis and reference, or historicism, of experimentalism), and of a relation of the 'formation of patterns' (the placing of things by their resemblances, by their similarities)" (30).

The basic ordering process of analytico-referential discourse assumes that the syntactic order of language "is coincident both with the logical ordering of 'reason' and with the structural organization of a world given as exterior to both these orders," such that the properly organized sentence "provides in its very syntax a correct analysis of both the rational and material orders, using elements that refer adequately through concepts to the true, objective nature of the world" (31). The exemplary formal statement of this mode is *cogito ergo sum;* "its principal metaphors will be those of the telescope (eye—instrument—world) and of the voyage of discovery (self-possessed port of departure—sea journey—country claimed as legitimate possession of the discoverer)."

Kepler is the transitional figure, indicating the way in which science is grounded in the "alien" discourse of patterning. Exemplifying Kuhn's argument that paradigm shifts are accepted or rejected for emotional and ideological rather than for logical "reasons" exclusively, Kepler elected the heliocentric theory of the universe because he thought of God "not in the Aristotelian manner as a self-contained and unmoved final cause of motion and endeavor in other beings, but chiefly as a generative and self-diffusive energy" (Donner, 25). The sun had to be in the center of the world since, for Kepler, the sun was the symbol of God. He wrote that the three regions of the universe corresponded to the three persons of the Holy Trinity: "the center, a symbol of the Father; the surface, of the Son; and the intermediate space, of the Holy Ghost. So too just as many principal parts of the world have been made— the different part of the different regions of the sphere: the sun in the center, the sphere of the fixed stars on the surface, and lastly the planetary system in the region intermediate between the sun and the fixed stars" (20). Out of this medieval system of beliefs combined with a knowledge of mathematics and a commitment to careful observation of the natural world came a major contribution to the scientific revolution. A basic feature of teletheory is that invention always includes an ideological dimension that is as important to the success or failure of research as is the disciplinary element. In euretics, it is not a question of eliminating or bracketing this ideology from thought, but of learning how to exploit it for the benefit of learning and discovery.

The word in an analytico-referential mode is arbitrary, allowing concepts to be serialized into a grammar. "Such an operation is impossible when noun (name) and object are perceived as essentially inseparable (as in the discourse of patterning). Paracelsus will be able to say that it is by the inherent signs (signatures) that 'one may know another—what there is in him.' One must understand that all things have 'true and genuine names' " (Reiss, 32). In this mode, reasoning is a search for resemblances, "the accumulation of patterns: thus the need for men who 'have had experience in the art of signature' and who can discover the 'genuine names' and nature of things" (44). Patterns allow verbal signs to be equated with any other kind of sign in nature "as valid manifestations of the relation between the universal and the individual."

Reiss finds that several modern thinkers have described, from within the dominant analytico-referential mode, the mode of patterning. Lévi Strauss's savage mind, the bricoleur, thinks by means of patterns—"an order of the formation of complexes, and it is a seemingly nonconceptualized ordering (because it does not seek to separate concept and object)" (46). Nietzsche's account of the "original split" between the Apollonian and the Dionysiac is relevant, as is Bachelard's distinction between the "formal imagination" based on discursive analysis, and the "material imagination" using "the immediate images of things as its code" (41). Reiss points out that all such accounts are limited by being themselves formulated within the analytico-referential mode, which, like Jack Goody, he suspects is excluded from the experience of the other style of cognition.

Kepler's application of quantitative arguments to celestial motion marks a moment of transition, passing from analogy to causality, giving rise to the separation of the public from the private, hiding the subject's enunciative responsibility, hiding the context of the production of meaning, the way the mediating discourse contributed to what it represented.

> A logic based on referential truth and internal (analytical) coherence, asserted by the discursive enunciating subject, and founded on the axiom of the excluded middle. The assertion in question is followed by the occultation of the subject, withdrawn from its own discourse. The discursive imposition of knowledge is concealed (it deals in "secrets"), and the authority and power openly assumed at the outset are gradually eclipsed, [concluding] in a discursive practice asserting discourse to be at once a mechanism transparent to the truths it transports and an ordering system whose coherence alone is responsible for the "value" of those truths. (223)

These are the secrets that contribute to the tomb and the crypt of the unconscious. From the point of view of discourse formation—the vantage point of teletheory—the unconscious is constituted by the suppression within the scientific paradigm of the claims to knowledge of all alternative styles of representation. The tendency in the twentieth century, symptomatic of the new instauration, to assign a "knowledge-effect" to the exposure of the production of meaning within a signifying system, may be seen as a direct response to the limitations imposed on discourse by the Enlightenment model of knowledge.

Reiss identifies Freud as the figure whose work marks the limits of the analytico-referential mode. Freud, he argues, internalizes, hypostatizes the galilean metaphor—the optical device—as a description of the relation of the psyche to the world. Here is Reiss's assessment of our moment:

> Whether or not the incorporation of occultations already proposes a passage into another discursive domain, only history will show. Freud may be right when he asserts at the end of [The Future of an Illusion] that the rule of "Logos" (a kind of science of which psychoanalysis would be exemplary) will indeed be "for a new generation of men" and foreseeable. The time is not yet that we could know it. But it is most certainly time to recognize the development of and a vital need for a new instauration. (380)

The term "instauration," of course, alludes to Francis Bacon's Renaissance project for a reorganization of all human knowledge, Instauratio Magna. As evidence that such an instauration may be in process Reiss cites Lewis Carroll "basing much of the nonsense of *Alice* on games with the law *tertium non datur*," comparable to C.S. Peirce "seeking to constitute a semeiotics on the basis of a tertiary relationship replacing the stasis of the true/false dichotomy with a continuous process of the production of sense" (381). Barthes's third meanings belong to this push beyond dualism as well, as do Derrida's differance, and Benjamin's dialectical images (as in his "Doctrine of the Similar").

Reiss's discussion is limited to Modernism, identifying the symptoms and the need for a new mode of discourse, a new conceptual order. He notes the relevance of Barthes and Derrida, among others, to this shift, but he does not see in them or in anyone else the signs of a new direction. "Derrida asserts that 'the Freudian concept of trace must be radicalized and extracted from the metaphysics of presence.' In view of what has been argued here, one wonders whether that is possible, whether the attempt is not bound to end up in just the same discursive space" (375). Reiss is stating these reservations at the end of a long and complex book in which he has provided both the rationale and the motivation for further work. Far from denigrating the achievements of the conceptual system that came to dominance in the seventeenth century, Reiss accepts that success as a model for our own time: "That it should have reached the limits of its useful and progressive action should only encourage us to undertake a work parallel to that of its founders" (379). This appeal is one point of departure for teletheory, which takes up the question of a new instauration called for but left undeveloped by Reiss, in the same way that White called for but does not himself produce a new historical discourse.

The task of *Teletheory* in particular is to outline a direction for this project— for the invention of a new cognitive model. I have more confidence than does Reiss in the possibility that everything needed to characterize the new discourse is already in place, even if these elements have not yet come together in an institutionalized practice. Reiss perhaps underestimates the value or significance of the clues he himself enumerates. Specifically, I want to reconsider his assessment of the relationship between the analytico-referential discourse and the discourse of patterning from which it emerged. Once it emerged, analytico-referential discourse opposed that which it could not accommodate: "By that time patterning was no longer a practice but an 'object' classified as a 'form of thought': 'ancient,' 'primitive,' 'mythical,' or later even, 'pathological.' Thus hypostatized it is no longer what was to be found in Kepler and his predecessors: it has become an *object* fit for analysis" (379). Patterning could coexist with analysis, but not vice-versa.

Patterning became distanced as "pre-scientific," but persisted on the margins, and constitutes "a kind of permanent ghost in the machine, posing a latent question to the signifying, denoting intentions of that discourse," contradicting "the logic of the dominant discourse in which it lies more or less hidden" (378). "That is not to say," Reiss adds, "that a discourse of *patterning* could ever function again as such for us." The "as such" is the crucial qualification, however, for I want to argue that patterning has come around again, as the ghost whose secret is buried in the crypt, as the pleasure of orality. But it returns not in the same place or condition. The crucial new element in the mix is electronic technology. It happens in the history of thought that a new step is made possible by a return, as in the case of Copernicus, who cited an ancient Greek as his source for the notion of a heliocentric universe.

Reiss underestimates Freud's importance for an electronic cognition, perhaps because he insists too much on the scientific claims Freud made, and too little on the artistic and speculative dimensions of Freud's writings. Psychoanalysis, Reiss argues, amounts to an internalization and hypostatization of the development of the analytico-referential discourse into "a universal human 'psyche' " (374). All of its concepts represent "the discursive means by which analytico-referentiality was installed."

> Psychoanalysis would affirm that this partial analysis has merely indicated the world-historical validity of its scheme, at least for the past three hundred years. I am affirming the reverse: that it is 'merely' the hypostatization of that history. That achievement and its internalization cannot but be seen as an ideological effort at maintaining the discourse in question, an effort quite similar to that of logical atomism, for example, to provide a new and more 'acceptable' foundation for an empirical science in logical and epistemological trouble. (376)

The relationship between analysis and patterning in Freud may be read differently however, by considering Freud as our Kepler, in whose texts may be found the emergence of a new discourse, as well as the ideology of the old one. It may be that Reiss is right about Freud's intentions, or the intentions of psychoanalysis as an institution. But, as White pointed out, we may confiscate a principle from a field without "treating the metaphors thus confiscated as inherent in the data under analysis." This approach is precisely the one adopted by Michel Foucault when he suggests that Freud's major discovery was not the problem of sexuality, the sexual aetiology of neuroses. Rather, "the strength of psychoanalysis consists in its having opened out on to something quite different, namely the logic of the unconscious" (Foucault, 1980: 212–213). With this description, the analytical account of the unconscious as a mode of thought—in short, with a new version of memory—method goes beyond itself and thinks its way into a new instauration.

Is it possible for academic discourse to work with the logic of the unconscious? Teletheory seeks an affirmative answer to this question.

3. After Method

If we are to hold to our experiment, applying the insights of contemporary science to the formation of a new historiography, we must consider the possibility of replacing method itself with an alternative conduct. The era of analysis is the era Derrida calls "logocentric," that emerged in Ancient Greece, became dominant in the Renaissance, and may be achieving closure in the era of electronic postmodernism. However crude such an outline is of a rich and complex historical evolution, it is useful as a context to grasp what is at stake in teletheory and the transformation of academic discourse— the shift away from method as such, as the exclusive mode of conceptual thinking, along with a transformation of memory and hence of the structure of learning itself.

Paul Feyerabend, in a study entitled *Against Method* (1975), helps us see the interrelationship between style and cognition and the appropriate level of generalization, focusing on the Ancient period in which emerged the ideology of depth. This ideology produced eventually, in our period, both in "depth of field" devices (technical and stylistic) of the cinema machine and the "depth" psychology of the unconscious: cinema and psychoanalysis are constrained by, but not limited to, the ideology of depth. By showing the inscription of this ideology in style, Feyerabend implies that the change in style that concerns us is similarly associated with a transformation of cognition and the subject.

Feyerabend's analysis of the contrast between the epic style of archaic Greece and the tragic style of classical Greece recalls Eric Auerbach's famous distinction between coordinating, paratactical, flat style, and subordinating, hypotactical, depth style. Feyerabend's comparison is between two epochs of Greek culture, whereas Auerbach's is cross-cultural, between the Greek and Semitic cognitive styles. As Auerbach notes, it is a question of two modes of realism. My interest is in the mobility of the contrast, which should be dissociated from a direct correspondence with the orality/literacy pair, as if the oral were inherently flat, and the literate inherently deep. It is a question, rather, not of essences but of change—the shift of epochs that entails a corresponding shift in cognition and style. Auerbach's use of the distinction reminds us that the two styles—flat and deep—combined in the synthesis we call the Western tradition, which teletheory now wants to reconstitute by including a third tradition whose features correspond to those of a non-Western, primal style.

In Feyerabend's account, then, the world of "archaic man" is "an open world":

> Its elements are not formed or held together by an 'underlying substance,' they are not appearances from which this substance may be inferred with difficulty.

They occasionally coalesce to form assemblages. The relation of a single element to the assemblage to which it belongs is like the relation of a part of an aggregate of parts and not like the relation of a part to an overpowering whole. The particular aggregate called 'man' is visited, and occasionally inhabited by 'mental events.' Such events may reside in him, they may also enter from the outside. Like every other object man is an exchange station of influences rather than a unique source of action, an "I" (Descartes' 'cogito' has no point of attack in this world, and his argument cannot even start). (248)

The contrasting negatives in the description, of course, allude to the cosmology that replaced the epic order. In the new order of depth, the soul and the I emerge. Feyerabend refers to the orders as Cosmos A (archaic) and Cosmos B (modern). "The transition from A to B thus introduces new entities and new relations between entities (this is seen clearly in painting and statuary). It also changes the concept and the self-experience of man. Archaic man is a puppet set in motion by outside forces such as enemies, social circumstances, feelings." (265) This puppet could be the one that Lacan said still exists in the unconscious.

In cosmos B, the world of depth, of which, Feyerabend says, linear perspective is one of the best exemplars, concepts are organized differently. Rather than the simple aggregate of elements and their relationships, in depth elements divide into two classes: essences and appearances. "Objects may again combine. They may form harmonious totalities where each part gives meaning to the whole and receives meaning from it. Aspects properly combined do not produce *objects,* but psychological conditions for the apprehension of *phantoms* which are but other aspects, and particularly misleading ones at that (they look so convincing). *No enumeration of aspects is identical with the object*" (264–265). In this account, the phantom haunting the modern paradigm has to do with "essence" and "meaning" and the unified ego.

Now the cosmology of depth is giving way to another one which it is part of our project to imagine. Timothy Reiss's concern with the new instauration comes within Foucault's delineation of an epistemic shift. The modern episteme that emerged as the analytico-referential style, "was bound up with the disappearance of Discourse and its featureless reign, with the shift of language towards objectivity," Foucault noted. "If this same language is now emerging with greater and greater insistence in a unity that we ought to think but cannot as yet do so, is this not the sign that the whole of this configuration is now about to topple, and that man is in the process of perishing as the being of language continues to shine ever brighter upon our horizon?" (Foucault, 1970: 385–386). "Man," that "as the archeaology of our thought easily shows, is an invention of recent date. And one perhaps nearing its end." "Man" is an invention—one of the inventions of some importance to euretics. We may suspend judgment on the question for which there is as yet no answer, according to Foucault—concerning the disappearance of "man." Rather, we locate our project within the conditions that have led to changes in the concept of the human subject—"change in the fundamental arrangements of knowledge" (387). The important point, in the context of the apparatus, is to realize that not only "method" (a practice), but "man" (an ideology) has a history. We are preparing to give up the ghost, then, the essence of Man and all that goes with it. But this may require a funeral and a period of mourning.

How to think our way into the new instauration? Could it be as direct, this change, as saying that we are adding one more dimension? That we are moving from a three to a four dimensional cosmology, just as the Ancient Greeks moved from a two to a three dimensional one? If we took that direction, we would draw together in an analogy a new nexus relating Einsteinian physics, vanguard collage, and the decentered subject, in order to generate from this mix a certain cognitive style. That enterprise is already well underway in contemporary culture, and provides a frame to which teletheory may allude while developing a distinct approach to the question.

As Hayden White noted, the problem with which one chooses to work plays a major role in the formation of theory and fact. Teletheory first of all is the name of a problem—"academic discourse in the age of television"— which this book and the seminars to which it refers attempt to solve. Or it may be that the problem itself is an invention. Feyerabend offers some advice about how to think in such circumstances. "Fundamental conceptual change presupposes new world views and new languages capable of expressing them" (256). The terms of this new language will become clear, Feyerabend continues, only when the process is fairly well advanced, so that the intercon-nections may be grasped and what seemed illogical or absurd resolves into something perfectly reasonable. One way to clarify the terms of such a process, he suggests, is

by incorporation into a language of the future, which means *that one must learn to argue with unexplained terms and to use sentences for which no clear rules of usage are as yet available.* Just as a child who starts using words without yet understanding them, who adds more and more uncomprehended linguistic fragments to his playful activity, discovers the sense-giving principle only *after* he has been active in this way for a long time . . . in the very same way the inventor of a new world view must be able to talk nonsense until the amount of nonsense created by him and his friends is big enough to give sense to all its parts. (256–257)

Such is my procedure, and the pedagogy that goes with the new academic writing—to approach the languages of knowledge the way a child learns language, not the way a foreigner does, using the video machine that writes the way a child thinks.

What is the pedagogy that might enact such a program? To glimpse it we must consider the invisible part of the dominant paradigm, the part suppressed by the ideology of analysis, the ghost. Feyerabend, that is, reviews the same historical developments as Reiss, except that for Feyerabend Galileo and his telescope are not a metaphor but the topic of study, which allows us to see not the scientist of received history (appropriately used in Reiss's assessment of the features of the dominant discourse) but the other side of Galileo—the side of the production or invention of Galilean science as practice, rather than as established principle (the former being the side occulted by the analytico-referential discourse). With the telescope of ideology, evidence closes the argument. In practice, however, Galileo brought together twenty-four of the world's leading professors, to have them look through the instrument and verify his own observations. Unfortunately, the group could not agree on what it saw (123).

The problem of the dissemination of scientific ideas is a useful one for the problem of pedagogy—for the dissemination of ideas in the university. Feyerabend complains that the analytic model has distinguished and separated two dimensions of science that should be kept unified—discovery and justification. The problem arose in part through the distortions created when the analytical discourse took itself as its object. Being ideologically habituated to the occultation of production, the empirical/logical description of science (represented by Popper) constructed an abstract account that ignored the actual practice of science. Indeed, if the concept of rules and "falsifiability" at the center of the logic of problem solving were actually applied to practice, Feyerabend argues, there could be no science. The ideology of method, that is, differs fundamentally from the practice of invention. Science, like cinema, is an apparatus, a machine, in which ideology plays an integral part. The same may be said for the university as an education machine.

How can one think about a new conceptual order from within the restraints of a given ideology? There is only one way to break the circle of percepts and concepts (both equally interdependent and equally laden with presuppositions): "it consists in using an external measure of comparison" (76). But where is such a measure to be found? "Ideological ingredients of our knowledge and, more especially, of our observations, are discovered with the help of theories which are refuted by them. *They are discovered counterinductively*" (77). In short, "we need a dream-world in order to discover the features of the real world we think we inhabit (and which may actually be just another dream-world). . . . We must invent a new conceptual system that suspends, or clashes with the most carefully established observational results, confounds the most plausible theoretical principles, and introduces perceptions that cannot form part of the existing perceptual world. This step is counterinductive. Counterinduction is therefore always reasonable and it has always a chance of success" (32).

"Truth," in this view, is part of the invention of the episteme of depth, and must be challenged in order to find a way into the new instauration. Again, the procedure will be dream-work, the operation of invention, of discovery. Now here we arrive at one of the crucial arguments of teletheory as a pedagogy, joining doing and telling, discovery and justification, with major consequences for educational practice.

> Reason grants that the ideas which we introduce in order to expand and to improve our knowledge may *arise* in a very disorderly way and that the *origin* of a particular point of view may depend on class prejudice, passion, personal idiosyncrasies, questions of style, and even on error, pure and simple. But it also demands that in *judging* such ideas we follow certain well-defined rules: our *evaluation* of ideas must not be invaded by irrational elements. Now, what our historical examples seem to show [Galileo and Copernicus] is this: there are situations when our most liberal judgments and our most liberal rules would have eliminated an idea or a point of view which we regard today as essential for science, and would not have permitted it to prevail—and such situations occur quite frequently. The ideas survived because prejudice, passion, conceit, errors, sheer pigheadedness, in short because all the elements that characterize the context of discovery, opposed the dictates of reason and because these irrational elements were permitted to have their way. (154–155)

Feyerabend does not want to invert the hierarchy in science from justification to discovery, but to bring them together as equal aspects of a whole endeavor. The false emphasis on justification led to the suppression of style as a feature of cognition. But style, Feyerabend says, is crucial to invention, and this is the point of similarity between the arts and the sciences. Style, which Feyerabend equates with propaganda, including especially "seductiveness of content" is essential in that it helps create and maintain interest in a theory that lacks "empirical fit." "It is of the essence because interest must be created at a time when the usual methodological prescriptions have no point of attack; and because this interest must be maintained, perhaps for centuries, until new reasons arrive" (157). Thus, when Sebastiano Timpanaro offers in place of Freud's spectacular explanation for his slip of tongue—a case of imperfect memory (in *The Psychopathology of Everyday Life*)—his own admittedly "pedestrian (but true)" explanation, we are encouraged to stay with Freud. For Timpanaro, there is nothing unusual or interesting about the slips that so exercised Freud.

> What is the explanation for this double error? The most mediocre of philologists would have no difficulty in giving one. Anyone who has anything to do with the written or oral transmission of texts (including quotations learnt by heart) knows

that they are exposed to the constant danger of banalization. Forms which have a more archaic, more high-flown, more unusual stylistic expression, and which are therefore more removed from the cultural-linguistic heritage of the person who is transcribing or reciting, tend to be replaced by forms in more common use. (Timpanaro, 30)

The oral and written transmission of texts is indeed our topic, but the banalization of explanations is not a helpful approach to our project. What does it mean, then, to be against method?

Inventing theories and contemplating them in a relaxed and "artistic" fashion, we often make moves that are forbidden by methodological rules. For example, we interpret the evidence so that it fits our fanciful ideas, we eliminate difficulties by ad hoc procedures, we push them aside, or we simply refuse to take them seriously. The activities which according to Feigl belong to the context of discovery are not just different from what goes on in the context of justification, they are in conflict with it. (Feyerabend, 167)

In practice scientists often choose to work inventively rather than method-ologically. If they did not, there would be no science. "Hence," Feyerabend concludes, "we are not dealing with an alternative either, we are dealing with a single uniform domain of procedures all of which are equally important for the growth of science. This disposes of the distinction [between discovery and justification]" (167).

It is possible to observe this split between discovery and justification that characterizes the era of logocentrism in the segregation of oral and literate representations of science. In their sociological analysis of scientists' discourse, *Opening Pandora's Box*, G. Nigel Gilbert and Michael Mulkay, focusing on a moment of a shift in accepted theory in a field of biochemistry, compared formal papers with interviews and other manner of talk by the same scientists, thus comparing the literate with the oral dimensions of scientific discourse. "We will examine two contexts of linguistic production, namely, the experimental research paper and the semi-structured interview involving biochemists and non-biochemists. We will show that participants' accounts of action and belief are systematically different in these two settings. This will enable us to identify two major interpretative repertoires, or linguistic registers, which occur repeatedly in scientific discourse" (Gilbert, 39).

One way to characterize the difference between the registers is that between a statement (formal) and its enunciative context (social, ideological). For my purposes, one of the insights of this study to emphasize is specifically that in the two registers what differs is the account of method, relevant to Feyerabend's critique of the separation between discovery and justification. "Whereas formal methods sections contain highly abstract versions of scientists' research activities in the form of impersonal rules, with no attempt to specify how these rules are interpreted in practice in particular instances, scientists' informal accounts emphasize that these rules depend for their practical meaning on the variable craft skills, intuitions, customary knowledge, social experience and technical equipment available to individual experimenters" (55).

A comparison of the empirical with the contingent registers reveals two conflicting views of method, which are embodied in different styles of representation. In the empirical, formal register, used in research papers,

> experimental data tend to be given chronological as well as logical priority. Neither the author's own involvement with or commitment to a particular analytical position nor his social ties with those whose work he favors are mentioned. . . . Although the content of experimental papers clearly depends on the experimenters' actions and judgments, such papers are overwhelmingly written in an impersonal style. By adopting these kinds of linguistic features, authors construct texts in which the physical world seems regularly to speak, and sometimes to act, for itself. Empiricist discourse is organized in a manner which denies its character as an interpretive product and which denies that its author's actions are relevant to its content. (56)

In the contingent register, the researchers no longer depict their actions as "generic responses to the realities of the natural world, but as the activities and judgments of specific individuals acting on the basis of their personal inclinations and particular social problems." In the empirical register, the theory, to the extent that it is made explicit, is said to be the result of the experiment. In the contingent register, the opposite is said to be the case—that alternative theories were never taken seriously, and that the experiment was designed on the basis of the theory it demonstrates. In this register, actions and beliefs are presented

> as heavily dependent on speculative insights, prior intellectual commitments, personal characteristics, indescribable skills, socialties, and group membership. Not only was the general style of the participants' informal discourse much more personal and idiosyncratic, but in certain passages they used the wider range of stylistic, grammatical and lexical resources to be found in informal talk to construct accounts of their own and others' actions and beliefs that were radically different in content from those appearing in comparable formal texts. (57)

The scientists claimed that no one in their profession was fooled by the empirical register, that they could all "read between the lines." Nonetheless, the disparity between the two representations is not without consequences. The harm that follows from this disjunction or deception may not affect science proper (as Feyerabend said, in practice scientists ignore the rules used to describe their discipline). The real victim is pedagogy, where it is precisely the formal rather than the informal, contingent, oral, discovery model of knowledge that is invoked and enforced. We know what is really going on, the scientists say, but we don't make it public (60). Such tends to be the relationship between the oral and the written registers of academic discourse in most disciplines, existing as they do in an institution organized by the dominant analytico-referential model of cognition.

Gilbert and Mulkay, then, provide further motivation for the convergence of styles in oralysis (literate orality), since in the context of Feyerabend their study shows that the discovery mode corresponds to the oral register, but this register consists of talk about justification, whose work in turn is represented in the literate mode. This overlap between cognitive styles and media of representation suggests the need for a review of education, opening up the curriculum to the private as well as to the public aspects of cognition.

Augustine Brannigan agrees with Feyerabend that these two contexts should not be kept apart, although for somewhat different reasons. She adds the valuable observation that psychological accounts of discovery fail to distinguish between invention and learning. They are really theories of learning, which is in fact precisely the context in which teletheory places them. Brannigan shifts attention from psychology to ethnography, noting that learning is not an achievement based on inherent and neutral intelligence, but a social phenomenon—the production of "an institutionally preferred response" (65). Schooling in the era of alphabetic logocentrism has preferred the analytical response of verification, while suppressing the playful response. It is time to bring these two responses into a relationship of interactive balance.

4. The Life Story

Research on science as an institution, especially with respect to the life experience of scientists, or of any professionals committed to a learned discourse, reveals the inmixing of the three levels (private, public, disciplinary) structuring mystory. Charlotte Linde, for example, investigated the interaction of the popular and schooled (contingent and empirical) registers of discourse by asking professionals to tell the story of how they chose their career. The method was the interview, soliciting an oral autobiography. "The interviews focused on the choice of profession since, at least for middleclass professional speakers, it is a necessary part of one's account of oneself" (346). She finds that the speakers relied principally on "explanatory models," which she distinguishes as existing in a register between common sense and expert knowledge. "An explanatory system is a system of beliefs derived from some expert system but used by someone with no corresponding expertise or credentials" (343).

The level of the explanatory system is exactly the one that E.D. Hirsch, Jr., refers to as the level of "cultural literacy": "cultural literacy lies *above* the everyday levels of knowledge that everyone possesses and *below* the expert level known only to specialists. It is that middle ground of cultural knowledge possessed by the 'common reader' " (Hirsch, 19). In terms of mystory, cultural literacy is carried in the public story, whose function in the society is "monumental," constitutive of the "national character," according to Hirsch. The explanatory or cultural register operates by means of stereotypes, whose important contribution to reasoning has been established by prototype theory (the cognitive psychology upon which Hirsch bases his argument). Teletheory departs from Hirsch, however, on the conception of the pedagogical consequences of this mediating level of thought. In a pedagogy of invention, taught through the genre of mystory, "Custer's Last Stand," for example, which is on Hirsch's list, would not be imposed universally as part of the vocabulary of a nationalist Imaginary community, but would be appropriated individually as a point of departure for a singular allegory. One use of Hirsch's list ("what literate Americans know") for teletheory might be as a partial inventory of public stories that a student might use in the mystory.

Interestingly enough, in our context, the predominant explanatory system used by the professionals to account for their choice of field was Freudian psychoanalysis, in a popularized version, assuming a split self, different levels of personality, with real causes assigned to childhood events. In general, the causal coherence of the life story was provided by the principle of "the unconscious" (356). The other levels of coherence in the story come from basic linguistic categories, and common philosophical assumptions (causality, accident, continuity). To the extent that teletheory involves the construction of a new expert system, then, it is one derived as much from this commonsensical Freud as from the disciplinary Freud. At the same time, it is important to remember that teletheory is designed to promote, within academic discourse, this communication between expert and popular thinking.

At least two aspects of Linde's study are important for teletheory. First is the observation, supported by research from areas as diverse as existentialism and artificial intelligence, that human identity is a function of a life story that people believe in and tell about and to themselves. The story operates less by referentiality than by coherence, has more in common with myth than with history, and is oral rather than written, consisting not of one fixed account but of the relationship among the various stories we tell in an ongoing practice (345). "Derrida at the Little Bighorn" is such a story.

The second, related aspect of Linde's study is her description of the interdependence of the different levels of models. The first step in the development of (invention of) a new expert explanatory system, she says, is the move from common sense and accepted theories, which provide the ground for the innovation (compare Reiss on the emergence of analytico-referential discourse). The new expert system will, at the same time, be in opposition to extant opinion and theory, and be constrained by them (in order to be recognized as a theory at all). Once the system has been articulated, there follows, in some cases, the diffusion from expert into general culture as an explanatory model (consisting of a selective subset of the original, taken out of context). "How this selection takes place is a fascinating question. It seems likely that the common sense of the period affects the selection so that the most radical and startling portions of the theory are *not* chosen" (363). Finally, the explanatory system is absorbed into common sense. Her example for this final turn of the cycle is "the Freudian slip, which seems to be a part of the general, common-sense body of accepted notions and which does not require the support of the Freudian explanatory system to be comprehensible."

The status of Freud here is relevant to my argument concerning the emergence of electronic discourse out of psychoanalysis. Linde's suggestion confounds Timpanaro's assumptions about the slip being a fallacy inconsistent with common sense (as if common sense itself never changed), as well as the notion that Freud's hypotheses need protection from empiricists. Linde herself adds that extensive research is needed to document the cycle she has outlined. "Such research is not currently available for any of the explanatory systems discussed in this paper, although there is some related research on the history of the development of Freud's ideas" (364). Such research might indicate that the diffusion of radical ideas occurs more often than Linde admits. For example, some of Freud's most radical theories about the logic of the unconscious (the logic of learning or invention that informs the pedagogy of teletheory) are conveyed in *The Psychopathology of Everyday Life*, concerning the slips, including, significantly, the processes of forgetting and remembering names. Nor does the assimilation of an explanatory system by common sense indicate the death or "wearing out" of the discourse at the expert level, given the continuing influence of Freud's psycho-linguistics in academic theory.

The point of stress for now is that the cycle evolves full circle, with expert systems deriving as directly from common sense as common sense derives from the explanatory models disseminated from expert systems. Freud is indeed a good case for researching this process, since his program is a thorough mix of materials derived from oral and literate cultures, from daily life and high culture. Especially relevant for euretics (critical invention or making) is the lesson to be learned from the way Freud used a toy—the magic slate—as a model for the relationship between the conscious and unconscious mind; the way he developed a description of dream work modeled after the rebus puzzles published in the daily newspaper.

The diffusion of Freud's discourse at all levels of culture offers an additional lesson for pedagogy as dissemination. Dan Sperber suggests that to survive in culture a representation must have certain qualities. In an oral culture representations must be easily remembered; more difficult representations must be translated into easier ones in order to survive (Sperber, 80). The structure of narrative is memorable, making the tale an optimal form for the storage of information. The technology of literacy removed to some extent this limitation, permitting the development of specialized concepts requiring formal teaching, and finally institutionalization, for their survival. "An institution is the distribution of a set of representations which is governed by representations belonging to the set itself. This is what makes institutions self-perpetuating. Hence to study institutions is to study a particular type of distribution of representations" (87).

Teletheory, approaching pedagogy in terms of the academic apparatus, must design a genre with this institutional frame in mind. Disciplinary concepts, as opposed to the basic concepts of common sense, rely on the cognitive ability, considerably enhanced by technologies of communication, to form meta-representations. Jack Goody stressed the development of criticism that results from this aspect of literacy, which Sperber formulates in his own way: "Doubting and disbelieving involve representing a representation as being improbable or false" (84). Goody's critics, such as Brian Street, in the post-literate context of electronics, call attention to the other aspect of meta-representation in the apparatus: "meta-representational abilities allow humans to process information which they do not fully understand, information for which they are not able at the time to provide a well-formed representation." Sperber's example of this ability to process half-understood concepts is the child who is told that someone has died, but who has no real understanding of "death." The child embeds the defective concept "in a representation of the form, 'it is a fact that Mr. So-and-so has "died", whatever "died" means.' "

Sperber's account may be extended to schooling, to describe the way a student acquires the concepts of a discipline. The problem in this context is that learning by means of the embedding of "defective" (half-understood) concepts gives rise to "conceptual mysteries": "With half-understood ideas, what is known as the 'argument of authority' carries full weight" (84). Whatever the rationality of such concepts, their success of survival, their dissemination or diffusion, depends on authority, and something else equally "irrational"—evocation.

> Evocation can be seen as a form of problem solving: the problem is to provide a more precise interpretation for some half-understood idea. This is done by searching encyclopaedic memory for assumptions and beliefs in the context of which the half-understood idea makes sense. . . . The most evocative representations are those which, on the one hand, are closely related to the subject's

other mental representations, and on the other hand, can never be given a final interpretation. It is these *relevant mysteries,* as they could be described, which are culturally successful. (85)

One of the tasks of teletheory is to turn this dimension of learning as gap-filling or coherence-making to positive account by working explicitly with evocative, relevant mysteries, to exploit their memorability as a feature of pedagogy. The tradition of criticism has attempted to promote one feature of meta-representation while denying the other—promoting doubt while suppressing the role of belief in the acquisition of knowledge. In teletheory both aspects of meta-representation are acknowledged and put to work.

Linde's outline of the cycle of invention—the circulation of concepts through the levels of common sense, expert discourse, and explanatory systems—clarifies a pattern that may be observed in the history of discovery. I want to pursue this notion of the cycle of invention, because it represents the interaction of levels that have to be made an explicit part of academic discourse. Howard Gruber's study of Darwin's "informal" thought, as recorded in his notebooks, supports the idea of the equal importance of the activities of justification and discovery, of what Gruber calls "secondary" and "primary" thinking, associated with the dichotomy of predominant aesthetic styles: classic and romantic. Cultural knowledge may be couched in either of two forms—proposition schemas and image schemas (active in each of the three conceptual registers). Propositional schemas involve causal chains, many details of which may be dropped when the schema is shared (as it is, for example, in the specialized field of biochemistry). The other form involves analogies and figures of all kinds. The choice of analogy, Linde notes, has consequences for reasoning and is as useful for thinking about logical relations as it is for physical or narrative relations. This is one important clue to the new academic discourse. Another such clue is the further role of image schemas in cognitive modeling—"mapping proposition-schemas and image-schemas in given domains onto corresponding structures in other domains" (Holland and Quinn, 27). In teletheory this act of mapping is a mode of translation, moving between expert discourses but also between expert systems and explanatory or commonsense models.

Gerald Holton expresses his insight into the role of personal themata in science in similar terms. He observed, based on a close study of the career of Albert Einstein, that in an invention or discovery "there is a mutual mapping of the style of thinking and acting of the genial scientist on the one hand, and the chief unresolved problems of contemporary science on the other" (Holton, 374). Just as there can be no creativity "in general," nor any science without a discipline of expert knowledge, neither can there be any invention without the dimension of "contingency," expressed in the oral life story.

Einstein's father gave him a compass when he was four years old, a compass that he never forgot, and that became for him a representation of the mystery of electromagnetism that guided him to the formulation of the theory of relativity. Einstein's compass is an emblem of his themata, identified by Holton as the balance between the relative and the fixed. This compass might serve teletheory in turn as an image of wide scope, demonstrating how such images, whatever they are for any given individual, must function. The image is not deterministic, setting a course of blind destiny, but, as with the compass, the very fact that the needle always points north is what allows the traveler to go in any direction, to always know his or her location. The compass and the image of wide scope are most useful when one is lost.

Gruber shows the role played in the invention of the concept of "evolution" by the "images of wide scope" active in Darwin's imagination—images derived from personal and popular culture. Gruber, in accord with Feyerabend's call for the joining of discovery and justification, notes that the mapping of data onto theory is a social, affective process as a methodological activity. Any one individual, as a part of the oral life story, will possess a small set of images of wide scope, four or five at most, that constitute that individual's personal cosmology, and to which he or she is committed by desire and value. If method is important to problem solving, the images of wide scope, with their emotional associations, are vital to the way the problem is represented in the first place. Such images organize the information into complex sets that direct the mapping or translation process of comprehension and learning, and finally of invention. Although Darwin's theory differed radically from the common sense of his day, the images he uses to think his way to that theory were perfectly familiar. The theory of natural selection, it could be said for our purposes, emerged out of an inmixing of Darwin's oral and literate repertoires. His reading of Malthus's *Essay on Population* brought to a level of explicitness the principle in nature Darwin had been working with in terms of such images as the branching tree, the tangled bank of a river, or human warfare (Gruber, 131). Nor are the images merely background, a feature of the discovery phase, but they appear in the formal, written treatise as well, forming an integral part of the theory. The image of the irregularly branching tree was central in the earliest formulations, for example: "'Organized beings represent a tree, irregularly branched. . . . As many terminal buds dying as new ones generated. There is nothing stranger in death of species, than individuals' " (126). The image, Gruber says, accounts for a number of items of theory: "the fortuitousness of life, the irregularity of the panorama of nature, the explosiveness of growth and the necessity to bridle it. And most important, the fundamental duality that at any time some must live and others die."

"An image is 'wide' when it functions as a schema capable of assimilating to itself a wide range of perceptions, actions, ideas. This width depends in part on the metaphoric structure peculiar to the given image, in part on the intensity of the emotion which has been invested in it, that is, its value to the person" (135). Gruber, too, complains about how little such imagery has been studied. He adds that the images are not just passively received, in some sort of deterministic way. They emerge as a part of the life story, but once so selected, "they are constructed, winnowed out, criticized, and reconstructed. They are the product of hard, imaginative, and reflective work, and in their turn they regulate the future course of that work. The scientist needs them in order to comprehend what is known and to guide the search for what is not yet known. He must represent to himself the possible unknowns. . . . The movement from such hypotheses to a conscious delineation of their source-images, marks an important turning point in the growth of any scientific thought process" (136–137). Gruber concludes with a caveat about this process, in a way that supports the goals of teletheory as academic discourse. "Although some images are shared, many are personal. They are so personal that even when the individual displays them openly they may go unnoticed. This is a gloomy picture. . . . But perhaps we have merely not yet lived in a world where thinking men and women really stop to listen to each other or to take long and loving looks at each other's images. Is this impossible?" (138).

One purpose of teletheory is to make personal images accessible, receivable, by integrating the private and public dimensions of knowledge—invention and justification. In the electronic age the academic apparatus may simulate the knowledge cycle that joins private, popular, and disciplinary cultural models, making explicit a situation that the dominant analytical model of pedagogy suppressed. Academic discourse in the new instauration consists of the translation or transference from one language to another. Ideology is understood in this context as the explanatory models used in both oral and literate culture to direct reasoning. The important point for teletheory is to develop a genre that brings these registers together, in which the folk models conveyed principally by oral culture are juxtaposed with the disciplinary models of schooling. The classroom is the mediating zone, of course, mixing oral and literate registers, with the instructions given to children, whether in the home or the school, being, we are told, the most explicit expressions of the models of thought at work in a culture.

To acknowledge Brannigan's point that such accounts are more useful as depictions of learning rather than of invention, since they don't distinguish between successful and unsuccessful ideas or "inventions," we might take note of a similarly original mixing of oral and literate systems that led not to the lionizing of a genius but to the martyrdom of a heretic. I am thinking of the case of the miller, Menocchio, recounted by Carlo Ginzburg, which is another instance of this interaction between the models of the different cultural registers that is a feature of teletheory. Living at the time of the

Counter Reformation, Menocchio produced some radically unconventional ideas in the field of theology, at a time when the decontextualized misrepresentations that characterize explanatory models were cause, if the topic were God, for arrest, torture, and even death. Menocchio's image of wide scope—the one that fascinated Ginzburg when he read the transcripts of the miller's trial by the inquisition—had its origins in the daily life of the period, and was used as the vehicle for Menocchio's oral culture. Indeed, much of the interest of Ginzburg's study has to do with what it tells us about the use a reader from a subordinate culture may make of the texts of the dominant culture, when the latter are read, as they inevitably are, through the models of one's subculture. In Menocchio's cosmogony, "all was chaos, that is, earth, air, water, and fire were mixed together; and out of that bulk a mass formed—just as cheese is made out of milk—and worms appeared in it, and these were the angels. The most holy majesty decreed that these should be God and the angels, and among that number of angels, there was also God" (Ginzburg, 1982: 6). Although the villagers wondered at his originality, and the inquisitors were curious enough about the image to inquire into its features in unusually thorough detail, Menocchio had no followers and founded no church. Nonetheless, Ginzburg's discussion of the interaction of Menocchio's readings with his peasant oral traditions, is valuable as evidence of this process of the cycle of invention in which expert, explanatory, and commonsense models are mapped one onto the other, a cycle to be operated in mystory. "Menocchio mulled over and elaborated on his readings outside any preexistent framework. And his most extraordinary declarations originated form contact with such innocuous texts as Mandeville's *Travels* or the *Historia del Giudicio*. It was not the book as such, but the encounter between the printed page and oral culture that formed an explosive mixture in Menocchio's head" (51).

Ginzburg notes that there was an interesting convergence between the oral tradition of peasant radicalism, the utopianism expressed in Menocchio's testimony, and the most progressive ideas of the Humanists of the period. Both expressed a materialism that was associated with important political and social attitudes. The circulation of books in the newly forming print culture gave Menocchio the boldness to speak out, Ginzburg says, and the oral tradition supplied him with the words. Why that particular analogy of the cheese and the worms? Ginzburg, from the vantage point of scholarship, observes that it has echoes in Dante's *Divine Comedy*; that the idea of spontaneous combustion, explaining the presence of the maggots in the cheese, was a widely accepted explanatory system of the period; that ancient myths describe the origin of the universe in terms of the coagulation of milk; that the myth is confirmed by astrophysics reporting the parallel between the thickening of cheese and of a nebula in the formation of a galaxy. In short, the analogy participates in a paradigm that, had Menocchio been free to work it, as Gruber suggests a scientist would, could have been a powerful guide to the formation of a new expert model. As it was, Ginzburg suggests that the choice of the cheese was motivated in part by the oral tradition in which Menocchio participated, with roots in a shamanistic or primal world view. Whether Menocchio's life story illustrates the role of popular images in learning or invention is perhaps less important, finally, than what it tells us about the role of institutions in the diffusion and suppression of relevant mysteries.

Silvano Arieti brings these various descriptions of the integration of justification and discovery back into the context of psychoanalysis and the primal style in relation to the secondary processes of intellection. In this context we can say that "secondary" orality refers to an orality put to the work of literate intellection. Arieti discusses ideation as a dialectical interplay oscillating between concepts and endocepts—between socially accepted, collective and public sets on one hand, and on the other hand private, inchoate drives— with the interchange mediated by a paleological dimension of primitive cognition that is organized by a non-Aristelian system of dream logic: primal thinking. An idea begins as the merest glimmer, a flash of awareness. To grasp the image, to bring it into awareness so that it may be worked, as Gruber recommends, requires emotional association. The semiotic-pragmatic notion of the "interpretant" suggests how this happens by indicating that our personal experience of things may serve as generalizations about the world—the image of one's pet dog may function as the sign of the concept, the category "dog." A concept thus registered in memory, however, carries an emotional overtone associated with the image and contributes to the operations of that image in thought. It would follow, for example, that Einstein's feelings about his father, associated with the compass, were an integral part of his cogitations on electromagnetism, just as much as were Freud's in his elaboration of the Oedipus complex. The investment, the love we have for such images, in lending palpability to vague formulations, contributes the high excitement, the motivation for the hard work, that sustains productive research (Gruber, 137).

Paleologic is an equal partner in cognition, then, not a lesser mode of thought. It supplements the analytical, conceptual style of thought (functional in the dimension of verification) with a reasoning that draws on the full range of rhetorical and aesthetic procedures. Arieti simplifies the matter by summarizing the two modes as logical and analogical. Analogy, he explains, is essential to invention, as demonstrated in synectics, "the joining together of different and apparently irrelevant elements." Arieti's discussion of Arthur Gordon's synectics includes a point important for teletheory.

Gordon distinguishes four types of analogy: personal, direct, and symbolic analogy, and fantasy. In personal analogy the individual imagines himself to be the material with which he works. For example, Kekulé identified himself in a dream with a snake swallowing its tail, and saw an analogy to the benzene molecule as a ring rather than a chain of carbon atoms. (Arieti, 376)

The exploration of personal analogy is one strategy for the mapping across domains needed in the pedagogy of teletheory, to help construct the themata of one's cognitive style—an element still excluded from the discourse of school. In fact, the Kekulé case is even more suggestive in this regard than Arieti implies, and provides an interesting example of the anecdotal dimension of reason. Meredith Skura, in her discussion of the implications of Kekulé's example for creativity in general, notes that the universal symbol of the snake with its tail in its mouth was invested in Kekulé's life with some powerful emotions. "There was a fire that destroyed the house next to Kekulé's when he was eighteen, killing the countess who lived there. The local investigators, decided that the episode constituted a deliberate murder, connected it with the simultaneous theft of the countess's jewelry—which included a ring in the shape of snakes biting their own tails. Eventually a trial was held, and Kekulé was called as an eye-witness" (Skura, 132).

At the time of the trial Kekulé was living through a disturbing conflict concerning his career choice (the critical plot of the life story), giving up his father's influence in favor of a mentor in chemistry (a continuation of mourning, and the loss of the parents). The story of mourning, that is, always comes up in the drama of men and their fathers. Skura speculates that since this particular conflict was an ongoing problem for Kekulé, it is possible that at the time he had the famous dream he was again experiencing personal difficulties which merged with his efforts to solve (as Holton would say), a major problem of the discipline (chemistry). As he stared into the fire, Skura says, alluding to the circumstances of this classic anecdote in the history of science, the countess's murder stirred in his memory. Skura's conclusion supports Arieti's notion of paleology—the discovery that the benzene molecule had the form of a ring was "the result of very personal, preconditioned, and eccentric ideas working illogically below the level of consciousness to reshape conscious thinking" (133). This story is usually invoked in the philosophy of science to indicate the impossibility of institutionalizing the discovery or invention process in formal schooling. My purpose is to show that the opposite conclusion is necessary—that we must learn how to include the dimension of invention if we are to have a complete education—and reasonable, now that we have a technology that does for the cognition of invention what alphabetic literacy does for critical analysis. Video is the prosthesis of inventive or euretic thinking, just as literacy is the prosthesis of hermeneutics. Such is the premise of teletheory (and one of my objects of explanation).

The murdered countess and her snake ring, associated with Kekulé's discovery, constitute what we will come to call a *mystory*—the contribution of personal anecdotes to problem-solving in a field of specialized knowledge. Kekulé's example includes the elements constituting the curriculum of tele-theory: not only the problems of a given discipline, but also the oral life story, and one more ingredient—a myth, legend, or other story from popular culture (the snake swallowing its tail). In this context we may see the specific lesson a pedagogy may draw from the invention of psychoanalysis, a lesson so basic it does not depend on whether or not Freud was "correct." What counts is the example he sets for the process of invention itself. Kekulé, Einstein, and everyone else, if Holton is right, could not have solved a single scientific problem without an inmixing of mystory with the history of a discipline. Freud is especially significant, however, as the first innovator to propose a system of knowledge and an institution (psychoanalysis) whose subject and object are one and the same: Freud's own story.

What is Freud's invention? It consists of the generalization of his peculiar, personal, familial story, mediated through a literary text (and myth) into an expert system of medical science. The example, joining strong emotional experience, associated most directly with the death of his father (the event that motivated his self-analysis and ultimately the writing of *The Interpretation of Dreams*), with a cultural text and an unsolved problem in a discipline of knowledge (sexual dysfunction, hysteria), may serve as a guide to our genre. What teletheory learns from Freud (and from all the other exemplars discussed in this section) has to do with the convergence of the styles and languages of general culture (in both its high and popular modes) and academic knowledge with a life story. What the examples show is that this integration of registers of thought and experience *happens*. Mystory brings this process into academic discourse so that it may be artificially developed, democratized, extended to normal schooling for everyday use.

Chapter 2

Conduction

1. The Voice of the Code

I am conducting an experiment, defined originally by Hayden White, to invent a new historiography. I have chosen to make this an historiography of learning, called "mystory." An experiment in mystoriography derives its guidelines from the sciences and arts of our time, just as "history" was invented based on the naturalistic tenets of nineteenth-century science and art. In the previous chapter we reviewed the history of method and a description of a mode of thought emerging or reemerging in our time. Especially important for mystory is the insight into the circulation through the oral and literate registers of sense that occurs in the social and psychological development of inventions, epitomized by Freud's invention of psychoanalysis, but equally manifested in the natural sciences. This new style of thought, called "oralysis," is writable in video, in the same way that analysis is writable in alphabetic literacy.

I do not want to move too quickly to a conclusion, nor will turning to the sample at the end stand in for the work of making the genre in general. Such is the pleasure of theory, fortunately, since so far we have only seen the features of electronic thinking from the outside, in terms of the arguments justifying the existence of teletheory. The next step is to specifically work out the features of the cognition that reasons oralytically. The assumptions directing this question, following the problematic of the apparatus, is that the age of television is emerging in pieces, separated and scattered through the domains of technology, ideology, and institutional practices—specifically in video, psychoanalysis, and postmodernist art and theory. The aim of teletheory is to assist this process, looking for leverage in the area closest to hand—academic discourse.

There is no need to assume that I already know how to tell a life story. First I need to focus more specifically on the problem of the new instauration, to locate and identify exactly how an electronic discourse might emerge out of psychoanalysis and the extant, dominant mode of cognition. The description of the codes of classic (readerly) narrative developed in Roland Barthes's *S/Z* is the point of departure for this specification. Taking a short story by Balzac as his tutor text, Barthes provided an analysis of the Realism that emerged as the narrative equivalent of the analytico-referential discourse. Barthes claimed no taxonomic privilege for his codes, but they have proven to be useful for the discussion of narrative in film as well as in print. They also allow us to identify the precise location best suited for grafting a new genre onto the old forms.

The five codes are distributed across the two axes of language, following a structuralist or alphabetic model of discourse—arrangement by columns and rows. Two of the codes represent the organization of the syntagmatic axis (the syntactical, linear movement of action and plot). The other three codes represent the organization of the paradigmatic axis (the selection of terms from a set of possible terms). Each of these codes (or "voices," as Barthes called them), turns out to be a formalization of a "simple" or "oral" form, a fact which, once noted, raises to an even higher power the explanatory function of Barthes's example.

The emergence of a new discourse is not something hypothetical, but a specific process operating in the material forms of culture. As Robert Scholes and Robert Kellogg explained, the forms of alphabetic literacy consist of unstable composites of simple forms.

> The novel is not the opposite of romance, but a product of the reunion of the empirical and fictional elements in narrative literature. Mimesis and history combine in the novel with romance and fable, even as primitive legend, folktale, and sacred myth originally combined in the epic, to produce a great and synthetic literary form. There are signs that in the twentieth century the grand dialectic is about to begin again [between the empirical and fictional impulses], and that the novel must yield its place to new forms just as the epic did in ancient times, for it is an unstable compound, inclining always to break down into its constituent elements. (Scholes and Kellogg, 15)

Like the novel, the essay is an unstable composite of simple forms (both oral and literate), its elements consisting of example, dialogue, proverb, letter, diatribe, quotation (Haas, 6). The essay and novel are the two principal forms of high literacy, invented to exploit fully the specific virtues of the print apparatus. Both are disintegrating in the culture of electronics, creating a reservoir of simple forms available for new combinations reflecting the capabilities of a new apparatus. The interplay of empirical and fictional impulses in the new instauration is producing a hybrid that crosses the received boundary separating fiction from non-fiction, novel from essay. Mystory, the genre to be invented in teletheory, demonstrates one version of this new combination of simple forms.

The first step toward organizing this new genre is to identify the simple forms associated with each of the codes Barthes used to describe the weave of the text in his tutor narrative, "Sarrasine," by Balzac. Barthes shared the view that realist fiction is a composite of simple forms, although he does not elaborate explicitly on this aspect of "text." Besides noting that the codes are "voices" (suggesting their "oral" nature), he did associate one code—the referential or cultural code—with one simple form—the proverb, an insight of the first importance.

> The utterances of the cultural code are implicit proverbs: they are written in that obligative mode by which the discourse states a general will, the law of a society, making the proposition concerned ineluctable or indelible. Further still: it is because an utterance can be transformed into a proverb, a maxim, a postulate, that the supporting cultural code is discoverable: stylistic transformation "proves" the code, bares its structure, reveals its ideological perspective. What is easy for proverbs (which have a very special syntactical, archaistic form) is much less so for the other codes of discourse, since the sentence-model, the example, the paradigm expressing each of them has not (yet) been isolated. (Barthes, 1974: 100)

The referential code is the one that dates most obviously. Thus, for example, the racist code organizing D. W. Griffith's *The Birth of a Nation* (1915) and its proverb ("would you want your sister to marry one?") is easily read off the surface of the film, although at one time its lesson might have seemed common sense, natural.

Once the parallel has been pointed out between a code and an oral form, it may not be as difficult as Barthes suggested to identify the sentence-model of each of the other codes: Code of Action = anecdote; Code of Enigma = riddle; Code of Semes = figures (metaphor/metonym); Code of Reference = proverb; Code of Symbol = joke. One implication of this juxtaposition of codes and simple forms is the possibility of identifying more codes by noting how some of the other simple forms organize dimensions of narrative. There is no need to try to demonstrate all these alignments systematically, nor to extrapolate from them to still further codes. The interest of the association for me is in the organization of the symbolic code by means of the joke.

The site of the emergence of an electronic discourse, I am proposing, based on the notion of a reorganization of learning discernible in Freud, is the symbolic code of narrative. As Julia Lesage reminds us, the symbolic code is based on the theories of structural psychoanalysis, or Lacan's reading of Lévi-Strauss and the latter's application of linguistics to a reading of social and cultural phenomena. Freud's discourse, psychoanalysis, the logic of the unconscious, may be transformed in the symbolic code of a mystorical text, translated from the analytico-referential paradigm into the new paradigm of electronics, becoming the basis for a new cognition. How is this code organized?

> According to Barthes one can enter the symbolic field of the text on any of three levels: language, kinship or sex, and commercial economy. Language operates on the basis of an economy that is "usually protected by the separation of opposites," i.e. paradigms. The major rhetorical device which carries the symbolic motifs of the text is the antithesis, each term of which is exclusive and fully meaningful in its own right. Middle-ground figures transgress the antithesis, "pass through the wall of opposites," and abolish difference. . . . In the classical narrative, representation depends on an order of just equivalencies, by means of which we can regularly distinguish contraries, sexes, and possessions. Yet it is only when an excessive element enters which interrupts the normal circulation of the antithesis, sexes, property relations, or contracts that the narrative begins. (Lesage, 494)

The location of this code within narrative, specifying the dimension of discourse that operates by and is the vehicle for the stylistic and cognitive qualities described by psychoanalysis (appropriated in teletheory as the logic of the unconscious), is a major assistance to my attempt to define a genre of the new instauration. It is relevant to teletheory first in that the symbolic in Lacan's theory names that register of law and institutions into which one gains entrance by the acquisition of language. The entry into language is associated with the process of mourning and all the other psychoanalytic concepts of the Oedipal stage. I want to suggest that the learning of an academic, specialized language replays the entry into language of the infant, reactivating, renegotiating the mourning process experienced in the original entry into everyday discourse.

This context helps clarify the possibility, noted in the discussion of Feyerabend, of learning the terms of a new cognition the way a child learns a first language. This learning involves in each case a passage from the imaginary to symbolic: "the symbolic realm involves a displacement away from this imaginary fix, a de-centering of the ego's place as the center of the self, to relationships, not of possession but of exchange" (Nichols, 1981: 32). At the same time this context reminds us of the "ideology effect" of cinema, of how, through the processes of recognition and identification with respect to both the content and the production of a text, the individual subject is positioned within the dominant belief system of the culture.

Barthes's codes also suggest a direction for the experimental invention of a new genre for academic discourse, which may be seen in the distinction between the readerly and writerly modes.

> The readerly text is a *tonal* text (for which habit creates a reading process just as conditioned as our hearing: one might say there is a *reading* eye as there is a

tonal ear, so that to unlearn the readerly would be the same as to unlearn the tonal), and its tonal unity is basically dependent on two sequential codes: the revelation of truth and the coordination of the actions represented: there is the same constraint in the gradual order of melody and in the equally gradual order of the narrative sequence. Now, *it is precisely this constraint which reduces the plural of the classic text.* . . . The classic text, therefore, is actually tabular (and not linear), but its tabularity is vectorized, it follows a logico-temporal order. It is a multivalent but incompletely reversible system. What blocks its reversibility is just what limits the plural nature of the classic text. These blocks have names: on the one hand, truth; on the other, empiricism: against—or between—them, the modern text comes into being. (Barthes, 1974: 30)

The readerly text is "tabular," which is to say that it is alphabetic, exploiting the full range of the columns and rows of print technology. The challenge of the writerly (modern) text is to imagine a discourse that functions without the code of truth (without the syntagmatic constraints on plurality of meaning). "Who," Feyerabend asked, "has the fortitude, or even the insight, to declare that 'truth' might be unimportant, and perhaps even undesirable?" (Feyerabend, 171). This question makes considerably more sense when it is posed in terms of Barthe's code of truth, the hermeneutic code (the code being replaced in teletheory by the euretic code). Is a euretic *code* a contradiction in terms? Can invention be codified and produced out of stereotypes? To imagine a text organized by euretics rather than by truth requires a reordering of relationships among the simple forms, producing a different event out of a different enunciation.

The point of departure for the invention of a new academic discourse, then, might begin with a dismantling (to remove the mantle of "his majesty the ego") of the dominant forms of narrative and argument fostered in the alphabetic apparatus. It is evident that narratives explain and that explanations narrate, so the formal symmetry between narration and exposition comes as no surprise. The comparison is clearest at the level of the simple forms. Labov's analysis of the parts of the anecdote, for example, includes:

1. *abstract:* a short summary of the story, encapsulating the point of the story and alerting the listener that a narrative is about to begin.

2. *orientation:* identifies the time, place, persons, and their activity or situation, occurring immediately before the first narrative clause.

3. *complicating action:* a temporal sequencing between narrative clauses involving the core of the story.

4. *evaluation:* interruptions in the story that reaffirm the tellability of the narrative or assess the situation, either in the form of an external commentary, or by statements embedded in the story itself.

5. *resolution:* the conclusion of the narrative.

6. *coda:* closes the sequences of complicating actions, completing the story such that everything has been accounted for. (Pratt, 45–49)

A standard description of the form of argument follows the same arrangement and strategy: an introduction of the thesis; an account of the relevant factors of background or context; the presentation of proofs, with specific evidence of how a solution fits the relevant facts; an epilogue, summarizing the implications of the presentation. The ingredients of a persuasive argument, that is, are similar to the makings of a good story.

A juxtaposition of Barthes's codes with the elements of classical rhetoric extend this parallel.

Narrative	Argument
Action Code—sequence of acts; initial situation destabilized due to excess or lack; locigal fallacy: post hoc, propter hoc.	*Reasoning*—demonstration, comparison and contrast, cause/effect, logical fallacies for persuasive effect.
Enigma—Code of truth: reader's desire to know how things come out; posing and delay of puzzles.	*Problem*—thesis: states a need for a solution to a difficulty, or for an explanation of a situation.
Semes—props that establish character; thematics, metonyms.	*Ethos*—moral appeal to character, authority; proof by analogy, image.
Reference—pragmatics, reception; commonplaces, receivedwisdom, doxa. Verisimilitude established by the correlation of representation with popular beliefs and stereotypes.	*Pathos*—verification by appeal to opinion, showing that the claims of the reasoning correspond to beliefs, couched in appeals to emotion.
Symbolic	*Logos*
1—ordering by antithesis; narratives pose and resolve contradictions or paradoxes (mythology).	1—contradiction: a principle resource of argument is to locate contradictions in a target text. enthymemes (suppressed premise).
2—ordering by exchange; contracts govern three levels of relationships among the characters: language, economics, kinship.	2—address: direct or indirect commentary, evaluation, favoring exchange of values; position reader dependent on expert.

One way to produce a writerly narrative, according to Barthes, is to drop the two sequential or syntagmatic codes—the codes of action and truth—a generative strategy that could be extended to the classical essay. The intended effect of the classical or readerly narrative—realism—corresponds, of course, to the effect of truth produced by the readerly essay. The above chart indicates that the equivalent in the essay for dropping the codes of action and enigma would be to somehow argue in the absence of the usual connectives of reasoning and without the statement of a specific goal (a problem to be solved). Formally in both cases the materials of discourse are delinearized, and one question might concern how a writerly essay would handle the diachrony of development. Julia Lesage's observation of the temporal dimension of the symbolic code offers one solution:

> To a large degree the semes can be read synchronically, on the level of the single image or on the level of the shot. The symbols, however, especially in the working out of the antitheses, mediations, and transgressions, proceed diachronically. Substitutions, such as those of figures serving as doubles, are worked out on the syntagmatic level, and are frequently metonymic substitutions in which the whole is represented by a related part. (Lesage, 497)

In other words, the temporal, sequential development of the text may be ordered by means of the symbolic code, in the absence of the syntagmatic narrative codes of Action and Truth, or the argumentative rhetoric of problem and demonstration. The usual defense of breaking with the code of realism in fact tends to be made in terms of the code of truth, as for example in Baudry's contrast between the ideology effect (identification and recognition of the social taken as "natural") with the knowledge effect (awareness of the production of meaning). Most critiques of realism rely, that is, on the concept of critical thinking which is as much a feature of the alphabetic apparatus as is the style of realism, invoking the values of distanced self-awareness. Teletheory is an experiment with a different approach to the critique of realism, attempting to represent the issue without depending itself on the same code as its target. (In this context most critiques of realism amount to parodies).

To drop the codes of action and truth for the organization of knowledge, then, will require the writer to find an alternative for the logic of classical reasoning, and for the interest of problem solving. This alternative may be constructed in the symbolic code, drawing on the formal and social features of the joke, the simple form organizing this code.

2. The Joke

The full importance to teletheory of the description of both the anecdote and the argument in terms of Barthes's codes may now be seen in the context of Jolles's description of the modalities or moods of the simple forms.

	Interrogative	Indicative	Silence	Imperative	Optative
Realist	Case	Saga	Riddle	Proverb	Fable
Idealist	Myth	Anecdote	Joke	Legend	Fairy Tale

The key insight provided by this table is the classification of both the riddle (the simple form organizing the code of truth) and the joke (the simple form organizing the symbolic code) in the modality of silence. The "realist" register refers to items designated as possible, capable of happening, while the "idealist" register refers to items that escape the concern for truth (Jolles, 8). For my purposes, that the joke operates within the same modality as the riddle, but without the constraints of truth, makes its ability to take over the direction of a euretic academic discourse all the more probable. In any case, one of the more fruitful legacies of structuralism is the insight, derived from folklore studies, that these oral forms mediate between the levels of the sentence and the level of literate forms; that they function as minimal units of organization at this intermediate level both for purposes of generation and of analysis of texts. The juncture of oral and literate forms in structuralism is in fact a symptom of the adjustments our culture is making to the electronic apparatus, which tends to be organized more by oral performance than by written forms.

What remains unclear in this classification is the precise nature of the mood of silence. In the absence of any clue from Jolles, we may speculate. The mood of a verb "refers to the way writers present their ideas and information," stressing either factuality or counter-factuality, wishes, commands, or questions. But what about the mood of silence? Does it suggest a statement free of the speaker's presence, that is, in which the position of enunciation is left unoccupied? Or, it is not that the enunciation is left unmarked, but that it comes from the culture itself, in the cases of the riddle and the joke, from the discourse of the Other (the Symbolic order of the unconscious). The ambiguity of this grammatical category opens an opportunity to develop in teletheory a linguistic allegory of the kind suggested by Barthes, who sometimes used

> a pseudo-linguistics, a metaphorical linguistics: not that grammatical concepts seek out images in order to express themselves, but just the contrary, because these concepts come to constitute allegories, a second language, whose abstraction is diverted to fictive ends: the most serious of the sciences, the one which is responsible for the very being of language and supplies a whole portion of austere names, is also a reservoir of images, and as a poetic language enables you to utter what is strictly your desire. (Barthes, 1977a: 124)

By way of example Barthes noted "an affinity between 'neutralization,' a notion which allows the linguist to explain very scientifically the loss of meaning in certain pertinent oppositions, and the *Neutral,* an ethical category which is necessary in order to erase the intolerable scar of the paraded meaning, of the oppressive meaning" (124).

Theoretical invention relies upon just such strategies in order to imagine a mystory. The linguistic allegory in our case concerns "mood," then, the mood of the Symbolic register, which Barthes described using Lacanian psychoanalysis, having to do with the entry into language, the symbolic order, and the Law of the Father. It tells the Oedipal story, in other words, the story of the Sphinx and its riddle. Its mood is that of mourning and melancholia. It is now possible to state directly the material event and task of teletheory, which is to devise a genre in which the entry into the Symbolic is conducted not in terms of the riddle (with its features of examination and catechism, as Jolles noted), but the joke (with its manner of "untying knots" and "loosening intelligibility" through play). It will still be the mood of silence, in this allegorical linguistics, but no longer inflected with melancholy, and no longer needing to mourn. Here we have the specific, immediate terms of the experiment. The project is not to do everything, to speculate on electronic cosmology or write science fiction, but to attempt something quite precise—to extract from the symbolic code of narrative, reordered from riddle to joke, the prototype of a new genre for academic discourse.

In teletheory Freud's *Jokes and their Relation to the Unconscious* is read as a treatise on one of the oral forms, indicating the special importance of the joke to psychoanalysis. The first thing most students observe about *Jokes* is how unfunny it is, both in its own style and in the examples it provides. This lack of humor is just the effect that needs to be explored in order to clarify the operations of joking in teletheory. Freud himself, in any case, called attention to the peculiar character of the wit that interested him.

> But where does this bewildering resemblance between dreams and jokes come from? This necessitated my making a thorough investigation into the question of wit itself. Wit originates as follows: a preconscious train of thought is for a moment left to a process of unconscious elaboration. While under the influence of the unconscious it is subject to the mechanism there operative—to condensation and displacement. But the unintentional "dream joke" does not amuse us as does an ordinary witticism: a deeper study of wit may show you why this is so. The "dream joke" strikes us as a poor form of wit; it does not make us laugh, it leaves us cold. (Freud, 1963: 210)

The joke in teletheory is not an embellishment but a textual structure, organizing the exchanges of the symbolic code, with a capacity for extension into the most complex workings of the academic apparatus. The virtue of the simple form is that it enables us to imagine more specifically the operations of this code, using the joke as a model of our invention in the same way Freud did in inventing "dream work."

One point to emphasize is the relation of the joke to logic—the joke as false reasoning, resulting in a form capable of evading the inhibitions and compulsions of reason and criticism. This evasion applies in everyday life to the inhibitions of common sense, a feature that teletheory adapts to an evasion of the inhibitions of expert systems. "We have already found from two groups of examples that the joke-work makes use of deviations from normal thinking—of displacement and absurdity—as technical methods for producing a joking form of expression. It is no doubt justifiable to expect that other kinds of faulty reasoning may find a similar use" (Freud, 1963a: 60). Freud's observation was anticipated by the ancient rhetoricians such as Quintillian, who noted that every mode of argument could also produce a joke (Olbrechts-Tyteca, 24). Many others since then have suggested that jests are structurally the equivalent of fallacies, including Jolles who stated that anything that logic tied wit could untie (Jolles, 199).

The joke, then, represents a certain kind of thinking, whose character has been described by John Allen Paulos.

> To get a joke, one must ascend, so to speak, to the metalevel at which both interpretations, the familiar and the incongruous, can be imagined and compared. . . . The various interpretations and their incongruity of course depend critically on the context, the prior experience of the person(s) involved, their values, beliefs, and so on.
>
> The necessity of this psychic stepping back (or up) to the metalevel is probably what is meant when people say that a sense of perspective is needed for an appreciation of humor. It also explains why dogmatists, idealogues, and others with one-track minds are often notoriously humorless. People whose lives are dominated by one system or one set of rules are stuck in the object level of their system. (Paulos, 27)

Paulos uses René Thom's "catastrophe theory" to graph the short-circuiting event of getting a joke.

> All these properties—catastrophic jumps between two layers, divergence, hysteresis, and an inaccessible gap—are sequence of the general shape of the graph; and the general shape is dictated by Thom's theorem, which stipulates that any quantity (behavior) that depends on two factors, is discontinuous, and satisfies certain mild general conditions must give rise to this shape. . . .whether the catastrophes are stock market crashes or recoveries, cathartic releases of anger or anxiety attacks, decisions to go to war or decisions to stop fighting, the cusp catastrophe model is often applicable. (84)

The cusp, then, is the *eidos,* the shape, of the joke.

This property of switching levels has been described in a variety of other ways. Freud stated the process as a "short-circuit between two sets" (Freud,

1963a: 119). Umberto Eco notes that metaphors and jokes function similarly by means of superimposing disparate frames or semantic fields, thus producing "a shortcut through the encyclopedic network, a labyrinth which would take away too much time if it were to be explored in all its polydimensional complexity" (Eco, 1984: 120). One of the best, and simplest, illustrations of this shortcut or switching between unrelated or non-contiguous domains— a principal feature of jokes—is the pun. The pun, of course, is said to be the least funny of all joke types. "A convenient way to conceive of puns is in terms of the intersection of two sets. A pun is a word or phrase that belongs to two or more distinct universes of discourse and thus brings *both* to mind. The humor, if there is any, results from the inappropriate and incongruous sets of associated ideas jarring each other" (Paulos, 61).

The nonsense generated by short-circuits in the encyclopedia of culture can be, as Susan Stewart explains, an essential part of learning, keeping in mind that "nonsense" is always relative to common sense, both categories being defined by social context. Learning about learning requires decontextualization, which may be achieved as much by play as by scientific taxonomy. The virtue of nonsense, especially of the "mistake-on-purpose" of joking and other forms of discursive play, for pedagogy is its familiarity as a mode of everyday life experience. These simple forms, that is, can be used for critical effect, exposing the location and manner of formation of our cultural frames and the shared assumptions of traditions. Nonsense is not a matter of content, but of relationships between domains, generated by the violation of boundaries.

Stewart's insight into the quality of nonsense as metacommunication is important to teletheory for at least two reasons. First, it identifies one way to move between the registers of thought in the cycle of knowledge dissemination described by Linde. The passage from common sense to expert systems to explanatory systems is not continuous—is not "rational" or logical—but nonsensical in the formal sense of the term used by Stewart. In the symbolic code nonsense organizes the transgression of antitheses in discourse.

The second reason that it is important to emphasize the role of nonsense in learning has to do with the politics of the institution. Secretary of Education William Bennett recently received national coverage in the newspapers of his charges that the curriculum of colleges and universities has been debased by the replacement of the classics by "trendy, soft-headed courses." "Some of these intellectual movements claim to spring from 'serious thinkers such as Karl Marx but look more like they spring from Groucho Marx in collaboration with Daffy Duck.' " Bennett cited George Orwell referring to "nonsense so bad only an intellectual could believe it. Welcome to some of our universities." Some of the college presidents at this talk defended the university as "an arena where nonsense could be spoken, debated and, conceivably, refuted." It is important to note the different senses in which the parties to this debate seem to be using the term "nonsense." In teletheory, in any case, nonsense is assigned a specific role for which Groucho Marx is indeed one of the principal tutors.

What is this role? Formally a joke constitutes a kind of false proof, an abuse of logic. Its particular attraction, for a project designed to integrate the cognitive styles of justification and invention, is that wit occurs precisely through the meeting of logical and paleological processes.

> In the creation of a joke, the creative process is based on the following: 1) primary-process mechanisms, or cognitive mechanisms that are usually discarded because of their faults, become available to the creative person; 2) out of the primary-process and/or faulty cognitive mechanisms that have become available, the creative person is able to select those which give the fleeting impression of being valid secondary-process mechanism. The amused response on the part of the listener occurs when he realizes the invalidity of the thought processes—when he recognizes the logic-paleologic discordance. The creative process of wit consists of putting together the primary- and secondary-process mechanisms and automatically comparing them. The comparison reveals the discordance and provokes laughter. (Arieti, 112)

Concept formation in paleologic does not follow "Leibniz's law," Arieti says: "'X is identical to Y if X has every property that Y has and Y has every property that X has.'" Rather, items are gathered into sets on the basis of Von Domarus's principle: "'X is identical to Y if X has at least one property that Y has and Y has at least one property that X has'" (117). This context gives new meaning to Barthes's statement that outside the paradigm of realist criticism it was not a question of subject/object but subject/predicate. As Arieti reminds us, jokes draw on the same cognitive mechanisms that occur in a range of related phenomena, including, besides logical reasoning itself, psychopathological discourse, paleological processes such as puns, the various fallacies such as reasoning with false premises, and logical thinking joined with additional facts that invalidate the premises.

Arthur Koestler was one of those who worked out in detail the relationship between wit and creativity, suggesting that the best simulation of the experience of original thinking, of having an insight, was getting a joke (similarly, the sense of *timing* required for an effective joke simulates the temporality of invention, of grasping the opportunity just when it presents itself). Koestler's discussion is relevant to teletheory, except that I would identify the activity in question not so much as "creativity" but as "learning" and "inventing" (in the rhetorical sense of supplying a reserve with raw materials for composition). The act of "creation," according to Koestler, involves a "bisociation of ideas," the juxtaposition of two semantic sets not previously related one to the other. The structure of juxtaposition producing tension within a single thought works, he suggested, in art, wit, and science alike. Some of the examples of the possibility that discoveries "are syntheses of commonplace events with theoretically important contexts" include Archimedes' bathtub, Gutenberg's application of the wine press to the task of printing, Kepler's joining of astronomy and physics, and even Darwin's application of Malthus to plant and animals species variation (Brannigan, 28). Bisociation, Brannigan notes, is valuable in learning, even if it is not a sufficient condition to explain discovery, since it may produce error as well as success. The distinction is important, however, only if one wants to maintain discovery and justification as absolutely separate dimensions of thought (which has been the case in the educational apparatus until now). The crucial point for teletheory, of course, is the association of the cognitive style of learning and invention with the form of the joke and wit.

There remains one more connection to make, in order to complete the rationale for teletheory as a search for a new academic discourse adequate to the age of television. If the learning process corresponds to the structure of wit, so too do the formal features of the video/film medium. In other words, there is an affinity, if not a necessary relationship, between the dream work of psychoanalysis and video representation, in the same way that there is an affinity between alphabetical technology and critical reason, as described by Jack Goody.

Charles Altman reminds us that the comparison between films and dreams goes back at least to Hugo Münsterberg (1916), and continues into the present in the later work of Christian Metz and other versions of psycho-semiotics. For his part Altman is suspicious of all reasoning by analogy in general, and specifically of the analogy between the psyche and cinema. In this analogy,

> The cinematic signifier is like the Imaginary Other of the mirror state [in Lacan's theory], the cinematic apparatus recalls that of dreams, the cinema-viewing situation makes each of us a voyeur witnessing the primal scene. Such analogizing performs an essential function . . . focusing cinema's various aspects around a single constitutive metaphor (the cinema apparatus equals the psychic apparatus), thus providing the cinematic experience with a unity which it otherwise would lack. . . . As a method of reasoning, analogy presents the constant danger that critical language will remain a prisoner of Imaginary relationships. (Altman, 530–531)

Altman may be right about the status of reasoning in alphabetic criticism, in which the subject and the object are kept apart. Bill Nichols, editor of the authoritative anthology, *Movies and Methods,* representing in two volumes the best or most representative work of film studies as a discipline, supports Altman's point in a way that indicates the unity, Imaginary or not, of film studies, on the matter of what counts as critical thinking. The knowledge effect tends always to be defined in terms of alphabetic and verificationist values, as in Nichols's praise for the films of Emile de Antonio. "The film's own consciousness (surrogate for ours) probes, remembers, substantiates, doubts. It questions and believes, including itself. It assumes the voice of personal consciousness at the same time as it examines the very category of the personal. Neither omniscient deity nor obedient mouthpiece, de Antonio's rhetorical voice seduces us by embodying those qualities of insight, skepticism, judgment, and independence we would like to appropriate for our own" (Nichols, 1985: 268). In short, de Antonio has managed to harness film to do the work of literacy, to create distance that demythologizes, playing the code of truth against the code of realism. At the same time, Nichols is well aware of the same limitations on alphabetic science noted by Jack Goody, which may not be overcome except by a change of apparatus: "the most recent appearances of self-reflexive strategies correspond very clearly to deficiencies in attempts to translate highly ideological, written anthropological practices into a proscriptive agenda for a visual anthropology (neutrality, descriptiveness, objectivity, 'just the facts,' and so on)" (272).

Nichols is interested in political films more than in scientific ones, which for him implies posing documentaries as a cinema of consciousness against the fiction narratives of a cinema of unconsciousness. The goal of teletheory, based on the premise that video must develop its own model of intelligence, is to formulate a new synthesis of fiction and nonfiction, of paleologic and logic, whose primary application will be in teaching. In this context it is necessary to stay provisionally with the analogy between psychoanalysis and film/video, and with analogical reasoning as such, in part because, as demonstrated at length by Susan Stewart, for example, the nonsense of paleologic is as powerful a strategy for decontextualization and reflexivity (the criteria for a cinema of intelligence invoked by Nichols) as are the procedures of analytical methodology. The other reason is that there is one more mode of movement between the registers of the knowledge cycle; one more besides nonsense—what Lacan calls, in a pun, bliss-sense (jouissance, jouis-sens). Bliss-sense names that affective unconscious involved in the logic of identification, transference, and the drives of desire that inform the subject of knowledge, the subject who wants to know, which teletheory also attempts not to strip from learning but to acknowledge and tap for the representation of invention.

The analogy between psychoanalysis and television in teletheory, continuing from the psyche-cinema relationship in film studies, should be specified as the borrowing of Freud's discovery/invention of the logic of the unconscious for the purpose of describing the logic most compatible with, most specific to, the format of video technology. Whatever the usefulness of the concept of the discourse of the unconscious might be in psychoanalysis, in teletheory it is adapted as a model for the language of invention scriptable in video. Historically it could be said that the discourse and the technology were invented more or less simultaneously and independently, and have only gradually come together in development that is still underway.

Freud's position in the history of method is that, with him, method— the achievement of analytico-referential discourse—was ready finally to recognize, to readmit, patterning to the status of knowledge. As Freud said in the introduction to his Dream Book, dreams at one time constituted a major element of knowledge, and he was prepared to reopen the question of that knowledge again. If the comparison between filmic language and the language of dreams or of the unconscious is as commonplace as is the relationship between primal and creative thinking, it is still worth remembering that cinema and psychoanalysis arose simultaneously as independent institutions, in a way that inevitably suggests participation in the same paradigm relevant to the new instauration. They may have arisen independently, but there has been considerable interinfluence ever since. On the side of film practice there is the example of surrealism, of course, but even more important for my purposes is the influence of Freud on Sergel Eisenstein, who was deeply affected by Freud's study of Leonardo. In his development of "intellectual montage"—a style that would be capable of putting on the screen and making available for the illiterate masses of Russia the theoretical writings of Marx, Eisenstein came to recognize the similarity of filmic logic, created through editing within and between shots, to primal (or primitive) thinking. Eisenstein believed that only in the new medium of film could the separation between science and the arts (we might say between science and the discourse of patterning) be resolved in a hybrid discourse. Drawing on the Soviet psychology of the day, including Vygotsky and Luria, and the concept of "inner speech" (whose description, again, shares the features of primal thinking), Eisenstein designed a style that represented the very movements or dynamics of thought, in which concept formation functioned in terms of story telling.

The forms of sensual, pre-logical thinking, which are preserved in the shape of inner speech among the peoples who have reached an adequate level of social and cultural development, at the same time also represent in mankind at the dawn of culture developmental norms of conduct in general, i.e., the laws according to which flow the processes of sensual thought are equivalent for them to a "habit logic" of the future. In accordance with these laws they construct norms of behavior, ceremonials, customs, speech, expressions, etc., and, if we turn to the immeasurable treasury of folklore, of outlived and still living norms and forms of behavior preserved by societies still at the dawn of their development, we find that, what for them has been or still is a norm of behavior and custom-wisdom, turns out to be at the same time precisely what we employ as "artistic methods" and "techniques of embodiment" in our art-works. (Eisenstein, 131)

Eisenstein's example suggests that the affinity of the film-psyche analogy influenced some filmmakers as much as it did certain theorists, such that it seems almost redundant to theorize film in terms of psychoanalysis. Or rather, psychoanalysis cannot serve as a hermeneutics of film, but only as a euretics. Film, that is, is psychoanalysis by other means. Walter Benjamin's comparison of psychoanalysis and film shows the optimistic side of the equation, holding out the hope for film as a cognitive medium.

The film has enriched our field of perception with methods which can be illustrated by those of Freudian theory. Fifty years ago, a slip of the tongue passed more or less unnoticed. . . . Since the *Psychopathology of Everyday Life* things have changed. This book isolated and made analyzable things which had heretofore floated along unnoticed in the broad stream of perception. For the entire spectrum of optical, and now also acoustical, perception the film has brought about a similar deepening of apperception. (Benjamin, 1969: 235)

Benjamin added that one of the revolutionary functions of film would be "to demonstrate the identity of the artistic and scientific uses of photography which heretofore usually were separated" (236). He also observed that the illiterate of the future would be one who did not know how to take a photograph.

Dream-work, as Lacan and the movement of structuralist psychoanalysis have shown, amounts to a generic codification of the organizing principles of a wide range of non-analytical texts, including dreams, jokes, myths, all the forms of everyday life, as well as of the arts. One of Freud's methods, that is, was to construct the operations of the unconscious by means of analogy with the forms and rhetoric of both oral and literate culture.

If the film is similar to dreams it is because of its mode of presentation. . . . Freud pointed out the essence of dream work: condensation and displacement. With this he may have alluded to dream's affinity to all artistic activity, for his entire psychoanalytic method may, in some respect, be considered the working out of the science of tropes: metaphors and their variations. Freud proved that consciousness can operate without logic but not without some guiding dream-image, which also controls the realm that gives birth to logic. The subconscious does not know "because," or "but," etc.—those peculiar conjunctions of syntactic logic—yet the order of relationships is expressed very clearly. Similarities and oppositions appear as images in the dream unifying the various elements. (Biró, 103)

Reiss pointed out that the development of the analytico-referential discourse actually involved the invention of conceptual thinking—it devised the form and style by which a certain way of representing and ordering thought could be systematized. Freud's project similarly reflects the invention of an alternative mode of thought, whose form, style, and function are still in the process of development. Taking dream-work as the logic of primal thinking, my argument is that the film or video media provide the technology for primal Writing. Such Writing functions as the representation of invention.

The point to stress first is that dream-work *is* a "logic," in that, as Yvette Biró notes, "every logic is the logic of *relationships*" (117). The relations specific to dream-work are those of figuration, which as the studies of Metz or N. Roy Clifton have shown, are fully representable in film/video. Biró's book, *Profane Mythology: The Savage Mind of the Cinema*, treats the "second film revolution." In the first film revolution, according to Christian Metz, film developed into a language by learning how to tell a story. The second revolution concerns the continuing evolution of the medium (extended by video now) into an intellectual instrument (similar to the emergence of philosophy out of mythology in Plato's time, or the emergence of analytico-referential discourse out of patterning during the Renaissance). The difficulty of her project, Biró says, is that talking about the intellectual potential of film includes putting into question our received notions of thinking itself. Her study synthesizes the analogies or comparisons between all the descriptions of primal or marginal thinking on the one hand (savage, child, madman) and the features of filmic representation, associated with the concrete, the sensual, emotional, action on the other.

One of the most important observations of Biró's study, in the context of my interest in academic discourse, is the systematic parallel she draws between filmic representation and children's thinking. Specifically, with that stage after the sensory-motor phase but prior to the development of conceptual thinking known as "experience-thought" characterized by a reliance on allusion to common experiences in a way that is powerfully evocative. "This experience-thought and cinematic expression have a great many similarities. In both, the stuff of presentation is made of sequences of action, islands of happenings, and remnants, discontinuous and fragmentary bits of events" (14). Such thinking, too, has a special relationship with memory. "It can be said that child-thought or archaic thought, that is, all modes of sensory, emotionally oriented thought, is myth-creating. It is an existential interpretation that produces a most tightly closed order with the help of its own powerful, emotionally charged symbols. These symbols, born of concentrated memories, behave like ancient gods" (13).

At the same time it is important to stress that in teletheory it is not a question of whether minds actually function in the way that the various psychologies claim, but that these converging descriptions of primal logic constitute the invention of a new discourse that can be learned and practiced as a calculus of composition, as an invention.

3. VITA—TV/AI

Teletheory is concerned with discovering and inventing the kind of think-ing and representation available for academic discourse in an electronic age. My working assumption is that the mode I seek is modeled in the simple form of the joke. This possibility is suggested in part by an opposition to the melancholy seriousness that has been associated traditionally with the emotional experience of academic work; and in opposition to the nostalgia that Jameson and others have identified as the predominant emotion of culture in the period of late capitalism. Why should wit be the best response to these moods? "At its birth, knowledge is happy, delivered natively from all culpability," Michel Serres states. "It is perhaps happy by nature. However, in the institutions which direct it, exploit and transmit it, for the individuals it overwhelms it fosters in fact the death instinct. Throughout my youth I believed I discerned on the walls of amphitheaters or on the brows of the learned the hideous word—sadness alone is fruitful. How the change came about I don't know. By whatever means its own nature might be restored it is urgent on pain of death to respond to this question" (Serres, 1974: 75).

Serres's formulation echoes a kind of Rousseauist pre-revolutionary insight into a disparity between our institution and its charge. Here we encounter a political dimension of teletheory, addressing the ideology of learning, the borders marking the inside and outside of discipline. Derrida is my guide to this question, exposing the joke in the claims to neutral objectivity upon which rests the authority of the scientific model of knowledge. This model excludes the non-serious, to which Derrida replies (referring to speech act theory):

> The necessity assumed by classical theory of submitting itself to the very norma-tivity and hierarchy that it purports to analyze, deprives such theory of precisely what it claims for itself: seriousness, scientificity, truth, philosophical value. Because the model speech act of current speech act theory claims to be serious, it is normed by a part of its object and is therefore not impartial. It is not scientific and cannot be taken seriously. Which is what constitutes the drama of this family of theoreticians: the more they seek to produce serious utterances, the less they can be taken seriously. It is up to them whether they will take advantage of this opportunity to transform infelicity into delight. For example, by proclaiming: everything that we have said-written-done up to now wasn't really serious or strict: it was all a joke: sarcastic, even a bit ironic, parasitical, metaphorical, citational, cryptic, fictional, literary, insincere. What force they would gain by doing this. But will they take the risk? Will we have to take it for them? Why not? (Derrida, 1977a: 211–212)

There are symptoms that something is happening in our culture, in the societies of Western capitalism. Teletheory is a response to these symptoms, taking them as guides for the formulation of a new approach to education. Consider the many endorsements of the theory-joke. "In the great majority," according to Nietzsche, "the intellect is a clumsy, gloomy, creaking machine that is difficult to start. They call it 'taking the matter seriously' when they want to work with this machine and think well. How burdensome they must find good thinking. And 'where laughter and gaiety are found' they say, 'thinking does not amount to anything': that is the prejudice of this serious beast against all gay science. Well then, let us prove that this is a prejudice" (Nietzsche, 1974: 257).

Wittgenstein suggested, as the "wit" in his name might lead us to expect, that a good philosophical work could be written that consisted entirely of jokes. Norman Malcolm's memoir of Wittgenstein's seminars reveal, however, that Wittgenstein was not yet prepared to let others in on it. Malcolm reports that Wittgenstein was often amused by his own examples, "grinning at the absurdity of what he had imagined." But if anyone laughed he reproved them, saying "no, no, I'm serious!" (Malcolm, 29).

Wittgenstein's goal was to show the fly the way out of the fly bottle, to put philosophy at rest or to free it from the false metaphysical questions with which it was bound up. No amount of argument, however, was capable of achieving such a closure. Yet in his *conduct* Wittgenstein demonstrated how this escape might be affected. After his lectures, Malcolm reported, Wittgenstein sometimes felt disgusted by what he had said over the course of the two hours of his seminar. "Often he would rush off to a cinema immediately after the class ended." He sat in the front row and *leaned forward*. "He wished to become totally absorbed in the film no matter how trivial or artificial it was, in order to free his mind temporarily from the philosophical thoughts that tortured and exhausted him. He was fond of the film stars Carmen Miranda and Betty Hutton" (27).

In teletheory we have to think these two sides of Wittgenstein's experience at the same time—*Philosophical Investigations* and a Carmen Miranda film. We need to imagine a monster text—"Wittgenstein meets Carmen Miranda"—in which we learn about the fate of method in video discourse. Olbrechts–Tyteca suggested that the juxtaposition of the specialized and everyday lives of the expert produces a joke, and has ever since the tales of Socrates' shrewish wife. Since my project assumes that learning depends upon both domains equally, and juxtaposes them in the same discourse, it is bound to the structure of the joke, albeit the unfunny kind. But this structure is capable of producing the knowledge effect, as well as the pleasure of entertainment.

Derrida has done the most to help me see how to go on from here—how to imagine the mode of reasoning that results from "oralysis" (a spoken-written hybrid). He shows in his strategies how to work electronically, even if he is the Plato of video, being just as suspicious of television as Plato was of writing. As Eric Havelock reminds us, conceptual thought did not arise "naturally," it had to be invented (Havelock, 1967: 302), and Plato's internalization of alphabetic writing played a major role in that process. Now Derrida is playing a similar role for us. Other grammatologists and discourse analysts are insisting on the commonality rather than the separation of orality and literacy. Derrida, however, has theorized this convergence in the register of language itself with the notion of *differance*:

> Elsewhere I have tried to suggest that this differance within language, and in the relation between speech and language, forbids the essential dissociation between speech and writing that Saussure, in keeping with tradition, wanted to draw at another level of his presentation. The use of language or the employment of any code which implies a play of forms—with no determined or invariable substratum—also presupposes a retention and protention of differences, a spacing and temporalizing, a play of traces. This play must be a sort of inscription prior to writing, a protowriting without a present origin, without an *arche*. From this comes the systematic crossing-out of the *arche* and the transformation of general semiology into a grammatology, the latter performing a critical work upon everything within semiology—right down to its matrical concept of sign— that retains any metaphysical presuppositions incompatible with the theme of differance. (Derrida, 1973: 146)

What are the consequences of differance at the more elaborated levels of discourse and logic? That is one of the motivating questions of teletheory. For now I must confine the answer to the question of logic, in which a new term is needed to replace induction, deduction, and even abduction, in order to identify the electronic properties of differantial reasoning. The term is conduction (which to Bennett, with his philosophical training, is going to sound like daffy-duction). How should we conduct ourselves in the age of television? Electronically. How might we keep current in education? Electronically. Conduction, that is, carries the simple form of the pun into a learned extrapolation in theory. When we pose the ancient question of the ground of reason in the context of teletheory we think first of all of the pun that gives us an electronic ground. *Ground:* a conducting connection between an electric circuit or equipment and the earth or some other conducting body. Reasoning by conduction involves, then, the flow of energy through a circuit. Later we will want to discuss this flow in terms of transduction. For now we should confine ourselves to the short-circuiting of this flow, which gives us a new definition of truth as "a relationship of conduction between disparate fields of information," as illustrated here in the conduction between the vocabulary of electricity and that of logic.

The ground of teletheory is the research pun, bringing together two unrelated semantic fields on the basis of one or more shared words. The terms of one field are treated as figures for the other, as an invention for problem-solving. The "duction" words shared by the fields of logic and electricity, for example, allow the description of a reasoning or generative procedure possessing figuratively the features of the electronic terms (conduction and transduction). Another way to view the strategy is as a style of thinking by means of an entire set or paradigm, rather than selecting the one unit of the set that apparently (by common sense) would be the "correct" choice. All the terms in the set may be considered relevant to the matter at hand (the invention stage of thought relies on nonsense). Derrida has demonstrated the productivity of this thinking in several areas. The received concept of "truth," for example, suggests that the truth of a proposition is determined by the existence of some one-to-one correspondence between the terms of the proposition and the elements of some fact. The issue in this situation has been the capacity of the proposition to represent or portray the fact. Derrida has altered the terms of this epistemology to read "epistle-mology," such that he reopens the problem of truth in terms of "correspondence" or letter-writing carried on by an author. The pun, he shows us, is as useful as the metaphor proved to be over the ages in the formation of concepts out of figures, for he does not stop with the joke in which someone, a student for example, might misunderstand the discussion of the abstract "correspon-dence" with a different everyday life usage. He studies, rather, the relation-ship between the structure of the family situation expressed in the letters of Hegel and Freud, with the theoretical structure of their specialized texts. The letters serve as a representation of the theories, but not their cause, and vice versa.

This addition of letters to the correspondence theory is appropriate for the revision of truth needed for the electronic paradigm, since the family situation provided an important metaphor in the original invention of conceptual thinking. As Havelock explained, Hesiod, in the *Works and Days,* composed a semi-abstract system of morality, mixing rule and precept (generalizations) with the concrete level of anecdotes. It is a book of conduct that contributed to Plato's insight that the kind of typologies identified by Hesiod could themselves be the "object" of intellection. "Family" provided the vehicle for this abstracting process.

The composer of the Theogony, seeking to rearrange and regroup narrative situations, had found great linguistic assistance for his task in the words for "family." Used with facile frequency in his composition, these then reappear in the *Works and Days,* to furnish the conception of a "type," at what would appear to be an increasing level of sophistication. Thus the author composes what he calls a *logos* of the five "families" of mankind, which as they succeed each other begin to demonstrate typologies of moral conduct, and the abstract possibilities of the same word are carried even further when, as he launches his poetised discourse, he draws a distinction between two "families" of strife, one beneficial and one destructive. (Havelock, 298)

With this history in mind, we are charged with looking to our family stories for further guidance in the invention of the next generation of concepts. "Conduction," that is, concerns the logic that links the histories of the literature of conduct (guidebooks for the culturally approved forms of desire) with the conduct of writing literature (Armstrong and Tennenhouse, 1). Foucault also marked "conduct" as the term whose elaboration might prove productive:

> Perhaps the equivocal nature of the term "conduct" is one of the best aids for coming to terms with the specificity of power relations. For to "conduct" is at the same time to "lead" others (according to mechanisms of coercion which are, to varying degrees, strict) and a way of behaving within a more or less open field of possibilities. . . . The word must be allowed the very broad meaning which it had in the sixteenth century. "Government" did not refer only to political structures or to the management of states: rather, it designated the way in which the conduct of individuals or of groups might be directed: the government of children, of souls, of communities, of families, of the sick. (Foucault, 1984: 428)

In the context of teletheory, Foucault did not go far enough in the latitude he allowed the term. When it is a question of invention, the term must be pushed not only where it has been in the past (its history or etymology), but also to where it might be in the future (catachresis), to name, in this case, the flow of significance from one semantic field to another.

Another example from Eisenstein motivates the use of conduction as a logic of passage from the particular to the general, which occurs in film texts in a way similar to that in pre-literate languages. The Klamath language, Eisenstein noted, citing Lévy-Bruhl, contains no concept of "walking" in general, but only different terms for each particular form of walking, yet these particulars can convey the general idea, which he compares to the way a Western actor or director works: "the details of walking and selected movements, however refined they may be, in a genuine master would always be, at the same time, also a 'conductor' of the generalized content which he produces in a particularized embodiment" (Eisenstein, 1957: 139).

The conduct portrayed in a "life story," whose outline may be glimpsed in a *Curriculum Vitae,* may be a conductor for generalized abstractions, leading to the formation of new concepts. The macaronics of conduction reveals that "vita" may be read as the diagnostic anagram of TV + AI, demonstrating at a stroke the need for an integrated relationship between television and artificial intelligence (which may have consequences for the composition of our life stories as well).

One research pun in teletheory is "program," concerning the change in memory that accompanies the hypomnemic capabilities of computer and video. Computer programming involves AI—"artificial intelligence." More-over, the computer has been explicitly counted as one of those technological prostheses, as an extension of the brain in this case. But what needs to be made clear is that the computer is the prosthesis only of what may be called the left brain, with its algorithmic features of analysis and linear sequence. The TV program (the colossal pun, for Derrida, is the one crossing between noun and verb), meanwhile, is similarly a prosthesis of the intelligence of the right brain, with its features of imaging and simultaneity. This analogy is important to teletheory: TV is to right-brain cognition what AI is to left-brain cognition. TV, or more specifically the technology of video, is a mnemonic technology available for information storage and retrieval, like every writing system that preceded it. The term "vita" as an anagram of TV and AI tells us the same thing a physician would tell us about a person in whom the right and left brains were disconnected: to be a sane and effective human being the two sides of the brain must work together. A culture that has split the two sides of its intelligence the way ours has is seriously disabled. The analogy suggests several lessons: that life, or rather, survival itself, depends upon the communication of these two parts; that one aspect of this intercom-munication concerns the technical invention of computer-video interface; that another aspect concerns the invention of a cognitive style integrating right and left modes.

This context clarifies an important point: that electronic thinking does not abandon, exclude, or replace analytical thinking; it puts it in its place in a larger system of reasoning. In fact, conduction gives rise to the following hypothesis, related to Foucault's observation that the important discovery of psychoanalysis was precisely the "logic of the unconscious." If we focus on just this logic, observing its features, we may notice the commonality of nearly all the descriptions of the "primal" mind developed in the various branches of the social sciences in our century and manifested in the vanguard arts as well. That the rationales accounting for the features of these non-objective styles of thought differ according to the disciplinary commitments of the source is irrelevant when we are scanning our paradigm for symptoms or oralysis. What matters is that the *descriptions* of the unconscious, the right brain, inner speech, the mind of the savage, child, or even "feminine style," all share similar features, which we recognize to have been generated for the most part in opposition to analytico-referential reason. From the point of view of teletheory, there is no need finally to make up a science-fictional reasoning; the cognitive style of the new instauration has already been invented out of the body of science itself.

The following list, distinguishing right- from left-brain features, is typical of the description to which I refer (Roukes, 1984).

Right Brain	Left Brain
Intuitive	Intellectual
Perceptual	Rational
Creative	Analytical
Experiential	Verbal
Felt Thought	Computation
Spatial/Pattern Recognition	Sequential/Linear
Simultaneous Processing	Routinization
Emotion	Reason
Active during dream state	Quiet during dream state
(and so forth)	

Thinking along these lines suggests further that the accounts of primal thinking also tend to line up symmetrically with accounts of creative or inventive thinking. Euretic cognition, in short, corresponds with these lists of creativity (keeping in mind the restrictive nature of lists noted by Goody). To mobilize creative thinking, Roukes suggests, for example, the following activities or attitudes are necessary, "and have been observed in all truly creative people regardless of profession":

- the training and practice of activities that largely involve right-brain functions.
- suspension of judgment; making disconnected jumps in thinking (lateral thinking).
- openness to new stimuli, new ideas, new attitudes, new approaches.
- willingness to take risks; making 'leaps of faith'; lessening inhibitions.
- freedom in subjective thinking; expression of emotions and personal realities.
- intuitiveness, 'playing hunches' to generate spontaneous ideas.
- rejecting destructive criticism, prejudices, indiscriminate praise.
- a childlike attitude of creative play, tinkering with ideas, materials, structures; a 'fun' attitude toward experimentation.
- freedom to fantasize, unconventional imagining.
- divergent thinking; simultaneous processing of ideas; fluency of ideas.
- acceptance of non-ordinary realities, contradictions; ability to tolerate and manipulate puzzles, ambiguities.

The first thing I notice about such descriptions of creative thinking is that this is not the kind of cognition promoted in the schools—at least not the schools I know anything about. Instead, institutionalized learning promotes the dominant analytico-referential style of thought. As Reiss noted, the analytico-referential discourse sets itself apart from and opposes all other styles of cognition, taking them at best as objects of study. These objects, however, are becoming subjects in the age of television, in which they must be used as well as studied. The ideology of science requires the separation of subject and object, and in its popular and professional expressions takes an aggressive stand against all challenges to its exclusive claims to the knowledge effect. Most of the attacks on video as a medium and on television as an institution may be seen as examples of the assumptions of alphabetic cognition used as the basis for the condemnation of primal thinking.

One example of this tendency is *Four Arguments for the Elimination of Television,* by Jerry Mander. Mander's objections to television are instructive in this context since he reiterates some of the same objections to video that Plato made to chirography, with even stronger warnings about the disaster that awaits a civilization in which television is the dominant medium (part of the lesson of this example is his failure to distinguish between television and video). His assumptions are that television, like other technologies, is not neutral, but involves an ideology that shapes a society to correspond to itself. As a medium video is inherently stupid, is anti-democratic, and is not reformable. The argument of the apparatus exposes the technological determinism of Mander's position, but his attitude is instructive because symptomatic.

Mander calls upon the analogy between video and psychoanalysis, but this time to support his condemnation of television. Unlike the reading process in which the reader is self-conscious and in control, watching television is a "kind of wakeful dreaming, except that it's a stranger's dream, from a faraway place, though it plays against the screen of your mind" (Mander, 201). This flow of dream images "bypasses thinking" and becomes an "influencing machine" to which people respond with zombie-like passivity. It simulates a kind of "sleep teaching," by implanting images in one's unconscious directly, without mediation by the conscious intellect. One of the best analogies for the mental condition produced by television, Mander argues, is schizophrenia. The accounts in psychoanalytic case histories of schizophrenic experience, in which an alien force communicates with a person by means of an "influencing machine," resemble, Mander says, electronic broadcasts. Freud's study of Schreber is a good example of one such case history. The principal symptom shared by the schizophrenic Schreber and the viewer of TV is the confusion of the inside and the outside of the self, the internal and external worlds, "the worlds of one's own thoughts and the concrete world outside the person" (110). "Doubtless you have noticed that this 'influencing machine' sounds an awful lot like television. The mystery is how the phenomenon could have existed in 1919 before the apparatus was invented. Dare I suggest that television was invented by people similarly preoccupied, as an outward manifestation of their minds?" (111). Mander is referring to an article published in 1919 by Victor Tausk, one of Freud's colleagues. "The influencing machine usually has gigantic wheels, gears and other paraphernalia," Tausk says. "It often has the ability to project pictures and invisible rays in some way capable of imprinting the brain. The pictures frequently emanate from a 'small black box' and are flat, not three-dimensional, images. The machine and its emanations can produce feelings and thoughts in the victim, while removing other ones" (109). Part of the argument of the apparatus is that ideology contributes to invention in part through the dreams and desires of a civilization. Mander joins in this line of thinking at least to suggest that video is a technology born of madness.

To reinforce this idea Mander borrows another model of madness, using the right brain/left brain to suggest that viewing television leads to a dysfunctional state similar to that experienced by people in whom the two sides of the brain have been severed. The passage manifests Mander's general bias favoring a "left brain" definition of reason. Citing a "technical treatise" on the effects of watching flickering light similar to that produced by video, Mander notes that the left brain (seat of cognitive and critical thought)

> "goes into a kind of holding pattern. . . . The right half of the brain, which deals with more subjective cognitive processes—dream images, fantasy, intuition—continues to receive the television images. But because the bridge between the right and left brains has been effectively shattered, all cross-processing, the making conscious of unconscious data and bringing it into usability, is eliminated." . . . If the Emerys are correct, then their findings support the idea that television information enters unfiltered and whole, directly into the memory banks, but it is not available for conscious analysis, understanding or learning. (207)

To put Mander's concern another way, he fears that when filmic/video discourse becomes the dominant mode, it will exclude analysis, the way analysis excluded patterning after the Renaissance.

Despite Mander's commitment to alphabetic literacy (he frequently praises the intellection associated with the reading process) he also is a critic of the excesses of science. His ideology, in fact, represents the Platonic preference for "natural" or "living" memory over artificial memory. Video is condemned as artificial, as producing an ersatz simulation of reality which cuts us off from organic, direct experience. The representatives of a natural, sane way of life are, for Mander, the American Indians. Against the "nether world of experts and abstractions" produced by the mediations of Western science, to the point that the common person has lost all confidence in his own experience, Mander invokes the "direct education" of the Indians who attained a detailed knowledge of nature without the artifices of specialization (72). Mander became convinced of the unreformability of television by watching the ineffectiveness of the Hopi Indians' efforts to use the medium to communicate their alternative point of view in a land usage dispute. In the four minute report that made the evening news, what the public got was a "formula story: Progress versus Tradition," and "a lot of old savage-looking types in funny clothes, talking about a religion which says that to dig up the land is dangerous for the survival of every creature on the planet" (40–41). The irony of the Hopi example is that video, in the line of invention traced in teletheory from Eisenstein to Biró, is becoming the conductor of primal thinking, of which Amerindian culture is one of the best models (Highwater, 1981).

Mander, then, is right to compare video discourse, and descriptions of the viewing experience, with the psychoanalytic description of schizophrenia. In our context, the conclusion to be drawn from Mander's account is not that TV is "evil" in need of elimination, but a clue to an emergent cognition, associated homeopathically with the dominant image and theme of our era— total catastrophe. As Robert Jay Lifton noted, the "end-of-the-world" imagery so prevalent in our time is related to three levels of experience:

> There is first the external event, such as the Hiroshima bomb. We could also speak of the plagues of the Middle Ages as an external event, so much so that there were some notable similarities in imagery between plague survivors and survivors of Hiroshima. Second, there is the shared theological imagery, or eschatology, that renders such imagery acceptable as a meaning structure. Finally, there is the internal derangement—the intrapsychic disintegration of personal Armageddon of psychosis, especially in certain schizophrenic syndromes. (Lifton, 33)

The similarity between the thought produced in schizophrenic and nuclear catastrophe, then, may be seen as a model for an invention best suited to dealing with our situation. Gilles Deleuze and Félix Guattari's development of a "schizoanalysis" (to be discussed later) is a more productive response to the electronic change in the apparatus than is Mander's foreclosure. The point is not that video causes schizophrenia, but that descriptions of schizophrenic cognition provide the best outline of the logic specific to video.

Whatever the fit between psychoanalysis and its object of study might be, in teletheory the descriptions of primary-process discourse serve as models for the "logic" suited to the video medium. In this context Mander may be seen as correct not at the level of the real, but at the level of discourse. The issue of collective sanity and intelligence (the American mind), continuing the split-brain analogy, according to teletheory, is that television is not the cause but the cure for our half-wittedness, a condition created by the dominance of analytical science. The privileging of the kind of intelligence identified as "left brain" in our schooling and civilization had to do, as we have seen, with the affinity of alphabetic literacy with critical thinking. Alphabetic technology allowed ordinary people, by means of schooling, to acquire and practice analytic reasoning "artificially," in the mode of remembrance and routinization, if not in the style of living memory necessarily. Alphabetic writing, whose dissemination required the existence of schools, democratized, rendered teachable and available, analytical reason. Perhaps this democratization is part of what Plato feared, given his conservative politics, when he expressed his opposition to writing. It was one thing for a "natural" genius like Socrates to possess the powers of logic, even if he was the son of a stonemason and a midwife. But what would happen to society if the power of argument became available to the common man generally? Such a dissemination would not be without political consequences.

Here we encounter a central thesis of teletheory, which brings together under one heading the description of three distinct processes—"primal" thinking (in all its variations), creative invention, and videography. The thesis is that the new electronic technologies relate to euretics the way alphabetic literacy relates to analytic thinking. Just as the features of alphabetic writing noted by Goody associated with the list, table, and formula provided the prosthesis of analysis, so is the prosthesis of invention available in video. The implication, and this is a premise, is that video permits the institutional dissemination of inventive thinking—its artificial simulation as a routine conduct by ordinary students. Until now we could not institutionalize invention in the way that we have institutionalized analysis, because we simply lacked the prosthesis needed to democratize it. Certainly invention existed in a wild state, in individual instances, and was practiced within the rhetoric of method. The premise is that a collective, artifical intelligence of the sort institutionalized as schooling requires, just as much as does the individual mind, the cooperative integration of the two modes of processing. We have a better chance of producing a sane, intelligent civilization if we reintegrate analysis with patterning rather than if we "eliminate" (disavow) the technology and institution that have made it possible to achieve a cognitively balanced culture. Teletheory seeks the genre that might be the bridge capable of conducting thought between the two technologies. What is at stake, then, involves not just the introduction of video into the classroom, but the formulation and practice of conduction, an electronic mode of reasoning that is already available, and necessary for using the full potential of our emerging apparatus.

By way of transition, let me say one more thing about "vita"—the interdependence of "programming" in conduction. A comparison of the two kinds of "program" indicate that AI is becoming more and more like TV. The programmers have abandoned their early efforts to simulate an abstract, logical description of intelligence (modeled on an analysis of reason, tree diagrams, and other book influences). In the alphabetic model, "concept" is understood as a classification system in which knowledge is organized in rigorous categories of shared properties. More recent efforts in AI programming, however, have been based on something that resembles an oral order of knowledge, in which quotidian native routines are organized by means of episodes and schemas. Roger Schank and Robert Abelson, for example, designed a "restaurant script" that dealt with intelligence not in terms of class-inclusion systems but by units of an event sequence—actions and changes of state, expectations and regularities that are episodic rather than "logical." If a computer is to interact with people—and this is the measure of its intelligence, just as the measure of any tool is its human fit—it must first simulate the repertoire of stories by which humans organize experience. How to negotiate a restaurant: enter; be seated; menu; order; eat; pay; leave. The difference between AI and the TV script—say a situation comedy—is that the AI programmer wants the routine to match the norm, to be typical and to pass unnoticed (if it is being tested by a native human), whereas the TV program foregrounds the deviation, the error, the mess of everything going wrong in the restaurant, as in the Monty Python skit in which the customer's benign observation of a dirty fork escalates into, yes, a massacre. We are prepared to recognize now that these two versions of the story are two sides of the same operation—logic and joke—and that it is difficult to find one's way without the constant interplay between the two.

The computer, we might say, has its memory filled with stories that aren't worth telling. I went to the restaurant, ate, and left. So what?, we want to know, and yet that things normally go right is the ground of attending to what happens when they go wrong. Teletheory takes its point of departure from this burgeoning of anecdotal material in modern texts, in relation to the VITA. As Andrew Tolson argues, "an anecdotal effect might, to some extent, be built into the structure of TV's discursive regime: both within particular program formats and in terms of the way many TV narratives are organized. Finally, this possibility, that television's *regime* is anecdotal, might account for some of its problematic pleasures" (Tolson, 24). Pursuing his thesis that the anecdotal structure is specific to television, Tolson finds that news shows, and by extension all uses of interviewing and the like in documentaries— the format of truth—fall within the anecdotal framing.

Michel de Certeau made a similar case, collapsing the distinction between scholarship and popularization that is of the first importance to the resituation of history in teletheory.

> Scholarly discourse is no longer distinguishable from that prolix and fundamental narrativity that is our everyday historiography. Scholarship is an integral part of the system that organizes by means of "histories" all social communication and everything that makes the present habitable. The book or the professional article, on the one hand, and the magazine or the television news, on the other, are distinguishable from one another only within the same historiographical field which is constituted by the innumerable narratives that recount and interpret events. (de Certeau, 205)

What remains to be explored, then, is the possibility of performing theory and all the other functions of academic discourse not only in the form of the anecdote and the other oral and simple forms as well, but most particularly in the form of the joke, for if that is feasible, then there can be no doubt that it is possible and practical to marry the institutions and apparatuses of education and television; to supplement analysis with oralysis in a pedagogy of invention.

4. Text

I want to turn to the elaboration of one example to show the practical possibilities of the theoretical joke—the capacity of the joke for the representation of theory, which should also indicate the possibility of translation across the levels of culture upon which the cycle of invention depends. The example comes from a suggestion first made by Barthes: "A Night at the Opera—a work which I regard as allegorical of many a textual problem" (Barthes, 1977: 194). This 1935 Marx Brothers film, in other words, provides a model for the difficult and controversial poststructuralist concept of "text." The immediate implication is that a teacher wishing to introduce textualist theory to a class might begin by showing A Night at the Opera to the students. This would be a step toward realizing Brecht's goal (to which Barthes frequently alluded) of integrating the realms of entertainment and intellect.

Barthes himself indicated what he had in mind with respect to this model in several asides alluding to Opera as an emblem of "text," in which laughter replaces melancholy as the mark of the sting or *punctum* (the sign of memory in cognition).

> Emblem, gag, What a textual treasure, A Night at the Opera! If some critical demonstration requires an allegory in which the whole mechanics of the text-on-a-spree explodes, the film will provide it for me: the steamer cabin, the torn contract, the final chaos of opera decors—each of these episodes (among others) is the emblem of the logical subversions performed by the Text; and if these emblems are perfect, it is ultimately because they are comic, laughter being what, by a last reversal, releases demonstration from its demonstrative attribute. What liberates metaphor, symbol, emblem from poetic *mania*, what manifests its power of subversion, is the *preposterous*, the "bewilderment" which Fourier was so good at getting into his examples, to the scorn of any theoretical respectability. The logical future of metaphor would therefore be the gag. (Barthes, 1977a: 80–81)

There are, then, at least two ways to model the operation of Text. One way, demonstrated in Camera Lucida, is by means of the sentiment or emotion generated by anecdotes told in association with one's family album (relevant to the generation of concepts out of the family structure in conduction). The accessibility of family anecdotes is a virtue for a pedagogy, but Marx Brothers' gags are equally accessible, although when it comes to his own practice Barthes never provided more than a few hints of how to operate in the dimension of the gag or joke, preferring finally to stay on the side of melancholy (and to dramatize in *Camera* a theory of mourning). The fragments of the film Barthes discussed indicate that the aspect of Text emblematized most forcefully in *Opera* has to do with the "fading of the subject." The "fading" refers to the current status of the problematic of the self—the shift away from a Cartesian to a Freudian notion of the person in common sense. In this context *Camera Lucida* (in which Barthes expresses his mourning for his mother, may be read as a dramatic exploration of the Oedipal problem. His hints about the Text as gag in *Opera* offer an alternative style of working through mourning, a style perhaps more suited for mourning for the father (the fact that Barthes never knew his father may have something to do with his failure to develop this gag). The cognitive style of teletheory—conduction—involves a reordering of the emotional experience of the entry into the Symbolic away from mourning and melancholia toward wit and humor.

In the Cartesian or "classical" conception, language is understood as "decoration or instrument, seen as a sort of parasite of the human subject, who uses it or dons it at a distance, like an ornament or tool picked up and laid down according to the needs of subjectivity or the conformities of sociality. However, another notion of writing is possible: neither decorative nor instrumental, i.e. in sum secondary but primal, antecedent to man, whom it traverses, founder of its acts like so many inscriptions" (Barthes, 1976: 40). Barthes's own sympathy is with the "modern" understanding: "He wants to side with any writing whose principle is that the subject is merely an effect of language" (Barthes, 1977a: 79). In the classic work the origin of the speaker is assigned to a consciousness (an author or character) or to a culture (a code). But even in a *work* the utterance may become pluralized, indeterminate: "the voice gets lost, as though it had leaked out through a hole in the discourse. The best way to conceive the classical plural is then to listen to the text as an iridescent exchange carried on by multiple voices, on different wavelengths and subject from time to time to a sudden *dissolve,* leaving a gap which enables the utterance to shift from one point of view to another without warning" (Barthes, 1974: 41–42).

Barthes finds in *Opera* two scenes that teach this lesson "in a burlesque mode." One of the scenes emblematizes his own experience of the fading of the subject in the act of lecturing to a class:

In the *exposé,* more aptly named than we tend to think, it is not knowledge which is exposed, it is the subject. The mirror is empty, reflecting back to me no more than the falling away of my language as it gradually unrolls. Like the

Marx Brothers disguised as Russian airmen (in *A Night at the Opera*—a work which I regard as allegorical of many a textual problem), I am, at the beginning of my exposé, rigged out with a large false beard which, drenched little by little with the flood of my own words (a substitute for the jug of water from which the *Mute*, Harpo, guzzles away on the Mayor of New York's rostrum), I then feel coming unstuck piecemeal in front of everybody. (Barthes, 1977: 194)

The other scene (part of the performance of *Il Trovatore* enacted during the film) is the one in which the stage backdrops rise and fall (marking Harpo's Tarzan-like progress swinging from rope to rope above the stage, working its machinery haphazardly) during the villain Lassparri's solo: "This hubbub is crammed with emblems: the absence of background replaced by the rolling plural of sets, the codage of contexts (issue of the opera's repertoire) and their derision, the delirious polysemy, and finally the illusion of the subject, singing its imaginary with the other (the spectator) watches and who believes to be speaking backed by a unique world (a set: a complete scene of the plural which derides the subject: *dissociates* it)" (Barthes, 1981: 111–112).

One reason why a Marx Brothers farce is a perfect emblem for the fading of the subject, for the "death of the author" has to do with the pun available in "gag" ("joke" and "choke") for naming the allegorical meaning of a Marx Brothers routine. In the next chapter this allegorical procedure itself will be elaborated. For now I want to focus on the possibilities of the research pun, on the cognition of "conduct" as "routine" in this Marx Brothers sense. "Gag," that is, is one of those "amphibologies" that Barthes found so appealing.

Each time he encounters one of these double words, R. B. on the contrary, insists on keeping both meanings, as if one were winking at the other and as if the word's meaning were in that wink, so that *one and the same word*, in *one and the same sentence*, means at one and the same time two different things, and so that one delights, semantically, in the one by the other. This is why such words are often said to be "precisely ambiguous": not in their lexical essence (for any word in the lexicon has several meanings), but because, by a kind of *luck*, a kind of favor not of language but of discourse, I can *actualize* their amphibology. (Barthes, 1977a: 72)

The gags in *Opera*, then, allegorize the other gag, the gagging or choking associated with the experience of the body of desire, revealed when the subject fades or dissolves. At one level the gag is provoked by the "writing machine," with the writer's desire for certain fetish words, certain binary oppositions such as "metaphor/metonymy" that provide one with "the power of saying something"—"Hence the work proceeds by conceptual infatuations, successive enthusiasms, perishable manias. Discourse advances by little fates, by amorous fits. (The coming of language: in French the word remains in the throat, for a certain interval)" (110).

At another level, however, the gag remarks the *disgust* experienced in the disgorging or exorcism of one's own image-repertoire (the "stupidities" of one's habits, *routines,* in short of one's ideology), which is related, no doubt, to the disgust Wittgenstein felt that caused him to rush out after his seminar to see a film starring Carmen Miranda. "How to question my disgust (the disgust for my own failures)? How to prepare the best reading of my self I can hope for: not to love but only to *endure fasting* what has been written?" (111). The "life story" in question in teletheory, that is, involves this fading of the subject, exposing the amphibological position of the subject formed by attraction and repulsion, pleasure and disgust—*joussance* or bliss-sense of the self, in other words. Against the stereotype, while acknowledging the contribution of the stereotype to concept formation, which Barthes under-stands as "discourse without body," the "grain" of the voice introduces the problem of judgment, value, taste, at the level of the inner body, emblema-tized for Barthes by Bernard Réquichot's collages and reliquaries (boxes representing open torsos displaying the "magma" of the body). Réquichot's interest in repugnance, Barthes states, resembles de Sade's, for whom "the body begins to exist there where it is revolted, disgusted, yet wanting to devour what disgusts it" (Barthes, 1973: 13).

This gag, too, has an affinity with the "laugh of the Medusa": "Write your self. Your body must be heard," declares Hèléne Cixous, (Cixous, 1981: 250). In the case of women, the disgust is imposed by the patriarchy, and must be overcome in order "to start scoring their feats in written and oral language." The theory of feminist *écriture* suggests how to design the text that makes bliss-sense: "Her speech, even when 'theoretical' or political, is never simple or linear or 'objectified,' generalized: she draws her story into history. There is not the scission, that division made by the common man between the logic of oral speech and the logic of the text, bound as he is by his antiquated relation—servile, calculating—to mastery" (251). As Cixous notes, men must write their own sexuality, so her project touches only obliquely on "man." For now I take note that the laugh of the Medusa is related to the unfunny joke, and to oralysis, and that it supports the potential of the gag as an alternative mode of cognition (as may be seen in a film such as Yvonne Rainer's *The Man Who Envied Women* [1985], organized as an expansion of a stand-up comic routine).

An allegorical reading of the film, then, names the obtuse meanings of Text by exploiting the amphibologies of certain key words. Another such pun is available in *Opera,* emblematizing perhaps the principal element of textuality—the sliding of the signified under the signifier, the infinite skid of meaning which replaces "signification" with "significance." If the "gag" as such emblematizes the "fading of the subject" in textuality, the specific content of the *Trovatore* sequence in *Opera* emblematizes the textualist sliding of the signifier:

> To decondition us of all the philosophies (or theologies) of the signified, that is, of the Arrest, since we others, "literaries," we lack any sovereign formalisms, that of mathematics, we must employ as many metaphors as possible, for the metaphor is a means of access to the signifier; lacking an algorithm, that which could discharge the signified, especially if one could manage to disoriginate it [the metaphor]. I propose today this: the scene of the world (the world as stage) is occupied by a play of "sets" (of texts): raise one, another appears behind it and so forth. (Barthes, 1981: 111)

The play of the "sets" or stage backdrops, as a metaphor, replaces the algorithms of mathematics (set theory, for example) used in the sciences, and achieves its own style of precision, which is equivocal rather than univocal.

If we keep in mind that "opera" literally means "work," we may see that *Opera* demonstrates the passage from "work" to "text" in the way that it *traverses* the classical opera *Il Trovatore*, by Verdi; that it shows something similar to what Barthes argues in the essay "From Work to Text":

> The Text is experienced only in an activity, a production. It follows that the Text cannot stop, at the end of a library shelf, for example; the constitutive movement of the Text is a *traversal*: it can cut across a work, several works. . . . What constitutes the Text is, on the contrary (or precisely), its subversive force with regard to old classifications. . . . Whereas the Text is approached and experienced in relation to the sign, the work closes itself on a signified. . . . The Text practices the infinite deferral of the signified: the Text is *dilatory*; its field is that of the signifier. (Barthes, 1979: 75–76)

The two scenes from the opera actually performed in the film are indeed two of the famous moments in the repertoire—the "Anvil Chorus" and the "Miserere." As one commentator put it, "*Trovatore* succeeds too well. Its melodies have been played and sung in every conceivable arrangement until their spontaneity has largely been worn away. Particularly is this true of the remarkable ensemble known as the 'Miserere,' really a most telling piece of dramatic music, but heard so often, that if we do not pause to give it thought we are likely not to appreciate fully its excellent qualities" (O'Connell, 1936: 509). The textual traversal, that is, operates with the stereotypes of its material, which is to say that it is an immanent critique, a deconstruction.

A brief plot summary will help establish the theoretical gag in these scenes. The "traversal" of *Il Trovatore* begins in the second act, when Fiorello (Chico) and Tomasso (Harpo) invade the orchestra pit, inserting the sheet music for "Take Me Out to the Ball Game" into the scores on the music stands, a substitution overlooked in the distraction provided by their "refunctioning" of some of the instruments (sword fight with violin bows). The music begins, shifting suddenly, with the turning of the page, from Verdi to "Take Me Out to the Ball Game" signaling Chico and Harpo to produce a ball and gloves and play catch while Groucho sells peanuts in the aisle.

To evade the Opera Director, Gottlieb, and the policemen sent to arrest them, Chico and Harpo move onto the stage, mingling with the actors, costumed as gypsies, performing the "Anvil Chorus" ("Who cheers the life of the roving gypsy? The gypsy maiden! The gypsy maiden!"). A constrained chase scene follows, mixing the plot of the film with the plot of the opera, leading to the hubbub of rising and descending decors to which Barthes referred. Gottlieb and the detective Henderson don costumes and join the scene themselves, hoping to disturb the action as little as possible. As Lassparri sings the effect of the chase is registered in the changing sets—the gypsy camp is replaced first by a forest scene then a railroad, a fruit wagon, a battleship, and so on.

The motivation within the film for the disruption of the performance has to do with the attempt by the Brothers to force the director to give the leading role to their friend Baroni, a talented but young and unknown tenor, in place of the famous Lassparri, hired by Gottlieb. At the beginning of the film Groucho's plan to exploit Mrs. Claypool (Margaret Dumont), playing on her desire to enter high society by promising to arrange for her to be a sponsor for the New York Opera company, is threatened by Gottlieb who secures her agreement to fund the hiring of Lassparri, reputed to be the "world's greatest tenor." Groucho, impressed by Lassparri's fee ($1,000 a night), makes a deal with Chico, Baroni's agent, to sign Baroni with this fee in mind, of which Baroni would get ten dollars and the agents would split the rest ("we are entitled to a small profit"). The invasion of the stage during the performance of *Il Trovatore* (near the conclusion of the film) is the final strategy to get Baroni into the leading role in place of Lassparri. The Marx Brothers refuse to quit the stage until Lassparri is dismissed and Baroni hired to take over the part of "Manrico."

The allegorical significance of the *Trovatore* sequence is signaled by the pun available in the word "tenor." Chico, Harpo, and Groucho may be read as *personifications* of the signifier (their antics represent the "field of play" mentioned in the definition of Text). This "signifier," of course may be translated into the rhetorical terminology of Ogden and Richards (*The Meaning of Meaning* being approximately contemporary with *A Night at the Opera*), who classified the parts of metaphor as "vehicle" and "tenor" (comparable to "signifier" and "signified"). The Marx Brothers, that is, are the agents or vehicles (signifiers) "representing" the *tenor* (signified) Baroni. Their disruption (which was not a complete interruption, however) of the performance, substituting one tenor for the other (forcing Gottlieb to fire

Lassparri and hire Baroni in the middle of the opera), is an allegory of the sliding of the signified constitutive of Text. The gag depends on the amphibology in "tenor," and also *singer* and *signified,* with sing suggesting anagrammatically the "sign."

I noted that the allegorical reading of *Opera* is directed by two puns—gag, which names the fading of the subject and the emergence of the body of desire; and *tenor,* associated with the sliding of the signified (displacement), the Marx Brothers themselves personifying the drive of the signifier. That Barthes should prefer *A Night at the Opera* to one of the other Marx Brothers films must be due in part to this operatic element, the same theme informing "Sarrasine," the story analyzed in *S/Z.* Such patterns refer finally to Barthes as subject, to his ideolect (a dimension of the life story to be pursued later). Suffice it to say here that the musical score as such served Barthes as a metaphor for the interaction of the codes or "voices" of the Text, with the readerly or classic work being compared to tonal music, and the writerly or modern Text being compared to atonal, serial music. More specifically, Italian opera is charged for Barthes with sexual connotation, associated with the theme of castration: "Italian music, an object well defined historically, culturally, mythically (Rousseau, Gluckists-and-Piccinists, Stendhal, etc.), connotes a 'sensual' art, an art of the voice. An erotic substance, the Italian voice was produced *a contrario* (according to a strictly symbolic inversion) by singers without sex" (Barthes, 1974: 109–110).

Barthes selected "Sarrasine" as a tutor-text because it possessed that double structure he required for his allegories, defined as "double" work, "a work apparently naive and in fact very cunning, as would be the story of a battle made conjointly and with a single voice by Stendhal's Fabrice and General Clausewitz" (Barthes, 1981: 51). The intertextual analysis of codes reveals how this double form occurs in "Sarrasine": the hermeneutic code, conveying the story of the castrato, Zambinella, manifests literally the symbolic code (involving the psychoanalytic, Lacanian theory of the entry into language figured in the Oedipal stage and the castration complex). The discourse mixes two codes: "Of these two codes, simultaneously referred to in the same words (the same signifier)," it is impossible to decide which one has priority, which one determines the meaning of the other. "Tenor" functions in *Opera* in the same way that "castration" functions in "Sarrasine," as an amphibology marking at this level nothing less than a pun of codes, capable of moving between levels of culture (high, popular) as well as between semantic fields.

The principle for using a story as an emblem for a theoretical concept, or for generating a concept out of a story, is an extension of Barthes's metaphorical approach, with the double structure of an exemplary work being achieved by the projection of any one of the vertical codes (semic, cultural, symbolic) onto either of the horizontal codes (action, truth), based on Jakobsen's notion of poetry as the projection of the paradigm onto the syntagm. "Just as a successful metaphor affords, between its terms, no hierarchy and removes all hindrances from the polysemic chain (in contrast to the comparison, an originated figure), so a 'good' narrative fulfills both the plurality and the circularity of the codes" (Barthes, 1974: 77). This capacity of the codes to fuse suggests the practical means for representing the research pun in a discourse, as well as how the symbolic code might take over the work of the code of truth.

The peculiar effect of such conjunctions distinguishes Barthes's allegorical procedure from such related operations as "illustration," "demonstration," and the like.

> To make *being-castrated,* an anecdotal condition, coincide with *castration,* a symbolic structure, is the task successfully carried out by the performer (Balzac), since the former does not necessarily entail the latter. . . . This success hinges on a structural artifice: identifying the symbolic and the hermeneutic, making the search for truth (hermeneutic structure) into the search for castration (symbolic structure), making the truth be *anecdotally* (and no longer symbolically) the absent phallus. . . . Which accounts for this story's perhaps unique value: "illustrating" castration by being-castrated, like with like, it mocks the notion of illustration, it abolishes both sides of the equivalence (letter and symbol) without advantage to either one; the latent here occupies the line of the manifest from the start, the sign is flattened out: there is no longer any "representation." (163–164)

A *Night at the Opera* includes this same flattening, such that it functions not as a sign but as a catachresis. Barthes avoids the logocentric trap of representation—the charge Derrida brought against Lacan when the latter used Poe's "Purloined Letter" to teach the truth of psychoanalysis—by stressing that his allegories are obtuse, structured not representationally as signs but as metaphor, metaphors that do not refer to preestablished truths, but themselves constitute the *significance* of Barthes's own Text. His discourse, that is, is composed not as metalanguage but as Text. "*Let the commentary be itself a text:* that is, in brief, what the theory of the text demands. The subject of the analysis (the critic, the philologist, the scholar) cannot in fact, without bad faith and smugness, believe he is external to the language he is describing" (Barthes, 1981a: 44). This relation of the writer to language and culture reduces reliance upon the subject/object polarity, producing instead "third meanings" whose referent may be only the subject of knowledge. "We can put it still more precisely," Barthes adds: "from its very principles, the theory of the text can produce only theoreticians or practitioners (writers), but absolutely not specialists (critics or teachers); as a practice, then, it participates itself in the subversion of the genres which as a theory it studies" (44). It may be that textual practice will not produce teachers in the analytico-referential mode, but it may be the basis for teachers working in the academic discourse of teletheory.

The next step in the invention of a new genre is to consider the possibility of generalizing Barthes's discovery—the possibility of generating intelligibility and understanding without recourse to the codes of argument. He demonstrated that the Symbolic code can do the work of the syntagmatic axis of narrative; that the joke can replace the riddle as the simple form organizing the drive of research.

Chapter 3

Mystory

1. Mystoriography

I am telling not only how to make a mystory, but why I want to make one. I do not expect to be able to persuade anyone by means of argument that conduction is an effective inventio, but it is important to note that this argument itself is constructed conductively, as well as inductively and deductively (as is usually the case in descriptions of genre).

It is now possible to begin to formulate the principles of the genre which it is the purpose of teletheory to invent. The emergence of a regionalized epistemology, the dysfunctioning of the grand explicating metanarratives, and the effectiveness of feminist appeals to personal experience are among the trends encouraging the development of mystory—a term designating the nexus of history, politics, language, thought, and technology in the last decade of this millennium. The mystorical approach to a topic such as the future of academic discourse involves a reworking of certain ancient problems—the relation of the particular and the general, the reality of change, the invention of the "subject," to name a few. Whether ancient or modern, it is not always easy to recognize the peculiar configuration of possibility in one's own moment, hence the use of neologism to name this movement, or this "mythical concept" (to use Roland Barthes's term for the historical, unstable dimension of myth).

> The concept is a constituting element of myth: if I want to decipher myths, I must somehow be able to name concepts. The dictionary supplies me with a few: Goodness, Kindness, Wholeness, Humaneness, etc. But by definition, since it is the dictionary which gives them to me, these particular concepts are not historical. Now what I need most often is ephemeral concepts, in connection with limited contingencies: neologism is then inevitable. (Barthes, 1972: 121)

The peculiar mixture of bells, rickshaws, and opium-dens that constitute "China" for a Frenchman Barthes dubs "Sininess," noting that the ugliness of the term is compensated for by the fact "that conceptual neologisms are never arbitrary: they are built according to a highly sensible proportional rule."

As a conceptual neologism, "mystory" is the title for a collection or set of elements gathered together temporarily in order to represent my comprehension of the scene of academic discourse. It is an idea of sorts, if nothing like a platonic *eidos,* whose name alludes to several constituent features (generated by the puncept of "mystory"):

A.   *History.* In her contribution to the authoritative (for an earlier generation) *Relations of Literary Study,* the late Rosalie Colie explained the difference between history and mystory:

> I have often been forced, by myself and by kind friends, to give up some beautiful theory which depended on material I happened to unearth. The words are important: that *I* happened to unearth, and that I *happened* to unearth. Though it is demonstrably true that chance favors the prepared mind, and serendipity is rarely arbitrary, one should not bank on the reliability of Pasteur's axiom in relation to oneself. After all, as medieval allegorists and Renaissance mythographers amply demonstrate, anything can be made to connect with anything: the trick is to distinguish the real from the illusory connection. (Colie, 1967: 20)

Colie knew about the tradition of patterning displaced and suppressed by the analytico-referential discourse of science, but she could not admit that the former constituted a legitimate model of cognition. Colie's attitude, admitting patterning as an object but not as a subject of knowledge, manifests the exclusionary ideology of referential cognition in the discipline of historiography. In teletheory, the two styles of cognition—analysis and pattern— are not mutually exclusive, but in alliance. Thus, mystory emphasizes precisely what *I happen* to unearth.

B.   *Herstory.* The progress from history to mystory is a classic example of the growth of language, of word formation by a certain mimesis. Feminism, in any case, makes mystory possible, and shows how to include race, class, region, nation in the formula along with gender and sex, while also manifesting the very limited ability of the received genres of criticism to represent alternative styles of thinking. The pun on *maistrie,* from *The Wife of Bath's Tale* ("And whan that I hadde geten unto me,/By maistrie, al the soveraynetee"), suggests the problem, shared with feminism, of finding an alternative to mastery and assertion as they are practiced in conventional academic discourse. How to think that which, being a scholar, scholarship takes for granted? What has been given to us, in what place, compromising every question we ask?

The feminist critique of film narrative addresses the patriarchal ideology at work in the philosopheme of theory as seeing. The convergence of theory and narrative in mystory makes this critique important for the formulation of teletheory. Barthes noted the connection among language, narrative, and the Oedipal story, such that narrative movement is directed by masculine desire. "The pleasure of the text is," Teresa de Lauretis says, citing Barthes, "an Oedipal pleasure (to denude, to know, to learn the origin and the end), if it is true that every narrative (every unveiling of the truth) is a staging of the (absent, hidden, or hypostatized father—which would explain the solidarity of narrative forms, of family structures, and of prohibitions of nudity)" (de Lauretis, 1984: 107–108).

Laura Mulvey, who posed the most extreme version of the sadism in the narrative drive, provided a description of male pleasure in cinema, based on a tension between a mode of representation of women in film and conventions producing the diegesis (the imaginary space and time of filmic realism):

> Each is associated with a look: that of the spectator in direct scopophilic contact with the female form displayed for his enjoyment (connoting male fantasy) and that of the spectator fascinated with the image of his like set in an illusion of natural space, and through him gaining control and possession of the woman within the diegesis. . . . By means of identification with him, through participation in his power, the spectator can indirectly possess her too. (Mulvey, 1977: 421)

The chief point for mystory in this argument is the display of unity joining the style of narrative realism and the apparatus of cinema with the cognitive style of science (both organized in Oedipal terms).

> Having divided the world into two parts—the knower (mind) and the knowable (nature)—scientific ideology goes on to prescribe a very specific relation between the two. It prescribes the interactions which can consummate this union, that is, which can lead to knowledge. Not only are mind and nature assigned gender, but in characterizing scientific and objective thought as masculine, the very activity by which the knower can acquire knowledge is also genderized. The relation specified between knower and known is one of distance and separation. (Keller, 79)

Keller's study of the language of science exposes the register at which film has access to the representation of theory. The rhetoric of scientific methodology, that is, draws upon metaphors of domination and control, aggression and assault upon nature, language that is shared by the cognitive styles of sadism, paranoia, and compulsion. Stories about the gendering of men and women, and their erotic relationships, then, may offer insight into relationships between subject and object at other levels of culture, including the practices of invention. Feminist critiques of method—especially those exploring the slogan "the personal is political" and the emotional foundations of reasoning—are an important model for locating the precise place of mystory as a genre of learning.

What kind of writing can replace the treatise which held the subject apart from the object of study? The search for a feminine aesthetic contributes to the intelligibility of an alternative, to the invention of a mode of knowing and representing knowledge that is not organized in terms of an object presented to a subject positioned as the observer of a spectacle. One expression of this project is "For the Etruscans," by Rachel DuPlessis. DuPlessis's essay takes note of the two issues of most importance for mystory—the function of personal experience in a discourse of knowledge and the value of formal experimentation as a strategy with political as well as epistemological goals.

Regarding the question of experimentation, DuPlessis notes that a feminine aesthetic is not an essentialist program: "We are making a creation, not a discovery" (DuPlessis, 1985: 281). In an essay that shows this creation while telling it, DuPlessis states the assumption that is also central to mystory:

> If it's really the forms, the language, which dominate us, then disrupting them as radically as possible can give us hope and possibilities. What I'd like to try to understand and explain to other people (*you yourselves are the riddle*) is how the form of women's writing is, if ambiguously (*of double, sometimes duplicating needs*) nonetheless profoundly revolutionary (as are, in their confusing ways, modernism and postmodernism, also written from positions of marginality to the dominant culture). (287)

She acknowledges, unlike some feminists, the commonality of the feminist project with other programs for change. "What we have been calling (the) female aesthetic turns out to be a specialized name for any practices available to those groups—nations, genders, sexualities, races, classes—all social practices which wish to criticize, to differentiate from, to overturn the dominant forms of knowing and understanding with which they are saturated" (285).

The problematic relationship between ideology and critique concerns the place of the individual in collective history, to which the feminists have contributed by insisting on the value of oral history and popular autobiography.

> In one domain, the modern Women's Movement well understands the process of silencing and is raising the "hidden" history of women's feelings, thoughts and actions more clearly to view. Feminist history challenges the very distinction "public"/"private" that silences or marginalizes women's lived sense of the past. But similar processes of domination operate in relation to specifically working-

class experiences, for most working-class people are also robbed of access to
the means of publicity and are equally unused to the male, middle-class habit
of giving universal or "historic" significance to an extremely partial experience.
(Popular Memory Group, 1982: 210)

Although it frequently takes the form of stories and autobiographies, then,
herstory is nonetheless representative and true "for women in a particular
historical phase," according to the Popular Memory Group, "because of the
personal character of women's oppressions" (238). The legitimation of the
personal and the popular as knowledge within the domain of historiography
is an important precedent for mystory, making available experience as an
alternative to the rule of method.

   C. *Mystery*. The function of narrative in historiography is a major question for mystory, which seeks an alternative to the manipulation of enigma
and delay, and the exploitation of identification and recognition, that informs
realistic narrative in fiction and history alike in the paradigm of referentiality.
Mystory continues to include narrative knowledge, but prefers to work with
forms such as the anecdote and joke in order to expose the way the grand
metanarratives position the subject in a particular ideology. The anecdote is
a more appropriate form in which to investigate the future of academic
discourse, about which there can be no authoritative account (mystory is not
science).
   To write a mystory about the future of theory is not to create an expectation
of resolution, the illusion of an explanation; not to predict, assert, or attack,
neither in the tone of science nor manifesto. Rather, the mystorical voice
derives from Freud's self-analysis more than from the peculiar institutionalization that followed from Freud's discoveries. Post-Freudian, it is less a
matter of learning a secret and more an effort to think outside living memory,
with the artificial or "dead" part of memory. The experiment exploits the
emerging middle voice in Western languages.
   Derrida is one of those who has attempted to articulate the middle voice
as a new condition of enunciation:

And we shall see why what is designated by "differance" is neither simply
active nor simply passive, that it announces or rather recalls something like
the middle voice, that is, speaks of an operation which is not an operation,
which cannot be thought of either as a passion or as an action of a subject
upon an object, as starting from an agent or from a patient, or on the basis
of, or in view of, any of these *terms*. But philosophy has perhaps commenced
by distributing the middle voice, expressing a certain intransitiveness, into
the active and the passive voice, and has itself been constituted in this
repression. (Derrida, 1973; 137)

In Derrida's differance, as we noted previously, the mode of oralysis seeks a notion of representation capable of electronic cognition.

Roland Barthes noted that, although most European languages did not have a middle voice, one was beginning to develop, originating in usage, in writing, marking the continuing evolution of the forms as well as of the technology. The appearance of the middle voice may also be seen as a symptom of the change in memory that accompanies a change in technology of communication. Deriving his definition form the linguists Meillet and Benveniste, Barthes explained the concept in relation to contemporary literature, in which "the instance of discourse" replaces the "instance of reality."

> In the case of the active voice, the action is accomplished outside the subject. In the case of the middle voice, on the contrary, the subject affects himself in acting; he always remains inside the action, even if an object is involved. The middle voice does not, therefore, exclude transitivity. Thus defined, the middle voice corresponds exactly to the state of the verb *to write:* today to write is to make oneself the center of the action of speech; it is to effect writing in being affected oneself; it is to leave the writer inside the writing, not as a psychological subject, but as the agent of the action. (Barthes, 1972: 164–165)

Mystory works in the middle voice, the voice of pedagogy foregrounded in the new instauration.

The element of mystery associated with the code of truth must derive in mystory rather from the symbolic code, in a way that shows its affiliation with some aspects of the conjectural mode of knowledge operative in hunting, divination, medicine, and psychoanalysis. As Ginzburg explains, "the hunter could have been the first 'to tell a story' " due to the particular kind of knowledge involved: "Its characteristic feature was that it permitted the leap from apparently insignificant facts, which could be observed, to a complex reality which—directly at least—could not. And these facts would be ordered by the observer in such a way as to provide a narrative sequence—at its simplest, 'someone passed this way.' Perhaps indeed the idea of a narrative, as opposed to spell or exorcism or invocation, originated in a hunting society, from the experience of interpreting tracks" (Ginzburg, 1983: 89).

Ginzburg adds that the disciplines practicing conjecture could never "meet the criteria of scientific inference essential to the galilean approach," being concerned, as they were, "with the qualitative, the individual case or situation or document *as individual.*" Such disciplines, including history, must make room for the element of chance while attending to the concrete, particular case, which is known through "signs and scraps of evidence" (92–93). Conjectural thinking, based on experience, is learned not from books but from "listening, from doing, from watching; their subtleties could scarcely be given formal expression and they might not even be reducible to words"

(100). Against the classifications of types that one might find in a treatise on physiognomy Ginzburg invokes the practice of horse dealers, card players, and lovers. The key term to identify the kind of knowledge that defies all rules, that enables a lover to differentiate the beloved as unique, is "intuition," which has its "high" forms, as in Arabic *firasa* ("the capacity to leap from the known to the unknown by inference on the basis of clues"), and its "low" forms (rooted in the senses) (98).

Ginzburg's article is included in the volume *The Sign of Three* collecting essays relating detective fiction to Peirce's theory of semiotics. The mode of detection ("the making of retrospective predictions"—"when causes cannot be repeated, there is no alternative but to infer them from their effects"— 103) dramatized in the characters of Sherlock Holmes and Auguste Dupin, manifests the abductive guesswork defined by Peirce. When read at this level, Jacques Lacan's seminar on "The Purloined Letter" constitutes an emblematic promotion of the conjectural (represented by Dupin's psychology) over the calculative (the reliance of the police on an empirical grid) paradigm. Freud's borrowing of the Oedipus story from Sophocles may be seen in this context less as the privileging of a particular content (the tragedy) and more as an affirmation of the mode of knowledge that psychoanalysis would reactivate against Platonic-Cartesian methodology. Indeed, keeping in mind that Lacan occasionally cited Jeremy Bentham, we can appreciate why Poe's story recommended itself to Lacan as an allegorical critique of method. Bentham, that is, associated method closely with logic, whose function of giving guidance to the mind he stated metaphorically as follows: if logic "were to be termed a *queen*, methodization, method, might be termed her *prime-minister*" (Buchler, 12). The Minister's attempt to blackmail the Queen in Poe's story, and his undoing by the conjectural Dupin, represents well the relationship among several styles of cognition.

D. *My Story.* The mystorian relates to the materials of a discipline in a way that Jean-François Lyotard describes as "pagan."

> What is very important is that among the pagans, these gods, even when they have the position of first speaker, are themselves narrated in narratives that tell what they are telling. This relation—an intradiegetic relation—means that the one who speaks is at the same time the hero of a story in which he is narrated himself; and these embeddings can be multiplied without end. It is, mutatis mutandis, the same situation as that of the Cashinahua narrator in relation to the story he tells since he narrates the story from a position where he is himself narrated. (Lyotard, 1985: 39)

A comparison with the quotations cited above show that Lyotard, too, is working with the middle voice, suggesting as a model for this voice the "pagan" or tribal story teller—the Indian, who has a place too as a hunter in that conjectural tradition.

Positioning oneself thus in a tradition suggests a rationale for the ghost-effect, as an alternative to the monumentality of academic mourning. In the pagan version, "every narrator presents himself as having first been a narratee: not as autonomous, then, but, on the contrary, heteronomous" (Lyotard, 1985: 32). The speaker is bound to retell the story heard, but not to the one from whom it was received. "I am obligated in the way of a relay that may not keep its charge but must pass it on" (35). This is the charge of mystory, reasoning in the mode of conduction.

Equally important is Lyotard's clarification of the relation to time reflected in the Cashinahua "tradition." It is not a relation of preservation that rejects the new, he notes. "The relevant feature is not faithfulness: it is not because one has preserved the story well that one is a good narrator, at least as far as profane narratives are concerned. On the contrary, it is because one 'hams' it up, because one invents, because one inserts novel episodes that stand out as motifs against the narrative plot line, which, for its part, remains stable, that one is successful." Like the pagan story teller, people in our culture, according to Lyotard, "get into language not by speaking it but by hearing it. And what they hear as children is stories, and first of all their own story, because they are named in it. This implies the very opposite of autonomy: heteronomy" (35). The middle voice is heteronomic, in which the teller designates him or herself as someone narrated by the social body and in which one has a place of one's own—a proper name. Such is the discourse of mystory. The student and teacher are the object of the explanation, engaging their own stories in the information set forth as scholarship. (The association of the middle voice with the "will to invent" will be discussed at the end of this chapter.)

E.   Envois: Mystory includes, then, history, herstory, maistrie, mystery, my story, paganism. Roland Barthes's novelesque of the intellect may be recognizable in the conceptual neologism elaborated here—"concepts that come to constitute allegories, a second language, whose abstraction is diverted to fictive ends" (Barthes, 1977a: 124). The embedding of the narrator within the narrative, such that the sender always speaks from the position of the receiver of the story for which one serves as a relay, may be associated with the "scene of writing" described by Derrida in terms of the envois (see The Post Card).

Derrida has investigated the peculiar temporality of theory, its already-not-yet structure, which, liberated from the metaphysics of teleology, may tell us something about the temporality of mystory. To understand the operation of theory we must remember, Derrida advises, that (for example) Freud, "the first and thus the only one to have undertaken, if not defined, self-analysis, did not himself know what it was" (Derrida, 1978a: 121). The question Derrida poses with respect to Freud's example—a founding question of mystory—is: "how can an auto-biographical writing, in the abyss of an unterminated self-analysis, give *its* birth to a world institution?" (121).

I want to take note of two aspects of this question. First, part of Freud's lesson for the genre of theory concerns the time of understanding for the writer or teacher *myself*. Theory as mystory is written with the apostrophe of self-address inherited from the essay tradition. A mystorical essay is not scholarship, not the communication of a prior sense, but the discovery of a direction by means of writing. It includes an assertion of comprehension that has more in common with the manifesto than with the essay. Consider Derrida's assessment of the status of *Beyond the Pleasure Principle*:

> Psychoanalytic theory exists. The first words imply an affirmation to that effect: "In psychoanalytic theory, we admit . . ." etc. We are not obliged to believe it exists, yet we must be sure that Freud means that it exists and that things happen in it. This statement is not a performative; it claims to ascertain and take note, but it takes note of a note whose speaker is also its producer. He is supposed to have been its producer, and those whom he associates with the movement of this production all accepted the contract which institutes him as producer. Thus when Freud puts forward a statement implying that psychoanalytic theory exists, he is in no respect in the situation of a theoretician in the field of another science, an epistemologist, or a historian of science. He takes note of a title of which the contract implies that it is his by right. He makes a contract with himself, he writes to himself, as if someone were informing himself by registered letter (on duty-stamped paper) about the attested existence of a theoretical history which he himself had launched. (Derrida, 1978a: 86)

The *envois,* in other words, concerns the invention of a theory and its institutionalization. Freud sends off a mystory couched as a contract and it comes back to him, to his name and credit, a science (or at least a discursive formation). This sending occurs in the middle voice (Freud is writing to himself via the apparatus) and in the register of the Symbolic code (which organizes discourse through the contracts governing exchange).

Teletheory seeks a pedagogy that positions the student and teacher in the relationship to knowledge that Freud had to psychoanalysis. Mystory, that is, intervenes on the side of discovery, within the problematic of the subject of knowledge. Derrida first raised this question in the context of Husserl's study of the origin of geometry, having to do with the problem of origins, of the foundation of a science on the ground of pre-science: the present of any idea is always pre-sent (*envois*). "Husserl repeatedly and obstinately returns to a question which is at bottom the following: how can the subjective egological evidence of sense become objective and intersubjective? How can it give rise to an ideal and true object, with all the characteristics that

we know it to have: omnitemporal validity, universal normativity, intelligibility for 'everyone,' uprootedness out of all 'here and now' factuality, and so
forth?. . . How can subjectivity go out of itself in order to encounter or
constitute the object?" (Derrida, 1978: 63). In asking how a unique, individual subject discovers, invents or otherwise gives rise to a system of knowledge, Derrida places the question of dissemination in the context of invention
and the apparatus—the conjunction of discovery and justification.

Derrida's extensive pursuit of this question is the basis for his interest in
psychoanalysis, which he takes as a potential model for a new order of
reasoning, suggesting how individual idioms may be generalized into theoretical formations. Freud is an excellent candidate for the study of euretics
(placing discovery in the context of rhetorical *inventio*) because of the nature
of the knowledge he sought: his application of method to the subject of
knowledge. Freud's texts are a point of departure for the mystorical integration of theory formation and autobiography. His texts are autobiographical,
"but in a completely different way from what was believed before," in a way
that will "force us to reconsider the whole topography of the *autos,* the self"
(Derrida, 1978a: 135).

In Freud's text, against the old model of "objective" science, "a 'domain'
opens up in which the 'inscription' of a subject in his text is also the necessary
condition for the pertinence and performance of a text, for its 'worth' beyond
what is called empirical subjectivity. . . . The notion of truth value is utterly
incapable of assessing this performance" (135). *Beyond the Pleasure Principle* manifests an inmixing of autobiographical and theoretical speculations,
as in the anecdote that Freud recited at the time of writing his text, recalling
his stay with his daughter, Sophie, and watching his grandson play a game
with bobbin on a string—the famous *fort/da* game. That Freud's consideration
of the Death Drive could be read as a kind of mourning, due to the untimely
deaths of the daughter and grandson, is not the autobiographical element
that most interests Derrida. In place of an existentialist "abyss," Derrida
explores the structure of embedding known as the *mise en abyme.*

In every detail we can see the superposition of the subsequent description of the
fort/da with the description of the speculative game, itself so assiduous and so
repetitive, of the grandfather in writing *Beyond the Pleasure Principle.* It's not,
strictly speaking, a matter of superposition, nor of parallelism, nor of analogy,
nor of coincidence. The necessity that links the two descriptions is of a different
sort: we shall not find it easy to give a name to it, but it is clearly the main thing
at stake for me in the sifting, interested reading that I am repeating here. . . .
The description of Ernst's game can also be read as an autobiography of Freud;
not merely an auto-biography entrusting his life to his own more or less testamen-
tary writing but a more or less living description of his own writing, of his way
of writing *Beyond the Pleasure Principle* in particular. (Derrida, 1978a: 119)

In Nietzsche's *Ecce Homo* Derrida finds another version of this mystorical *envois* that clarifies the status of the *auto* in the scene of writing. "This account that buries the dead and saves the saved as immortal is not *auto*-biographical because the signatory narrates his life, and the return of his past life, he is the narration's first if not only consignee. Within the text. And since the 'I' of this account only constitutes itself through the credit of the eternal return, the 'I' does not exist, does not sign prior to the account qua eternal return" (Derrida, 1982: 25). The *auto* of anecdotal invention here merges with the apostrophe of the *envois*. We are admonished not to mistake Nietzsche for another, not to confuse the once living, now dead person with the text signed "Nietzsche," or Freud with "Freud." The anecdotes embedded in the abyss of a theoretical discourse have a different status. They are told not for informational interest, not in reference to a prior life, but as part of a "speculative" organization, the *mise en abyme*, a double-take in which the narrative development of the event has formal, conceptual, explanatory consequences (the movement of the bobbin, away and back, is the organizing cadence of the pleasure principle, repulsion and attraction). The anecdotes, that is, are conceptual conductors.

Freud, then, demonstrated, especially in his case studies, the new status of conversion in an electronic culture, as well as the new semiotic importance acquired by everyday life in the context of science attempting to extend itself to every aspect of culture. As Lacan noted, in psychoanalysis the everyday life citizen finds a personal scribe who will record every utterance as once only a King's words would be recorded. The interest of psychoanalysis as a support for mystory is that it treats the spoken word as if it were written—oralysis. In it speech is recorded and studied using the fullest powers of hermeneutics, marking the complete integration of speaking and writing. This microanalysis reveals or makes accessible the extraordinary complexity of oral discourse. Nor is this complexity simply a feature of the dysfunctional status of therapeutic conversation. "Some speakers are convinced that they use very little indirection and limit themselves to plain and direct expression," William Labov and David Fanshel observe.

> But even a brief analysis of our own conversations shows us that we deal with others at roughly the same level of complexity and indirection as the therapeutic sessions analyzed in this book. We also use a wide range of mitigation and aggravation in modifying our utterances; we also construct long chains of indirect speech actions. We also use our intimate knowledge of rights, duties, and obligations to support, put-off, defend, or retreat from our actions in the course of conversation. (Labov and Fanshel, 360–361)

One of the arguments of teletheory in the construction of mystory is that conversation in the classroom operates with at least this degree of complexity, and that it has to be performed in its construction and reception with the kind of awareness manifested in the analytic situation. Noting that the therapeutic session is a kind of interview, Labov and Fanshel add that it is one kind of interview among others, which include the classroom. "We can subdivide interviews along two dimensions: according to who initiates the event, and who is to be helped by it. . . . In all these cases, the perceived benefit has a strong influence upon the type of verbal interaction which takes place, and so does the degree of compulsion that surrounds the event. Examinations given in school, text questions, and classroom quizzes are all kinds of interviews that produce very limited and constrained types of verbal response from the client" (31).

It has been noted that the interview is one of the predominant forms of our time, both in daily life, the popular media, and specialized research. Teletheory attempts to open up academic discourse to the broader reaches of this form, including some of the therapeutic dimensions, while reducing some of the policing functions, as is appropriate in the context of euretics. In the oralysis whose invention is still in progress, the functions of the analyst and analysand could be combined. Thierry Kuntzel has suggested that film is structured in just this oralytic way, as becomes apparent when cinema is understood in terms of dream work. Borrowing from the structures of allegory, in which the text tends to be an expansion on a pre-text. Kuntzel understands the development of a film as an explanation of an opening shot or sequence, often the credit sequence, which has all the features of a dream (condensed and displaced). "The spectator is *not* to be taken as homologous with the dreamer alone, as in previous film/dream analogies, but with two separate subjects: at first analogous to the dreamer (the introductory sequence representing the dream), the spectator subsequently becomes analogous to the analyst (the remainder of the film representing an explanation of the introductory 'dream' material)" (Altman, 527).

Oralysis is a discourse in which are merged the oral and literate modes of thought and representation, producing a new style of academic communication. Part of Freud's importance for us is his demonstration of the interrelationship and equality among the different registers of discourse, producing texts in which are integrated personal, popular, and high culture documents. Labov and Fanshel describe the therapeutic conversation in terms of an embedding of the patients' conduct in a series of concentric fields of discourse, which are in turn framed by the institution of psychoanalysis. The three principal fields of discourse are manifested in three different styles: "One is the style of everyday life, in which the patient tells about the events of the preceding days in a fairly neutral, objective, colloquial style." That style is embedded in the interview proper, used by both parties, marked by the specialized terminology of psychoanalysis, in which "emotions and behavior are evaluated as objects in themselves" (emotions are not expressed but discussed). The third style, framed by both of the others, is the family style—highly emotional outbursts, utilizing the idioms actually used in one's family situation (35–36).

A similarly embedded structure framed by the institution of education may be observed in academic discourse. My use of this analogy is facilitated by Labov and Fanshel's own use of a film metaphor. "Our primary interest must be in the coupling of one utterance with another, in the succession of cross sections, in the assembly of still frames into a moving picture" (69). The metaphor may be taken literally, since their study was facilitated, if not made possible, by the use of video tapes (the optical analysis praised by Benjamin). Their chief innovation or insight, as they explain, is that the locus of coherence of therapeutic conversations (and by extension of all conversations, including classroom discussions, I would add) is not at the surface level (regardless of the misleading effects of secondary elaboration). Rather, "the sequencing rules operate between abstract speech actions" arranged in a complex hierarchy (350). These propositional events are scattered or disseminated widely through the interview, and perform the drama of transference (about which more later). This performance dimension is activated also in teletheory, which draws upon the associational arrangement of poetics as much as it does upon the ordering of narration and exposition.

The embedded registers of the interview, especially as manifested in the psychoanalytic conversation, provide an important model for the representation of the cycle of invention in mystory. The three registers of discourse in mystory, that is, will be articulated according to the *mise en abyme* of the *envois* sent to myself.

2. Allegory as Post-Meaning

The recent insistence in discourse analysis on the interdependence of orality and literacy is one of the symptoms of the emergence of a new apparatus that includes a technology capable of writing orally (oralysis). One function of teletheory is to devise a genre integrating the features of oral, literate, and video discourse. This hybrid calls attention to the imaging (and imaginative) dimension of academic discourse, overlooked and even suppressed until now by the verbal or abstracting priorities of literacy. When video is integrated with the other media practices of pedagogy, academic discourse will rely as much on allegory as on allegoresis.

Roland Barthes is one of the theorists who has done the most to show how such a project might be realized. He is one of those, that is, who demonstrated how to adapt allegory to the functions of academic discourse, how to replace allegoresis with allegory for the representation of knowledge. One of his strategies was to appropriate certain texts by the act of writing introductions or prefaces that designated them as emblems of his own concepts and concerns. The collages of Bernard Réquichot, for example, who reworked preformed materials not as a realist would "in order to see better," but as a textualist, "in order to see something else," became, according to Barthes, "the emblem of my own work now" (Barthes, 1973: 22, 29–30).

One of the most important appropriations of this sort, in which Barthes signed the work of another artist, is the preface to the paintings of Arcimboldo. The innovation of Arcimboldo's portraits, Barthes said, is to devise for painting something similar to the double articulation of language (the point applies to the collage method in general, with Barthes's texts exemplifying one version of an adaptation of collage/montage writing to the critical essay): Arcimboldo's paintings function as if they were "written." "All is metaphor in Arcimboldo. Nothing is ever *denoted*, because the features (lines, forms, scrolls) which serve to compose a head have a sense already, and this sense is détourned toward another sense, thrown in a certain way beyond itself (that is what the word 'metaphor' means etymologically)" (Barthes, 1978: 37–38).

Arcimboldo's portrait heads, once constructed, function allegorically, and model what Barthes meant by "third meanings." the heads are composed at the first level of sense out of "nameable things: fruit, flowers, branches, fish, plants, books, children, and so forth," which are in turn nameable (at the second level) as, on the one hand, "heads," and at the same time as something completely other—a third sense—from a different region of the lexicon: "Summer," "Winter," "Calvin," "Fire," and the like. The names for this third level sense are derived from the viewer's general cultural codes: "I need a metonymic culture, which makes me associate certain fruits (and not others) with Summer, or, still more subtly, the austere hideousness of the visage of calvinist puritanism: and as soon as one quits the dictionary of words for a table of cultural meanings, of associations of ideas, in short for an encyclopedia of received ideas, one enters into the infinite field of connotation" (54–55).

Barthes's description of his own writing reflects an intellectual version of Arcimboldo's allegorical collages: "One could conceive *The Fashion System* as a poetic project, which consists precisely in constituting an intellectual object with nothing, or with very little, fabricating before the reader's eyes an intellectual object that develops gradually in its complexity, in the ensemble of its relations" (Barthes, 1981: 67). What happens with the articles of clothing in *The Fashion System* is possible with any cultural object: "Where it's understood that the cultural object possesses, by its social nature, a sort of semantic vocation: in itself, the sign is quite ready to separate itself from the function and operate freely on its own, the function being reduced to the rank of artifice or alibi . . . it likewise favors the birth of more and more complex lexicons of objects" (Barthes, 1983: 265).

In principle, then, every object is available, capable of being separated from its original justification or context and remotivated as part of a new discourse. Thus the semiologue may draw on the encyclopedia of a society the same way a poet makes use of a dictionary. Barthes's lesson for the teacher or popularizer is a lesson in allegorical writing, in which the elements of everyday life and of science may be introduced into a discourse to serve the ends of a third meaning, the nature of which may be associated with what Lacan characterized as bliss-sense (*jouis-sens*). Bliss-sense, as distinct from sense or common sense, concerns the pleasure of the text, the love of learning, the subject's desire for knowledge, which is grounded not in a specialized discipline but in the family story and everyday life. Bliss-sense manifests itself in mystory as the aleatory associations formed by the juxtapositions of the three levels of discourse—private, popular, and expert. Bliss-sense is a function of the circulation among the three levels, productive of discovery. The surprise it produces in the writer first of all is the academic equivalent of the uncanny, marking the place of the inmixing of self and other in the unconscious.

The film or video camera makes it possible for anyone to be an Arcimboldo—to write with the objects of the world. "That film should be the primary vehicle for modern allegory may be attributed not only to its unquestioned status as the most popular of contemporary art forms, but also to its mode of representation. Film composes narratives out of a succession of concrete images, which makes it particularly suited to allegory's essential pictogrammatism" (Owens, 230). What one receives in a film is not the world but a discourse on/of the world. We may discern in Barthes's allegorical procedure the model for an essayistic or pedagogical equivalent of filmic writing, demonstrating one version of academic discourse drawing on the features of film/video. Against the conventional pedagogy that attempts to represent the object of study in its discourse, an allegorical pedagogy works by figuration. "Similarly, and even more than the text, the film will *always* be figurative (which is why films are still worth making)—even if it represents nothing" (Barthes, 1975: 56).

Barthes's best-known discussion of third meanings concerns film stills. In the images from Eisenstein's *Ivan the Terrible* (1945–46) Barthes remarks not only an informational level and a symbolic level, but a third meaning, an "obtuse" meaning which "disturbs, sterilizes" metalanguage, because it is "discontinuous, indifferent to the story and to the obvious meaning (as the signification of the story)" (Barthes, 1977: 61). *Camera Lucida* develops the notion of the *punctum,* the wound, to work with the emotional nature of these third meanings. But the essay on Eisenstein offers several suggestions which are not pursued in the later book, but which may be equally useful for articulating that which inherently resists the naming process in the obtuse. Even though he is discussing images, Barthes indicates in a note that his third meanings have to do with the "vocal writing" mentioned in *The Pleasure of the* Text (which may be associated with his interest in the "voices" of the codes). Barthes found that the best image for the level of writing that interested him was precisely the cinema: "A certain art of singing can give an idea of this vocal writing; but since melody is dead, we may find it more easily today at the cinema. In fact, it suffices that the cinema capture the sound of speech *close up* (this is, in fact, the generalized definition of the 'grain' of writing)" (Barthes, 1975: 67). Barthes clarified the nature of this "close up" when he noted that "in the classical paradigm of the five senses, the third sense is hearing (first in importance in the Middle Ages). This is a happy coincidence, since what is here in question is indeed *listening*" (Barthes, 1977: 53). Barthes's intermixing of the categories of writing and speaking manifested in these remarks place him fully in the dimension of oralysis.

One listens to writing or images to hear something like the key names Saussure heard in Latin poetry. "The obtuse meaning is not situated structurally, a semantologist would not agree as to its objective existence (but then what is an objective reading?); and if to me it is clear (to me), that is *still* perhaps (for the moment) by the same 'aberration' which compelled the lone and unhappy Saussure to hear in ancient poetry the enigmatic voice of anagram, unoriginated and obsessive. . . . The obtuse meaning is a signifier without a signified, hence the difficulty in naming it" (60–61). The meanings that emerge out of the juxtaposed elements in a mystory are similarly *obtuse*, in that they are not intended, not *sent* as messages, since the Other cannot be said to "communicate" in the usual sense.

The clue to note is that the obtuse meaning may be nameable if one listens in the right way, attending to the peculiar situation of the third sense: "I even accept for the obtuse meaning the word's pejorative connotation: the obtuse meaning appears to extend outside culture, knowledge, information; analytically, it has something derisory about it: opening out into the infinity of language, it can come through as limited in the eyes of analytic reason; it belongs to the family of pun, buffoonery, useless expenditure. Indifferent to moral or aesthetic categories (the trivial, the futile, the false, the pastiche), it is on the side of the carnival" (55). This passage indicates first that the obtuse may be located, its operations identified, not only by the punctum of emotion, but also by the laughter associated with carnival. Barthes noted a model for this possibility in Bataille's approach to third meanings: "Bataille does not counter modesty with sexual freedom but . . . with *laughter*" (Barthes, 1975: 55). The second point to be stressed in Barthes's notion of the obtuse as carnival is that the third meaning may enter into language and be named by means of the pun. The pun is what may be heard in the close-up of a film or text considered at the level of vocal writing, as we heard in the example of the Marx Brothers in the previous chapter.

The next step is to consider the implications of Barthes's obtuse linguistics as a strategy of discourse. Barthes maintained a dialogical relationship with the three major sociolects, all of which share one common feature: "I suffer three arrogances: that of Science, that of the *Doxa*, that of the Militant" (Barthes, 1977a: 47). He described his career as a continuous attempt to scandalize the reigning discourse in each domain, a project carried out by posing a paradox in reaction to the endoxal, to popular opinion. The dependence of his paradoxes on the doxa indicates the ambivalence of his attitude toward opinion, and his recognition of the extent of his own complicity with ideology: his displeasure is also a desire, making his critique function also as a "reaction formation," a defense, in which he experienced his pleasure in the form of a displeasure (the very definition of repression). Alluding to his interest in television and radio programs, for example, Barthes had this to say about "la bêtise"; "It's lovely, it takes your breath away, it's strange; and about stupidity, I am entitled to say no more than this: *that it fascinates me*" (51).

Barthes described his relationship to science in the same terms of exclusion and fascination used to identify his attitude to popular opinion ("I am constantly listening to what I am excluded from"—51). His relationship to the episteme, to specialized "jargons," in other words, is not itself scientific: "What is an idea for him, if not a *flush of pleasure*? 'Abstraction is in no way contrary to sensuality' (*Mythologies*). Even in his structuralist phase, when the essential task was to describe the humanly *intelligible*, he always associated intellectual activity with delight" (Barthes, 1977a: 87). Here we have the essence of Barthes's strategy—not to pose an alternative thesis nor to repeat himself one of the modes of arrogance, but to operate their articulation, to "write" with them in order to discover what *else* might be said through them—hence the notion of "post-meaning," whose *significance* is bliss-sense.

To review the operation of post-meaning is to glimpse some of the possibilities of mystory. Post-meaning, of course, may be associated with the notion of "third meanings," the "obtuse" angle of sense which Lacan also exploited in his pedagogy: "You can make use [of the wall of language] in order to reach your interlocutor," Lacan observed, arguing against traditional didacticism, "but on condition that you understand, from the moment that it is a question of using this wall, that both you and he are on this side, and that you must aim to reach him along it, like a cue-shot along the cushion" (Lacan, 1981: 71). Barthes's image for the indirection required by his alternative discourse is also a game, "prisoner's base" ("or capture the flag"). The way young Roland played the game was not to provoke the other team, but to "free the prisoners—the effect of which was to put both teams back into circulation. . . . In the great game of the owners of speech, we also play prisoner's base. . . . In the conflict of rhetorics, the victory never goes to but the *third language*. The task of this language is to release the prisoners: to scatter the signifieds, the catechisms" (Barthes, 1977a: 50). The alternative discourse, in short, exploits the indirections of metaphor, supplementing science and opinion (the opposing teams) with aesthetics.

> The new discourse is perhaps built on a particular metaphor of which one rarely speaks, but which, personally, interests me greatly: catachresis. Modern discourse is "catachrestic," because on the one hand it produces a continuous effect of metaphorisation, but on the other there is no possibility of saying the thing in terms other than the metaphor: this conjunction of the image and a denotative void accomplishes a kind of heterology of discourse: intellectual discourse is as strange as a poetic discourse. (Barthes, 1978a: 438–439)

Post-meaning, then, attempts an approach to understanding and cognition quite distinct from the certainties and classifications of science, opinion, and politics, all of which constitute, however, the reserve out of which a third sense may be invented. Barthes suggested that this third language works not just with metaphors, but with emblems and allegories: "In relation to the systems which surround him, what is he? Say an echo chamber . . . he *invokes* notions, he rehearses them under a name; he makes use of this name as of an emblem (thereby practicing a kind of philosophical ideography) and this emblem dispenses him from following to its conclusion the system of which it is the signifier (which simply makes him a sign)" (Barthes, 1977a: 74). Barthes's linguistic allegory, noted earlier (when he used the linguistic concept of "neutralization" as the vehicle for addressing the ethical category of the "neutral" (Barthes, 1977a: 124) is a good example of using a discourse of knowledge allegorically. The procedure involves investing a theoretical or scientific concept with a value, or with a personal significance, such that the final *signified* of the discourse is not the general abstraction, but the "personality," the "imaginary" of the signer, "of the subject who speaks, of his affect, of his profound pathos" (Barthes, 1978a: 439).

Barthes's notion of the theoretical allegory expresses a formula for a new approach to academic discourse which still awaits its application—in mystory—suggesting exactly how to compose simultaneously with learned and quotidian orders of sense. Such a practice constitutes one side of Barthes's double orientation, the other part of which concerns the way certain items from everyday life enter his discourse as images for that which cannot be defined: "Text is never approached except metaphorically: it is the field of the haruspex, it is a banquette, a faceted cube, an excipient, a Japanese stew, a din of decors, a braid, some Valenciennes lace, a Moroccan wadi, a broken television screen, a layered pastry, an onion, etc." (Barthes, 1977a: 74). Just as the scientific concept may be an allegorical image, so may the quotidian item, a detail from daily life, be an "intellectual object":

> Different from the "concept" and from the "notion," which are purely ideal, the *intellectual object* is created by a kind of leverage upon the signifier. . . . It is a

good thing, he thought, that out of consideration for the reader, there should pass through the essay's discourse, from time to time, a sensual object (as in *Werther*, where suddenly there appeared a dish of green peas cooked in butter and a peeled orange separated into sections). A double advantage: sumptuous appearance of a materiality and a distortion, a sudden gap wedged into the intellectual murmur. . . . (Thus, sometimes, in Japanese haiku, the line of written words suddenly opens and there is the drawing of Mount Fuji or of a sardine which delicately appears in place of the abandoned word). (135)

The details thus introduced into the discourse, these intellectual objects (quotidian items charged with value), constitute what Barthes called the "novelesque," signifiers of the "lived" as opposed to the "intelligible" domain. These details are also identified as the "biographemes" of the subject of knowledge, the one who writes, so they ultimately have the same "global meaning" as the scientific emblems. To read for the biographeme, or to write one's own, is another example of the juxtaposition and recombination of doxa and episteme, relating to both in terms not of knowledge but of pleasure. "I hope to dissipate or elude the moral discourse that has been held on each of them," Barthes said in his study of Sade, Fourier, and Loyola; "working, as they themselves worked, only on languages, I unglue the text from its purpose as a guarantee: socialism, faith, evil" (Barthes, 1976: 9). Reading Amiel in this way, Barthes noted his "irritation that the well-meaning editor (another person foreclosing pleasure) had seen fit to omit from his journal the everyday details, what the weather was like on the shores of Lake Geneva, and retain only insipid moral musing: yet it is this weather that has not aged, not Amiel's philosophy" (Barthes, 1975: 53–54). The third language, in other words, tends to add moral value to theoretical concepts, and strip it from moralistic rhetoric.

The novelesque, then, described as the novel without the plot or the characters, consists only of the details of everyday life, of the setting or situation. "In daily life, I feel for everything I see and hear a kind of curiosity, almost an intellectual affectivity of a novelesque order. . . . For me, the problem will be to find little by little the form which will detach the novelesque from the novel" (Barthes, 1981: 192). Related to his desire to be the ethnologist of the modern, and to write a semiology of semiologies, *Roland Barthes* exemplifies a hybrid mode, the "intellectual novelesque," displaying the biographemes and emblems of his image repertoire (those things, personal and scientific, with and by which he is identified . "I am put on stage as the character in a novel, but without a proper name and to whom will happen no novelistic adventure properly speaking" (211).

What happens when Barthes plays off the two levels of language against each other, in the context of the three arrogances of discourse, in order to achieve a post-meaning (which translates doxa into intellectual objects and episteme into emblems) may be understood in terms of Jakobson's notion that poetry is created when one of the axes of language (paradigmatic axis) is projected onto the other (syntagmatic axis). In Barthes's case, the projection involves the relations between two second-order languages—connotation and metalanguage. "In connotative semiotics, the signifiers of the second system are constituted by the signs of the first; this is reversed in metalanguage: there the signifieds of the second system are constituted by the signs of the first" (Barthes, 1970b: 92). He observed that "*ideology* is the *form* (in Hjelmslev's sense of the word) of the signifieds of connotation, while *rhetoric* is the form of the connotators" (92). At the same time, metalanguage is an *operation,* "a *description* founded on the empirical principle."

The double inscription of Barthes's post-meaning, then, involves an oscillation between connotation and metalanguage. Against the doxa Barthes imposes a metalanguage on connotation, as in *Mythologies* or *The Fashion System.* "We have seen that the signified of this system (the rhetorical) was not easily controlled on the level of the system's users: latent, general, it cannot be *named* in a uniform manner by those who receive the connoted message: it does not have an assured terminological existence, except on the level of the analyst, whose proper function is precisely to superimpose a nomenclature on latent signifieds, which he alone has the power to bring to light" (Barthes, 1983: 292).

Against science, at the same time, Barthes explored the *connotations of metalanguage,* the effect in the life-world of scientific systems or concepts, which can only be designated metaphorically, by catachresis, as in *A Lover's Discourse* (which images the Lacanian system). Post-meaning is a continuous juxtaposition of and movement between these two directions, between taxonomy and emblem, metalanguage and connotation, tendencies that may be associated with two distinct literary modes: "One dares not leave the fact in a state of in-significance; this is the movement of fable, which draws from each fragment of reality a lesson, a meaning. A converse book is conceivable: which would report a thousand 'incidents' but would refuse ever to draw a line of meaning from them; this would be, quite specifically, a book of haiku" (Barthes, 1977a: 151).

In teletheory Barthes is read as symptomatic of literacy responding to the influence of the new media. The place he opens in discourse—the novelesque—makes thinkable a new intellectual design, a new genre called mystory, in which the fable and the haiku are written at once, putting post-meanings in the service of invention.

3. Theory Diegesis

The novelesque in teletheory makes theory filmable, a capability that follows in any case from the integration of oral, literate, and video media.

The filmable dimension of theory is discerned most readily by means of the pleasure of narrative, as defined, for example, by Bill Nichols:

> Narrative dangles a lure before us; it promises to unfold in time, yet not run down or dissipate; to take form, to in-form. Desire—the desire to recognize a return, a closure, to enjoy pleasure as the subject-who-knows when we recognize the repetition/transformation of the beginning in the ending—snares us in these unraveling coils of events loosely called the story. Delay teases and tantalizes, like foreplay, with its promise of things to come. . . . If we take the lure, we yield to the tale. It carries us, transports us into a fictional world (the diegesis) where the desire invoked will be satisfied. Pleasure is not wholly deferred. Various puzzles, little enigmas are continually posed, deferred, and resolved; partially resolved; repressed or forgotten, replaced by new enigmas. Narrative plays upon a retrospective or retroactive principle in which the partiality of the moment is suspended only to be engaged by a later influx of supplemental significance. (Nichols, 1981: 74–75)

I want to focus on the manipulation of the diegetic effect in one example of a theoretical essay (the way an essay, like a novel, "transports us into a imaginary space and time"), in order to show that mystory does not impose narrative on theory, but simply expands or elaborates on the narrative codes and their simple forms already available within theoretical discourse.

Nichols noted that narrative, documentary, and experimental modes of filmmaking are not entirely distinct, but share certain structuring principles. The explanatory effect of a documentary, thus, may be described in terms of diegesis, especially if it uses a mode of indirect address. But the diegesis in exposition, as distinct from narrative, according to Nichols,

> is no longer a spatio-temporal universe plausibly maintained in its autonomy, but rather a conceptual universe. . . . This removes diegesis from its close association, in Metz's writings for example, with the image track and the projection of an illusionistic universe; it makes diegesis a notion more closely linked with the sound track, primarily with speech and the logical universe of its ordering. In other words, exposition does not require the fabrication of an imaginary spatio-temporal universe so much as the fabrication of an imaginary rhetorical universe where demonstration, apparent or real, takes place. (Nichols, 183–184)

Exposition may not *require* a diegesis, but it frequently uses one. I want to show that theoretical exposition sometimes does include a subordinated, imaginary spatio-temporal universe, recognizable as like our own, but which functions rhetorically as a figure (allegorically). Ludwig Wittgenstein provides one example of how an argument may create a diegetic effect. He does not in fact eliminate the narrative spatio-temporal world in favor of a rhetorical order, but retains this imaginary order and exploits it for conceptual effects, as part of the rhetorical demonstration. The possibility of narrative diegesis as a common feature of theoretical writing is a major issue for mystory both because it suggests that all the theory couched in the alphabetic forms of the treatise and essay are translatable into film, and because from such translation projects we can learn how to compose theoretical research directly in a video format.

In classical narrative, committed to realism, the diegesis is unfragmented, closed, illusionistic; affords the pleasure of recognition (familiarity) and allows identification (of ourselves as subjects); takes on thematic resonance through the use of symbols (signifiers already charged with meaning) and markers (items of daily life with fewer connotations), directed by the five codes presented in *S/Z* (Nichols, 85). Although oriented in its own way by the code of truth, the diegesis in theoretical writing, in some cases, tends to be writerly and modern, relying for its closure on the rhetorical register (which suggests an exercise: to produce a writerly text by extracting from an essay only its diegetic materials, thus identifying the essayistic equivalent of the novelesque—the essayesque?). Wittgenstein's *Brown Book,* read in the context of Barthes's novelesque, demonstrates the organizing power of the anecdote and the seme for representing conceptual themes.

Wittgenstein is the master of the theoretical seme, whose musical nature is noted in Barthes's definition of this code:

> The seme is "cited"; we would like to give this word its tauromachian meaning: the *citar* is the stamp of the heel, the torero's arched stance which summons the bull to the banderilleros. Similarly, one cites the signified to make it come forth, while avoiding it in the discourse. This fleeting citation, this surreptitious and discontinuous way of stating themes, this alternating of flux and outburst, create together the *allure* of the connotation; the semes appear to float freely, to form a galaxy of trifling data in which we read no order of importance: the narrative technique is impressionistic: it breaks up the signifier into particles of verbal matter which make sense only by coalescing. (Barthes, 1974: 22)

Wittgenstein's reliance upon the semic code allows me to observe in his style an analogy with filmic writing: *The Brown Book,* with its numbered fragments, consisting of scenes and descriptions of material or concrete examples, already presents an effect of editing, of a shot list organized by montage. That he should favor the paradigmatic over the syntagmatic codes is a corollary of his belief that it is possible to show more than one can tell. Wittgenstein may have learned something about writing from watching those Carmen Miranda movies, as well as from reading the detective magazines he was fond of, in that he tends to provide a continuity for his fragments as if they were shot sequences, relying on a pattern of repetitions and matches that "gathers" significance through juxtaposition and arrangement, rather than through direct metacommentary.

The first number of *The Brown Book* is a scene: "Imagine this language— Its function is the communication between a builder A and his man B" (Wittgenstein, 1965: 77). The scene concerns the enigma, "what is knowing?" A shouts, "Now I can go on." "What was it that happened when suddenly he saw how to go on?" (112). With the accumulation of such scenes, a diegesis begins to form; I accept the lure of examples and begin to identify an imaginary space and time of a particular situation. As an analogy for the reading process, for example, a pianola is introduced into the scene, playing a roll of music, and I begin to think as much, if not more, about this instrument and its connotations as about the argument or enigma it purports to illustrate. "The mechanism which immediately suggests itself when we wish to show what in such a case we should call 'being guided by the signs' is a mechanism of the type of a pianola. Here, in the working of the pianola we have a clear case of certain actions, those of the hammers of the piano, being guided by the pattern of the holes in the pianola roll" (118).

Part of the effect is due to the insistence on the example itself, the extension of the analogy at length, almost forgetting about the tenor in order to work through the details of the thing: the formula for the allegorical effect. But the argument also reinforces this effect: "We could say that the notches and teeth forming a key bit are not comparable to the words making up a sentence but to the letters making up a word" (119). I want at first to know, if I am reading with desire, what that word is. Then I realize that the example is itself this "word," that the example conveys a meaning which I must name myself (a connotation). At the same time I am being taught how to read this text, its means of providing sensible things to represent intelligible ideas. The concept is accessible through a modeling of quotidian situations and objects; it is not hidden as a private psychological event. Moreover, he has opened up a critique of method—of the semiotic, conjectural method of following signs. The teeth of the pianola biting into the roll of music as something to do with artificial memory, with mechanical reproduction, and so I pay special attention.

How are we to read the models? "It was not the function of our examples to show us the essence of 'deriving,' 'reading,' and so forth through a veil of inessential features; the examples were not descriptions of an outside letting us guess at an inside which for some reason or other could not be shown in its nakedness. We are tempted to think that our examples are indirect means for producing a certain image or idea in a person's mind,—that they *hint* at something which they cannot show" (125). We are tempted to think, that is, that Wittgenstein is himself thinking within the paradigms of calculative or conjectural truth, both of which are equally concerned with a world of depth and of realism. But this is precisely the mode of cognition for which mystory seeks an alternative. "Our method," Wittgenstein continues, "is *purely descriptive;* the descriptions we give are not hints of explanations" (125). So, if we are not dealing with explanations, neither are we following a conventional narrative. How to describe or show a concept (for example the concept of "familiarity") is the stylistic challenge taken up in *The Brown Book.* The experimental solution is to describe a concept in the same way one might describe a thing, thus mingling the sensible and the intelligible:

> I gave the circumstances of recognizing the man as a means to the end of describing the precise situation of the recognition. One might object to this way of describing the *experience,* saying that it brought in irrelevant things, and in fact wasn't a description of the feeling at all. In saying this one takes as the prototype of a description, say, the description of a table, which tells you the exact shape, dimensions, the material which it is made of, and its color. Such a description one might say pieces the table together. There is on the other hand a different kind of description of a table, such as you might find in a novel, e.g., "It was a small rickety table decorated in Moorish style, the sort that is used for smoker's requisites." Such a description might be called an indirect one; but if the purpose of it is to bring a vivid image of the table before your mind in a flash, it might serve this purpose incomparably better than a detailed "direct" description. . . . These considerations should warn you not to think that there is one real and direct description of, say, the feeling of recognition as opposed to the "indirect" one which I have given. (181)

The connotations are beginning to pile up. A reader of Sherlock Holmes might associate the table used for smoking requisites as belonging in the apartment of the famous detective. Wittgenstein, we learn, includes in his descriptive method the use of novelesque detail as well as of empirical measure. This table inevitably suggests the other ones discussed by Jack Goody as representing the specific properties of alphabetic writing. His argument will be carried in part then by a vivid image, an active image in terms of the mnemonic tradition, selecting an object from the category of familiar things, rather than of ridiculous or violent things, the former being appropriate to the theme of the essay, which is memory.

Is Wittgenstein still conjectural, semiotic? "This example showed us one of the family of cases in which this word is used. And the explanation of the use of this word, as that of the use of the word 'reading,' or 'being guided by symbols,' essentially consists in describing a selection of examples exhibiting characteristic features, some examples showing these features in exaggeration, others showing transitions, certain series of examples showing the trailing off of such features" (125). He is showing us how items may be gathered into sets on the basis of similarity or resemblance, interrelated by fine distinctions of difference. Is this then how we comprehend the world, by reading connotations off the surface of a picture, by means of signs?

To approach knowledge from the side of not knowing what it is, from the side of the one who is learning, not from that of the one who already knows, is to do mystory. What is the experience of knowing, of coming to or arriving at an understanding, characterized as following a path or criss-crossing a field, if not a narrative experience, the experience of following a narrative? Narrativity as knowledge has a processual character: "the reader's attitude is a teleologically guided form of attention, always enlivened by the promise of additional insights. Following a story is very much a temporal process, not a logic sequitur" (Holdheim, 1984, 238–239). To the extent that a journey through a landscape is an adequate metaphor for theoretical method, the classic structure of narrative acts or functions—departure, interdiction, rendezvous—constitute a figure of comprehension, suggesting that it may be possible to "calculate" a theory by means of narrative.

Hayden White noted the unity of narrative and explanation at this universal level of high generalization: "far from being a problem, narrative might well be considered a solution to a problem of general human concern, namely, the problem of how to translate *knowing* into *telling*" (White, 1980: 1). To support his point he adds a footnote on etymology: "the words 'narrative,' 'narration,' 'to narrate,' and so on derive via the Latin *gnārus* ('knowing,' 'acquainted with,' 'expert,' 'skillful,' and so forth) and *narrō* ('relate,' 'tell') from the Sanskrit root *gna* ('know')." In more specific terms, I noted that the two codes describing the forward movement of narrative—action and enigma—have an equivalent in argument—demonstration and question. Narrative pleasure, as Nichols observed, derives from the simulation of an explanation: "things change. Yet the end refers us to the beginning. The middle gives us an account of this change. But it is more than simply a chronicle. Narratives are also a way of accounting *for* change. That is, they are a form of explanation and the great bulk of explanation takes place in the middle of a narrative" (Nichols, 1981: 76). How is this change *experienced* in a theory?

To learn the lesson of Wittgenstein's style we need to be clear about what is at stake in his narrative. First, his insight is that cognition includes an *emotional* experience, a certain feeling—a feeling of *recognition* or *familiarity*. To be more precise, *The Brown Book* describes something that, as Heidegger might say, has never yet come into appearance, whose very nature is not to appear—ideology. Narrative pleasure is one way to locate the pleasure-in-recognition central to the maintenance and persistence of ideological identification. Bill Nichols, in fact, focuses his study summarizing the insights of film theory, on just this phenomenon—the click of recognition by which meaning arises and boundaries are organized. "Instead of seeing the activity of our own perceptions and the construction of an image's meaning, we see through our perceptual habit and the image's construction to an already meaningful world (without, in this case, 'seeing through' the deception that is involved, the actual production or fabrication of meaning" (Nichols, 1981: 38). Such is the diegetic effect. Nichols cites Althusser's insights into the ideological operation of recognition: "It is indeed a peculairity of ideology that it imposes obviousnesses as obviousnesses, which we cannot *fail to recognize* and before which we have the inevitable and natural reaction of crying out: 'That's obvious! That's right! That's true!'" (39).

Part of the importance of *The Brown Book* for mystory is that it makes visible the goes-without-saying dynamic of pleasure-in-recognition ("Now I can go on," in Wittgenstein's expression of the explanatory effect). Not only that, but it shows us how to teach this elusive illusion upon which is based the *misrecognition* "that traps us within an imaginary realm of identity and opposition governed by desire to be what we are not and to possess what cannot be 'had' " (42). The "imaginary" to which Nichols alludes is Lacan's Imaginary register of identification with ego ideals. The embedding of the imaginary in the symbolic is a useful way to think about the structuration of the *mise en abyme* or embedding found in the psychoanalytic interview as described by Labov.

Meanwhile, let's observe how Wittgenstein accomplishes a demonstration with his central example, one that appeals to the imagination, and to the imaginary space and time of narrative diegesis. "Imagine that someone wished to give you an idea of the facial characteristics of a certain family, the So and so's, he would do it by showing you a set of family portraits and by drawing your attention to certain characteristic features, which, e.g., would enable you to see how certain influences gradually changed the features, in what characteristic ways the members of the family aged, what features appeared more strongly as they did so" (Wittgenstein, 1965: 125). In the diegesis, I find him thinking about his own family, growing old, looking at the Wittgenstein family album as seme.

The connotations of the album as seme are meant to remind us of the abstract problem—concept formation, gathering particulars into a set, anthology, or album (continuing the association Havelock noted between the familial and conceptual registers). "We see that a vast net of family likenesses connects the cases in which the expressions of possibility, 'can,' 'to be able to,' etc. are used. Certain characteristic features, we may say, appear in these cases in different combinations" (117). The difficulty is to communicate (represent) what the items in a set have in common. "Suppose I had explained to someone the word 'red' by having pointed to various red objects and given the ostensive explanation. . . . If he has really got hold of what is in common between all the objects I have shown him, he will be in the position to follow my order. But what is it that is in common to these objects?" (130).

Wittgenstein is describing the operations of quotidian categories. In mystory the formation of quotidian concepts and the formation of disciplinary concepts are related in the manner of a translation between two languages. Part of the value of Wittgenstein's example is that it figures this relationship by way of a family album, a memory book, as the vehicle for the tenor of concept formation, associated with the memory formation of philosophy. The experience of understanding is the same as the feeling of familiarity one has in recognizing the faces of family members in the photo album. An explanation, thus, consists of noting such similarities and differences. And the fundamental similarity established by the end of *The Brown Book* is that between recognizing the expression on a face, and understanding expression in words (the articulation of the sensible and the intelligible). "I am impressed by the reading of a sentence, and I say the sentence has shown me something, that I have noticed something in it" (178). There follows a discussion of which "expression" best conveys the experience of "meaning": "'Look at the line of these eyebrows' or 'The *dark* eyes and the *pale* face!', these expressions would draw attention to certain features. . . . 'The whole face expresses bewilderment' " (179). As Barthes said, "the pensive (in faces, in texts) is the signifier of the inexpressible, not of the unexpressed. . . . At its discreet urging, we want to ask the classic text: *What are you thinking about?* but the text, wilier than all those who try to escape by answering: *about nothing,* does not reply, giving meaning its last closure: suspension" (Barthes, 1974: 216–217). Wittgenstein, too, is describing the classic text, of which *The Brown Book* is a counter-example.

Despite the illusion of allusion, of something more left unsaid (promising further explanations of something withheld or hidden), a narrative, Barthes suggests, only explains itself. To perceive the productive process of the system is the one knowledge-effect of the text, against the ideology effects of identification and recognition (positioning the subject in the dominant ideology).

> Cinematographic specificity thus refers to a *work,* that is, to a process of transformation. The question becomes: is the work made evident, does consumption of the product bring about a "knowledge effect" [Althusser], or is the work concealed? If the latter, consumption of the product will obviously be accompanied by ideological surplus value. On the practical level, this poses the question of by what procedures the work can in fact be made "readable" in its inscription. (Baudry, 533)

In teletheory this distinction is problematized by means of a conduction between these two effects.

Wittgenstein in his own way discouraged us from looking for the more of surplus value; or rather he showed this more in its emergence, using music as his example: "It has sometimes been said that what music conveys to us are feelings of joyfulness, melancholy, triumph, etc. . . . To such an account we are tempted to reply 'Music conveys to us *itself!*" (178). As Barthes put it, the discourse itself is the protagonist of the narrative. In the essay, as in the narrative, we begin to glimpse the possibility of an argument or of a story without enigma: "The question itself keeps the mind pressing against a blank wall, thereby preventing it from ever finding the outlet. To show a man how to get out you have first of all to free him from the misleading influence of the question" (169). We are reminded here of Barthes's suggestion for a writerly narrative that would operate without the syntagmatic codes, dropping the codes of Action and Enigma. Wittgenstein makes thinkable the possibility of a writerly essay that could reason in the absence of argument and problem.

What then becomes of the anecdote? At the same time that he has been arguing against the narrative impression, however, Wittgenstein has been building a diegesis, to show us its effects, and how easily we become lured by its easy recognitions. Yet, when organized by the repetitions of semes, the anecdotal scene can effectively communicate a theory, as he shows us by entrusting his own theory of language to an anecdote. Whose dark eyes and pale face have we been shown (whose photograph in the album is he thinking of)? Just as it was Freud's own grandson who played the *fort/da* game in *Beyond the Pleasure Principle,* so is this album Wittgenstein's own. The music used to refute the reality effect of discourse is charged with what Barthes might call a "third" meaning that gathers in the pianola playing a particular roll with the photograph in the album. The music functions within the semic code, whose connotations are disseminated throughout the text. We may ask: in this theory of expression, what is being expressed? Can a theory express an emotion? It can if cognition itself is emotional (in its ideological register). And this emotional dimension of comprehension is precisely what is in need of exposure, such that to tell us about cognition without making us at the same time experience it emotionally would be to give a false account. And there is the further question, still delayed, concerning the dominant emotion of contemporary thought.

"The pleasure of recognition, among other things," Nichols observes, "may provide at least one point of entry in an attempt to explain the aesthetic experience, a line of thought pursued quite often in traditional aesthetics, which will be replaced here by a greater emphasis upon the ideological implications of aesthetic experience" (Nichols, 41). When he shows us the analogy between "understanding a sentence" and "understanding a musical theme," Wittgenstein contributes to this investigation of the effects of knowledge and ideology to which Nichols devotes his book. Wittgenstein withholds until the very last moment the crucial scene of the diegesis, which, following the feedback loop of narrative temporality, gathers the semes into a situation, an imaginary space and time.

But isn't there also a peculiar feeling of pastness characteristic of images as memory images?. . . I will examine one particular case, that of a feeling which I shall roughly describe by saying it is the feeling of "long, long ago." These words and the tone in which they are said are a gesture of pastness. But I will specify the experience which I mean still further by saying that it is that corresponding to a certain tune ("Davidsbündlertänze"—"Wie aus weiter Ferne"). I'm imagining this tune played with the right expression and thus recorded, say, for a gramophone. Then this is the most elaborate and exact expression of a feeling of pastness which I can imagine." (184)

This scene is an exact representation, in the form of an image, finally, and not a story (we are not told the story associated with this emotion) of the integration of emotions and concepts. It is important to mystory not only for the general strategy it demonstrates of reasoning by semes, but also for the specific concept of the scene—"pastness." We have been shown Wittgenstein paging through the family album, coming upon the photograph of his mother, shall we say, thinking of Barthes's *Camera Lucida* and the way he refused to show the snapshot of *his* mother; in the background, playing on the phonograph, is "Wie aus weiter Ferne." The scene is informed by a powerful sentiment of "pastness" that we might identify as "nostalgia" or "melancholy." We can admire this scene on one hand, learning how such personal elements may be put to work in thinking about disciplinary questions—in Wittgenstein's case the problem of concept formation in Philosophy. On the other hand, we can be provoked to reconsider the quality of the relation to the past in mystory, which depends upon such recollections and albums as the support for disciplinary discourse. Wittgenstein, that is, has shown us the emotion of nostalgia associated with reasoning in traditional philosophy. To show the fly the way out of the fly bottle, or to put philosophy at rest, is to be rid of that emotion, the melancholy of reference to an imaginary past.

Mystory, as an alternative historiography, positions itself in a different way in relation to the historical past and present. Barthes, again, helps us read Wittgenstein in terms of our project of an electronic discourse, by calling attention to the fact that Wittgenstein's seme is precisely a photo album filled with pictures of everyday life. This image and the words of the fragments in the numbered sections make *The Brown Book* a kind of film. Barthes in *The Lover's Discourse: Fragments* worked with "poses" that he took as representing the "figures" of a new rhetoric, in a way that reflects cinematic thinking. The "figures" of the discourse, that is, consist of "the body's gesture caught in action . . . what in the straining body can be immobilized" (Barthes, 1978: 4). The punctum is a mnemonic technique similar to "recognition" in Wittgenstein, in that the sting is an emotional response to certain details "expressed" in an image, calling to mind an experience of time. The effect often is not felt until later—it remains latent, emerging as an after-effect (having the quality of being *unforgettable*). While the source of the sting may be located in a detail of the scene, the punctum is motivated by a supplement, a surplus value of more that I add to the object as seme—the thoughts arising out of memory.

The referent of this sting cannot be denoted, but only connoted—hence the reliance on the seme. Barthes, too, relied on psychoanalysis to situate the peculiar features of this practice, noting that the body was the site of the unconscious, involving the drives of both life and death. "I understood that it was necessary from now on to interrogate the evidence of photography not from the point of view of pleasure, but in relation to what one romanti-cally calls love and death" (Barthes, 1980: 115). The punctum, informed by the intuitions of love and death, turns out to be a guide to the historical imagination.

Barthes's figures, that is, suggest how to apply Benjamin's "Theses on the Philosophy of History" to the mystorical project. "To articulate the past historically does not mean to recognize it 'the way it really was' (Ranke). It means to seize hold of a memory as it flashes up at a moment of danger" (Benjamin, 1969; 255). Such memories as Benjamin supplies and speaks of come as gifts or promises, appearing in a way that only the punctum can capture for further theorization. How should we experience the past? "The past can be seized only as an image which flashes up at the instant when it can be recognized and is never seen again. . . . For every image of the past that is not recognized by the present as one of its own concerns threatens to disappear irretrievably" (255). There is a major role for recognition, for the emotions of ideology, for the ideology effect itself, in an act of knowledge alert to the interactions of the past and future with the present. Here we have one crucial difference distinguishing the project of mystory from the traditions that rely on critical distance. In mystory, the punctum of emotional recogni-tion is put to work in the service of invention, bringing to bear on disciplinary problems the images and stories of autobiography.

Benjamin was working at a particularly terrible moment of history, address-ing the problem of fascism. Thus the image of history that he formed for himself may be a guide for us, a mnemonic image, as we generate the convergence of private and public events in an electronic historiography. History is represented in the "Theses" by a Klee painting named "Angelus Novus," showing an angel, the angel of history Benjamin said, turned toward the past: "where we perceive a chain of events, he sees one single catastrophe which keeps piling wreckage upon wreckage and hurls it in front of his feet" (257). The lesson of mystory is not to accept Benjamin's angel as History itself, but to observe the power of joining Klee's painting to the sense of time that Benjamin named "catastrophe." The emotion of reasoning now has something to do with catastrophe more than with nostalgia—with the forward movement of time, not the backward look. In mystory I ask, after Benjamin, what image, what tableau, what scene, and also what story from history stings me into an awareness of the temporality of catastrophe. The fragments of the three stories articulated in the mystory form a constellation, in Benjamin's terms ("the constellation which his own era has formed with a definite earlier one"—Benjamin, 1969: 263). This montage or filmic procedure, juxtaposing fragments from widely dispersed places and times, has a critical value, bringing into the composer's awareness hidden features of the present as well as of the past (Jennings, 40). The past moments thus rescued are not a spectacle for nostalgic contemplation, but tools for opening up the present.

The catastrophe of history refers precisely to "lost opportunity" (this is the flash, when the image must be recognized or lost). And here is the pedagogical challenge of catastrophic history: "From what are phenomena rescued? Not just or not so much from the ill-repute and contempt into which they've fallen, but from the catastrophic way in which they are very often portrayed by a certain form of transmission, by their 'value as heritage.'—They are rescued by the demonstration of the fissure in them. There is a form of transmission that is catastrophe" (Benjamin, 1983: 21). Mystory attempts to be the genre of this transmission, which comes into proper perspective in relating catastrophic time to the time of invention. Consider Benjamin's "definitions of fundamental historical concepts: catastrophe—to have missed the opportunity; the critical moment—the status quo threatens to hold firm; progress—the first revolutionary measures taken" (23). Such is the temporal character of absolute invention in history when it is thought not in terms of succession but in terms of invention, as Eric White notes in his term "kaironomia"—naming the "will-to-invent." Invention depends on timing, intervening or improvising at the right moment (Eric White, 1987: 13). With respect to this term, Cornelius Castoriadis observes that, according to the Hippocratic writings, "'time is that in which there is *kairos* (propitious instant and critical interval, the opportunity to take a decision), and *kairos* is that in which there is not much time.'. . . Time is only as that in which there is occasion and opportunity for acting" (Castoriadis, 212). That which emerges in an invention, Castoriadis reminds us, is not in what exists (the *given* for Benjamin), not even *logically* (190). Teletheory, in the practice of the mystory, brings this catastrophic temporality into the student's experience, and makes it thinkable, by means of the conduction between the mathematical catastrophe theory of the joke, and the catastrophe theory of history.

In Part Two we will begin to explore the qualities of the diegetic dimension of theory, which turns out to be a "rhetorical diegesis" in the literal sense. The space and time used in teletheory to tell a theory rather than a story turn out to be not imaginary but historical, memorial, mnemonic, in the way of a catastrophe.

Part 2
Models and Relays

Introduction

Fragments

Teletheory calls for a text capable of bringing into relationship three levels of culture that contribute equally to the cycle of invention: personal, popular, and disciplinary discourse. The nature of this text has been outlined under the rubric of "mystory." Part One provided a rationale and motivation for the invention of mystory, along with a description of conduction, the logic or paleologic directing both the making of the mystory and the mystory itself. The next step, in keeping with our experimental response to "the burden of the historian," is to collect some examples that may already exist in the contemporary arts of the mystorical genre, in order to get an idea of the formal solution to the problems of such a representation, and to develop further the theoretical guidelines for mystoriography.

Given the importance of Barthes in the formulation of the theory of mystory, it is not surprising to find that he also produced a model for the construction of a multitrack text—*A Lover's Discourse: Fragments*. Keeping in mind that one example noted of intuitive conjectural abduction was a lover's knowledge of the beloved, I want to read Barthes's *Fragments,* to the extent that Barthes separates himself at one level from the lover he describes at another level, as a critique of the conjectural, semiotic, interpretive style of cognition. *Fragments,* that is, offers an alternative way to represent reason by contrasting the lover with modern textuality. The text puts in relief and abolishes the image-repertoire within which the lover is positioned.

In the text, the fade-out of voices is a good thing; the voices of the narrative come, go, disappear, overlap; we do not know who is speaking; the text speaks, that is all: no more image, nothing but language. But the other is not a text, the other is an image, single and coalescent; if the voice is lost, it is the entire image which vanishes (love is monologic, maniacal; the text is heterologic, perverse). (Barthes, 1978b: 112)

What attitude is Barthes recommending? In the register of the doxa the lover performs what the psychoanalyst reenacts in the register of the episteme—for both of them everything is meaningful, everything is a sign to be interpreted. Not so for the text, which does without decipherment or concept, leaving the object of study (the beloved) as an affirmation: "I love, not what he is, but *that he is*"; "And what would best resemble the loved being *as he is, thus and so,* would be the Text, to which I can add no adjective: which I delight in without having to decipher it" (222). In short, he is performing the work of mourning for hermeneutics that prepares the way for a euretic approach to making a text.

With this attitude goes a refunctioning of narrative. The mystorian most needs to understand what happens to narrative in the post-conjectural text, and *Fragments* offers one option. It is in fact an application of all Barthes's previous research on writing across the divisions of discourse. When Barthes wrote the opening section of *Fragments*—"How this book is constructed"— he did not intend to found a genre, anymore than he intended to fix the codes of narrative when he wrote *S/Z*. Nonetheless, the five codes proved to be generalizable and have enjoyed a career of their own in a variety of new contexts, including teletheory. The future of mystory is based as well on a generalization of the strategies of both these books as means for theorizing academic discourse in the age of television.

The first feature of the generic model has to be inferred from the fact that *Fragments* opens with a set of instructions for making the fragments of a discourse—for any discourse whose purpose it is to put narrative in a textual frame. Here we have an answer to the puzzle that prevented many a willing experimenter from taking up the project of theory. If one was not to undertake close formal analyses as in the mode of calculation, nor to decipher signs as in the conjectural paradigm, then what else was there to do? The mystorical answer is, to make a text: invention.

Barthes provides specific instructions for generating the fragments, divided into three parts—figure, order, and references. Let me begin with a discussion of "references," a crucial aspect of the multi-track text. The fragment draws equally upon three levels of cultural experience: 1) Reading, which in turn breaks into two levels: a) "Ordinary reading"—Goethe's *Werther,* generalizable as any primary work of literature, or of high culture; b) "Insistent reading"—Barthes mentions Plato's *Symposium,* Zen, psychoanalysis, etc., generalized as the learned, epistemic background of the writer's context. 2) "Occasional reading"—popular culture, newspapers, magazines, and the like. 3) "Lived experience"—including conversations with friends, personal events, oral culture.

The first point to make with respect to the order of references is that it excludes nothing, but integrates the realms of knowledge and opinion, general and particular, specialized discourse and commonsense experience.

The second point to note is the instructions Barthes added regarding how to use these materials, how to select from an extensive collection of possibilities: the references "are not authoritative but amical: I am not invoking guarantees, merely recalling, by a kind of salute given in passing, what has seduced, convinced, or what has momentarily given the delight of understanding (of being understood?). Therefore, these reminders of reading, of listening, have been left in the frequently uncertain, incompleted state suitable to a discourse whose occasion is indeed the memory of sites (books, encounters) where such and such a thing has been read, spoken, heard" (9). In place of the authoritative citations of the treatise, the fragment offers "site-tations"—telling what I happened to find convincing in terms of the punctum (from *Camera Lucida*), the anecdotal memory I have of my experience—in my case of learning teletheory: the site, place, location of the general in association with my particular encounter falling under that name. It is a matter of memory, that is, relevant to the transformation of memory in the changing apparatus of education.

The section on figures offers a more detailed outline of how to generate the site-tations. The text will actually consist of a series of figures or poses that are typical or characteristic of a discursive practice (it is the compilation of a rhetoric, a commonplace book, an archive for a given practice). The general figures are called poses to suggest the way in which when I use a specialized language I am constrained to take up certain positions, as in a choreographed production. The text will consist of as many of these *topoi* as I care to provide, all of which are to be identified and produced according to the following procedure: the "heading" of each figure refers to something the subject of that discourse says (not to something I am) upon encountering that pose, figure, still, stereotype (oralysis—the oral register of literacy). Beneath the figure lies a sentence, or perhaps, Barthes adds, merely an "articulation" that is more affective thàn syntactic, although it always has a verbal dimension.

A figure is established if at least someone can say: "that's so true! I recognize that scene of language." For certain operations of their art, linguists make use of a vague entity which they call linguistic feeling; in order to constitute figures, we require neither more nor less than this guide: amorous feeling. (4)

To generalize *Fragments* as the model for a genre, of course, requires me to find the equivalent for that amorous feeling relevant to the specialized language in question. In academic discourse, I must ask, what is the feeling that goes with the sentences of insight, polemic, refutation, research? The exclamation—"that's so true!"—is the twin of the emotional sentence that identifies ideology (that-which-goes-without-saying), the stereotypes of a discursive formation being the vehicles of ideology in a specific practice: the effect of truth carries a certain feeling that may be used to sort out and name the figures of a given discourse.

An unusual aspect of this composition then is that it enters a practice at the oral level (the oralysis mentioned above). The headings being something said when the pose is encountered (the position struck) suggests that a literate practice always carries with it an oral accompaniment. A tension arises between the ordinary language of the speaking academic situated contingently and the specialized discourse of the written argument as legitimized knowledge, a point of exchange between oral and literate styles to the point that the mystorian tells anecdotes about concepts. Barthes is showing us how to articulate the private, public, and learned spheres of culture.

What are these instructions asking us to do? Mystory learns from them to approach a discourse formation, a knowledge practice, from the angle of a personal experience in which a general science exists as a collection of stereotypes and as an idiom; at the level of practice these two dimensions cross and exchange properties, such that the life story may become the vehicle for theoretical research, and the disciplinary concepts operate in terms of the prejudices of common sense. The figure, then, is a stereotype of a collective practice for which the reader (and the writer of a mystory is positioned as a reader/viewer) is expected to supply the instantiations. "Each of us can fill in this code according to his own history; rich or poor, the figure must be there, the site (the compartment) must be reserved for it. . . . Now the property of a Topic is to be somewhat empty: a Topic is statutorily half coded, half projective" (5). "Ideally," he adds, "the book would be cooperative." The text is literally a fragment, not only because it is composed in a discontinuous manner, but because half of it, the instances of the figures, are to be provided during the reading as enactment. The numbered sections under each title and heading, meanwhile, are Barthes's own instances of the types, suggestive only of one practice. Such a production foregrounds the demand placed on the reader to write in turn another text—a mystory.

The last part of the instructions—"order"—reveals the peculiar existence of narrative in textual mystory. The text as a whole, obviously, is not narrative. The figures collectively constitute an "encyclopedia" or a "thesaurus" organized alphabetically, as a list from which could be generated any number of individual accounts. The paradigmatic axis of alphabetic literacy, the axis of selection, is given predominance over the syntagmatic axis of combination in the construction of the poses, leaving the narrative for particular enactments of mystorians. The structuralist critics worried about the way in which the paradigm—the set of possible meanings or terms—influenced the specific term selected in a sentence. Hence they directed their attention to what a work did not say but could have (and this "unsaid" part of the linguistic process became confused with the romantic notion of the "unthought," even the "unthinkable," in ideological criticism). The basic unit of meaning in mystory, that is, is not the specific selection from the paradigmatic set but the whole paradigm (in this linguistic sense). In the case of *Fragments* we are not offered any particular lover's story, but all such stories with one instance embedded within it as model, in a way that reorganizes the traditional opposition between the particular and the general.

Barthes's instructions indicate that at least two different operations are involved in the composition of a fragment. The text explicitly provides, in numbered sections following each heading, a series of asides or soliloquies. These are the composer's comments on the narrative that is itself never told (although indirectly, as we will see, a certain scene tends to emerge dramatically from the anecdotes of instances provided by the reading writer). At the same time, there is also an implied narrative, *the* "love story":

> Every amorous episode can be, of course, endowed with a meaning: it is generated, develops, and dies; it follows a path which it is always possible to interpret according to a causality or a finality—even if need be which can be moralized ("I was out of my mind, I'm over it now" "Love is a trap which must be avoided from now on" etc.): this is the *love story*, subjugated to the great narrative Other, to that general opinion which disparages any excessive force and wants the subject himself to reduce the great imaginary current, the orderless, endless stream which is passing through him, to a painful, morbid crisis of which he must be cured. . . . The love story is the tribute the lover must pay to the world in order to be reconciled with it. (7)

The great narrative Other in mystory is the metastory of the verified and institutionalized disciplines—the grand metanarrative—to which the mystorian accedes in order to have the text recognized and counted within a discipline. This story may be glimpsed, overheard, in what is said about a given field or sub-discipline, about "deconstruction" for example ("it is only literary criticism"; "it is irreducible to any pedagogy"; "it is without an effective politics"; "it corrupts the young"; "it is nihilistic").

One way to approach the multi-track representation of the levels of invention, then, is to relate the tracks to Lacan's Symbolic, Imaginary, and Real (keeping in mind that the symbolic code—identified in teletheory as the point of emergence of electronic discourse—as Barthes develops it is based on Lacan's psychoanalysis). Indeed, the relationship between structuralism and poststructuralism could be couched in these terms, as Jameson observed in the late seventies: "at a time when the primacy of language and the Symbolic Order is widely understood—or at least widely asserted—it is rather in the underestimation of the Imaginary and the problem of the insertion of the subject that the 'un-hiddenness of truth' (Heidegger) may now be sought" (Jameson, 1977: 383).

In bringing into representation the relationship between the Imaginary and the Symbolic Barthes was interested in learning how oedipalization produced effects of authority and subjection. *Fragments,* that is, reflects the "politics of the Imaginary" that emerged after the May '68 events in France. Like the Romantics before them, the new "naturalists" (in the rousseauist sense) believed in the power of language to affect reality (with the talking cure of psychoanalysis as a kind of corroboration). The revolutionary effect is created, according to Julia Kristeva (whose *La révolution du langage poétique* is listed in the bibliography of *Fragments*), by introducing into the Symbolic Order of meaning and law the pre-social or extra-social energies of the Imaginary (Turkle, 82). The ethical function of the confrontation of the Imaginary and the Symbolic, Kristeva says, is not to promote the Imaginary Order as such, but to subvert domination and dissolve all narcissisms (Kristeva, 1974: 203). To be revolutionary a text must create an a-topical space that prevents the subject from being absorbed wholly by the Father (Symbolic) or the Mother (Imaginary). The lover's discourse is the best one in which to represent this effort since Lacan stated that the phenomenon of love operates precisely at the junction of the Imaginary and the Symbolic (Lacan, 1975: 298). Barthes attempted to perform this junction in his writing and teaching. Mystory too adapts a version of this interaction by juxtaposing the discourses of specialized disciplines, popular culture, and autobiography. *Fragments* in this context may be seen as the adaptation to academic discourse of the psychoanalytic interview, with the embeddings or *mise en abyme* structuration described by Labov and Fanshel. In short, it performs the analytic experience of "transference."

Technically transference "is the enactment of the reality of the Unconscious (Lacan, 1978: 146). Taking place between the analyst and analysand during treatment (but operating in other institutional settings as well, such as education, between teacher and student), transference involves the patient's unconscious wishes (a phantasm), is an immediate reexperience (in figurative form) of repressed infantile relationships with parental figures (Laplanche and Pontalis, 455–461). Although the activation of the phantasm serves at first as a resistance to therapy, its very exposure in analysis, manifesting forgotten or repressed impulses, ultimately contributes to the patient's release from compulsive repetition of behavior. The analyst's role in this situation is to remain silent—cadaverized, representing death—to withhold response to the patient's "demand," couched in terms of both attraction and aggression. Uninterrupted and thus free to flow into its compulsive patterns, the patient's (lover's) discourse ultimately reveals all the secrets and disguises of the Imaginary (Lacan, 1977: 251–256).

Adapted to academic discourse, this procedure is directed not to the object of knowledge but to the "subject," the one who wants to know. *Fragments* is an experiment testing the changing status of the "subject of knowledge" in the apparatus, relevant to the project in teletheory to consider together a new technology and a different notion of the subject. Lacan approached the question of the "subject of science" from "within," putting in question his own position as researcher. He established the problematic of the "double inscription"—the relation of the discourse of science (which produces knowledge) to the discourse of the Unconscious, the Other (which produces truth). He gains access to the two inscriptions present in any work by studying the function of the analyst's own desire in the analytic situation (counter-transference) in order to take into account "the desire that lies behind modern science" (Lacan, 1978: 160). The contribution of psychoanalysis to the field of science, Lacan said, is its concern for the "subjective drama of the *savant.*"

An example of the double inscription is listed in the bibliography of the *Fragments* (its "Tabula gratulatoria"), bearing a telling title: *Fragments of a Great Confession,* by Theodor Reik. In this "psychoanalytic autobiography" Reik returns to his study, written some twenty years earlier, of Goethe's romance with Friederike Brion (as told in Goethe's autobiography and commonly associated with the experiences that led to the writing of *Werther*). Reik discovered that the study, which at the time it was written he considered to be an objective application of his science, is filled with (expressive of) his personal conflicts: he has been a scientist and a writer at the same time. Reik discovered that his desire to know (about Goethe) is linked to certain unconscious desires. He explains the projection of his own conflicts into Goethe's situation (which does not, he says, alter the validity of the study) by pointing out that Freud named Goethe as one of the Great Men of Western Culture whose status is linked thus to the parental images in the Unconscious. With this association the critical discourse takes on the structure of transference. Reik related to Goethe, in other words, as to an "idealized object," and in Freudian terms such idealizations are the result of a narcissistic process that begins in infancy with the child's choice of love-objects—the image of the child's own body, or of the Mother. In ordinary criticism, by extension, the critic (unconsciously) identifies with the artist, relates to the object of study as to a love-object, in the same way that critics of the apparatus say in everyday life moviegoers identify with movie stars. The critic's values or motives are open thus to the Hegelian master-slave dialectic which serves Lacan as a model for the workings of the ego (formed out of this identification process) and which accounts for the aggressive struggle for recognition as well as for the over-valuation (fetishizing) of authors that characterizes much academic writing.

Normal criticism, because it ignores the possibility of transference, is in fact "neurotic" in this context because governed by repetition compulsion (specialization on one figure). Barthes's intention in appropriating therapeutic method for theory is "to practice that imaginary in *the full awareness of what it is doing*" (Barthes, 1970a: 414). *Fragments* is the most complete realization of Barthes's efforts to open a "third front" in criticism, referring to the three levels at which literature may be approached—science, criticism, and reading. Neither a science of literature (articulating the intelligibility of a work by setting forth the rules by which meanings are generated), nor the criticism of literature (generating specific interpretations) is a substitute for reading: "for of the sense that reading gives to the work, as of the signified, no one knows anything, perhaps because this sense, being desire, maintains with it a rapport of desire. To read is to desire the work, is to want to be the work" (Barthes, 1966: 78–79). Dismissed by classic criticism as mere "projection," reading in Barthes's sense is a "new epistemological object," involving not only the "consumption" dismissed by academics but also production: a textual reader "is one who wants to write, giving himself to an erotic practice of language" (Barthes, 1968: 1016). The "reading" Barthes has in mind is not trained academic reading but everyday life reading, of the kind practiced by Mark Chapman, for example, who explained his murder of John Lennon by reference to Salinger's Catcher in the Rye.

The erotic pleasure in the production of a reading takes place "whenever the 'literary' Text (the Book) transmigrates into our life, whenever another writing (the Other's writing) succeeds in writing *fragments of our own daily lives,* in short, whenever coexistence occurs" (Barthes, 1976: 7–8). He cautioned, (showing that his approach is not tied to the "mimetic" realism that characterizes normal criticism), that the (erotic) reading does not include an imitation of the program traced in a book (the way Goethe's readers imitated Werther's suicide). Barthes makes explicit the specific way in which the meeting between reader and text (lover and beloved) is to take place: "to be with the one I love and to think of something else: this is how I have my best ideas, how I best invent what is necessary to my work. Likewise for the text: it produces, in me, the best pleasure if it manages to make itself heard indirectly; if, reading it, I am led to look up often, to listen to something else" (Barthes, 1975: 24). The effect of this distraction from the book is due to the productive entry into the reading process of the reader's fantasies (phantasm): "our daily life then itself becomes a theatre whose scenery is our own social habitat" (Barthes, 1976: 8). The precise nature of this mediation, of this link between the read and the written, is crucial to teletheory, and will be explored further in the next chapter, with the help of some other theorists.

Meanwhile, Barthes manifests his own use of the anecdotal order of simple forms in an adaptation of theoretical diegesis. Besides stating his method—"*The Book/Life* (take some classic book and relate everything in life to it for a year)" (Barthes, 1977a: 150)—he dramatizes it in a portrait of a reading in progress, of the writer without his books, not writing but fantasizing. Fantasy, he says, is "a kind of pocket novel you always carry with you," and which you can open in a cafe while waiting for a rendezvous (the very setting of

Fragments). As opposed to the dream, the fantasy opens a double space—that of the internal fable, and that of conscious reality—the cafe. The result is a kind of fugue: "something is woven, *braided*—without pen or paper, there is an initiation of writing" (88).

The dominating (the only) scene of *Fragments* is a representation of the ideal-ego, of an image that *lies* at the source of Barthes's desire to write (prior to all writing). This scene displays the amorous subject seated at a cafe, perhaps wearing dark glasses, alternately reading a pocket edition of *The Sorrows of Young Werther* and pausing to reflect while observing the people who enter the cafe. The "plot" of *Fragments*, then, exemplifies the collapsing or "projecting" of one code or axis onto the other, of a kind of literalization or allegory in which the theory of the Symbolic is performed as an enigma—will the beloved arrive? In the cafe the lover waits for a phone call from the beloved, meditating while he waits on the relation of his situation to Werther's and to psychoanalytic theory (Lacan). Finally, disappointed, the lover departs having decided to end the affair. The scene in the cafe creates the theoretical diegesis, the novelesque of the essay, an imaginary (performing Lacan's sense of the term—a personal mythology) space and time productive of allegorical effects.

Barthes is right to deny in his introduction that his fragments can be reduced to this "histoire," because the real significance of the scene, with regard to the mirror-stage identifications, is clarified by recalling the fragment in *Barthes by Barthes* entitled "The Writer as Fantasy."

Surely there is no longer a single adolescent who has this fantasy: to be a writer! Imagine wanting to copy not the works but the practices of any contemporary—his way of strolling through the world, a notebook in his pocket and a phrase in his head (the way I imagined Gide traveling from Russia to the Congo, reading his classics and writing his notebooks in the dining car, waiting for the meals to be served; the way I actually saw him, one day in 1939, in the gloom of the Brasserie Lutetia, eating a pear and reading a book)! For what the fantasy imposes is the writer as we can see him in his private diary, the writer minus his work: supreme form of the sacred: the mark and the void. (77, 79)

The image of the amorous subject at the cafe is this image of Gide at the Brasserie Lutetia, is Barthes playing Gide, performing the want-to-be of the ideal-ego. Barthes suggested that everything he had written was a concealed attempt to reproduce "the theme of the Gidean 'journal' ": "the origin of the work is not the first influence, it is the first posture: one copies a role, then, by metonymy, an art: I begin by reproducing the person I want to be. This first want (I desire and I pledge myself) establishes a secret system of fantasies which persists from age to age, often independently of the writings of the desired author" (99). In *Barthes* and *Fragments* this secret book finally comes into appearance.

The projective-productive style of reading/writing puts the author in the position of analysand whose writing is a deliberate effort to expose his/her own Imaginary Order. Barthes dramatizes the implications of this experiment by adapting as the generating principle of *Barthes* and *Fragments* Lacan's theory of the mirror-stage, the phase in child development that gives rise to the alienating images of the ego. He uses Lacan's theory euretically, that is, and not hermeneutically—to make a scene, not to explain it. *"Myself by myself*? But that is the very program of the image-system! How is it that the rays of the mirror reverberate on me? Beyond that zone of diffraction—the only one upon which I can cast a glance . . . there is reality, and there is also the symbolic. For the latter, I have no responsibility (I have quite enough to do, dealing with my own image-repertoire!): to the Other, to the transference, and hence to the reader. And all this happens, as is obvious here, through the Mother, present next to the Mirror" (Barthes, 1977a: 153).

Both *Barthes* and *Fragments* stage Barthes's image-system, then, but with different emphases. One way to distinguish this emphasis would be to relate each one to one of the three passions Lacan associates with his categories—ignorance, love and hate. It is useful in teletheory to think of ignorance as a passion, rather than as a mere void or lack of information, and as a quality first of all of the subject of knowledge. Ignorance, which functions at the junction of the Real and the Symbolic, refers to the subject's relation to the "discourse of the Other" (the Unconscious): "If the subject engages in the search for truth as such it is because he is situated in the dimension of ignorance" (Lacan, 1975: 298, 306). In analysis, that is, the lies the patient tells about himself reveal his truth. The book of the passion of ignorance is *Barthes*: "this book consists of what I do not know: the unconscious and ideology, things which utter themselves only by the voices of others" (Barthes, 1977a: 152).

In this context Barthes's review of his own book (Barthes, 1975a) takes on added significance (supplying the hermeneutics missing in *Barthes* and *Fragments*). In the review he describes *Barthes* as a "refusal" of sense, the goal of the book being to discover the fundamental and irreducible "non-sense" of the subject, "non-sense" referring in this instance to the formula of the phantasm that is unique to each person (the Imaginary involves precisely what is specific to the embodied individual, a personal vocabulary or reservoir of myths). A mystory is non-sensical in just this way, so that its articulation of the levels of discourse may be understood in Lacanian terms as representing the inmixing of the Imaginary and the Symbolic (with bliss-sense marking the effect of the Real, produced out of the materiality of language). His book, he says, debates at this individual level with two "figures"—Value (likes and dislikes) and Stupidity (*Bêtise*, described as "the internal thing which he fears, in brief, 'La Chose,' " alluding no doubt to Freud's *das Kleine*—the fear being castration anxiety, the emotion of passing between the Imaginary and the Symbolic). *Barthes* is concerned with the Mirror, Barthes states—those deceiving modes under which he imagines himself, under which he wants to be loved: his ideology. The photos in the text deliberately feature himself and his mother, in order to offer "silently, in a stoical manner" in these banal or embarrassing materials evidence for the contaminating power of ideology—"the way petit bourgeois ideology speaks in me" (all those outmoded or unfashionable themes—reflection, amour-propre, sincerity—that appeal to his taste).

One lesson of the exposure of the Imaginary is that "truth" in science is bound up with another dimension of truth that has to do with one's fascination for science. Truth is a woman, Neitzsche said, describing the rhetorical system of Western science. More specifically, Barthes discovers, the woman is his mother/Mother and her substitutes (the *objet a,* other with a small "o"). One thinks about truth the way an infant thinks of its mother, a Zen story counsels (the implicit fable in Barthes's many references to Zen). Barthes cites a passage from the *Tao Te Ching,* in which the sage says, "I alone am different from other men, for I seek to suckle at my Mother's breast" (Barthes, 1978b: 213). In the same vein, the amorous subject experiences a "sensation of truth" thinking of the beloved (229). In the conjectural paradigm this sensation models the insight of intuition upon which abduction depends. But *Fragments* does not advocate conjecture any more than it advocates calculation. It is rather a model of conduction, conductive reason, associated with textuality and practiced in mystory.

"As a specular mirage," Lacan says, "love is essentially deception," because what one loves in the beloved object is one's own image(s), so that, in transference, "the analysand says to his partner, to the analyst, what amounts to this—*I love you, but because inexplicably I love in you something more than you—the objet petit a—I mutilate you*" (Lacan, 1978: 268). Barthes too shows the lover as a fetishist, "mutilating" the beloved: "I am searching the other's body, as if I wanted to see what was inside it, as if the mechanical cause of my desire were in the adverse body (I am like those children who take a clock apart in order to find out what time is)" (Barthes, 1978b:71). He uses the same analogy in *Barthes* to describe his attitude to intellectual systems which he says he plays with like unfamiliar gadgets to see how they make the "click of sense." His pursuit of the *objet a* in the beloved is the simulacrum of the scientist's objectivity—"this operation is conducted in a cold and astonished fashion;. . . I was fascinated—fascination being, after all, only the extreme of detachment" (71–72). The desire for knowledge is associated with fantasies about the Mother, in psychoanalysis, as in Freud's interpretation of his own dream of the botanical monograph, in which he associated his mother with all books: "The unconscious wish to commit incest (to be a passionate discoverer of his mother) is sublimated thanks to the gift of the Bible [from his Father] and the scene of tearing up the book, into a passion for reading and scientific discovery" (Lemaire, 172–173).

Fragments includes, then, a critique of science as a kind of sadism, but conducted through displacement, in the story of the lover. He asks the critic: "What is a piece of 'research'? To find out we would need to have some idea of what a 'result' is. What is it that one finds? What is it that one wants to find? *What is missing?*" (Barthes, 1977: 197). Psychoanalysis holds that the desire to know, to be a critic, to write, are expressions of the demand for the impossible object (sublimated). From these theories Barthes learns that his own inclination to transgress the known, his preference for novelty, are manifestations of repetition compulsion, for what the unknown promises him is knowledge of the desire of the Other. Not that these theories are accepted as fact. Rather, Lacanian theory is assigned the same status as the anecdote of the lover in the cafe, with each level of discourse being a commentary on the (O)ther. The text as a whole is constituted by the articulation among the levels, the passage or leap from one to the other, displacing the solution to a problem from one to the other, depending on which register at the moment offers the best opportunity for a representation (it is the flash of Benjamin's constellation).

Fragments has one more lesson to give related to the operations of transference in academic discourse. This lesson has to do with mourning, borrowed from Freud's description of the gradual process by which one copes with the loss of (detaches oneself from the memory of) a loved one. Barthes uses the concept as it is applied in the analytic situation: "I then go into mourning for my beloved, as the patient goes into mourning for his analyst: I liquidate my transference, and apparently this is how both the cure and the crisis end up (Barthes: 1978b: 108). When he gives up the "amorous condition," the subject is exiled from his image-repertoire. At the level of method this means: "to understand the Imaginary of expression is to empty it, since the Imaginary is misunderstanding" (Barthes, 1972a: 5). As in the analytic situation, each image is brought into consciousness, exposed, in order to be exorcised. Consisting often of those things that are an "embarrassment" (that only a mother listened to willingly, without benefit of "forepleasure"), the Imaginary exposed in *Fragments* represents Barthes's "attachments"—to Gide, bourgeois literature, the family.

This context, the sacrifices of the images, puts into perspective the dilemma of pronouns used to refer to the beloved and to himself. In *Barthes* he struggled with pronoun usage in the subject of the sentence: "I can say to myself 'you' as Sade did, in order to detach within myself the worker, the fabricator, the producer of writing, from the subject of the work (the Author. . .and to speak about oneself by saying 'he' can mean: *I am speaking about myself as though I were more or less dead*" (Barthes, 1977a: 168). In *Fragments* the problem shifts to the predicate, but the reference is the same—

the beloved object ("she," "him,") is Barthes's "self." The drama is *intra-subjective*, corresponding to the theory of narcissism, supported by the myth of the androgyne (the desire to merge with the other, to which Barthes alludes several times) which, according to Lacan, represents the effort of the split psyche to regain (impossible—Imaginary) unity. In the predicate, too, then, he is speaking about himself "dead"—the mourning is for the "death of the author," for the unified subject of Western metaphysics, and for the "person" of his ego.

There are several lessons for academic discourse in this work of mourning. For one thing, according to the transference (therapeutic) model, the primary effect of writing is registered *in the writer*—one writes for and to oneself as a kind of ethical and didactic exercise (Jack Goody pointed out the important role of alphabetic writing in producing the experience of the individual self through interaction with a text). The exposure of anaclisis in *Fragments* (the object-choice based on dependency, in which the sexual instincts rest upon the instincts of self-preservation), may be read as an "allegory" of the critic becoming a writer, leaving the security of the Mother, speaking finally in one's "own" voice (without authority), rather than with the voice of the agency formed through identification with parent figures (the imbrication of the Imaginary in the Symbolic of the institution). Throughout his career, Barthes says, "he worked successively under the aegis of a great system (Marx, Sartre, Brecht, semiology, the Text). Today, it seems to him that he writes more openly, more unprotectedly" (Barthes, 1977a: 102).

And yet the feeling of solitude, exclusion, that accompanies this autonomy is itself a dependency, a final dependency on the psychological image-system: the Imaginary, constituting the individual's uniqueness, states this very scene of exclusion (it is the feeling of the "I am," of the ego, the Apollonian). Hence he writes a book of anaclisis to escape even Lacan by playing with the psychoanalytic categories, dropping the quotation marks: to pose deliberately the figure of his image-system alters it, makes it a kind of *kitsch* (125). He displaces the category of narcissism by stealing its language, along with the literary language of *Werther*, and the scientific language of Lacan, which is the double tactic of Text: "it is necessary to posit a paradigm in order to produce a meaning [this counters *Doxa* which insists that meanings are natural, not produced] and then to be able to divert, to alter it [which counters Science's need for identity, consistency]" (92).

To translate a discourse into textuality, all that is required, the *Fragments* shows, is a change of attitude. Since science itself is finally an attitude one adopts toward an object of knowledge, to change science requires first of all a different attitude. It cannot be a question of annihilating desire, nor of living without an image-repertoire, but of a different style of conduct within these Orders. No more will to power over the object. The lover decides to love not what the beloved is, but *that* he (she, it) is, thus exiting the realm of value ("every judgment is suspended, the terror of meaning is abolished") (222). The mode of writing that corresponds to this manner of loving, Barthes says, is the Text—a mourning process that lifts repressions that mask the seductions and aggressions of signification. It has no designs on the reader, and is not a mode of communication in the conventional sense, emptying itself of love and hate, fetishes and aggressions, nullifying the struggle for pure prestige in which the desire to know is interchangeable with the desire to be known.

Mystory is a kind of lover's discourse, displaying the transference that binds education as an ideological institution to the community in which it exists, but intervening in the mourning that academic discourse, in its monumental mood, has never been able to complete.

Documents

Barthes's *Fragments* exemplifies the hybrid mix of theory and art that the mystorical genre is designed to generalize into a replicable practice. A brief comparison with another text, but one produced in the institution of art rather than of criticism, sharing some of the same features and a similar psychoanalytic problematic, may help clarify those aspects of the model with generic value. I am thinking of Mary Kelly's *Post-Partum Document,* which could have been subtitled "A Mother's Discourse: Fragments" (Kelly actually began her project before Barthes). The intertitles of *Document,* that is, refer, as did Barthes's "headings," to something the mother says, an everyday discourse of love ("What have I done wrong?" "Why don't I understand?"). Each of these headings organizes a multi-level set of multi-media documents relevant to a period in the mother-child relationship.

> The work, begun in 1973 with the birth of her child, covers the first six years of the child's development and is divided into six sections including, in all, approximately 135 pieces. Each section examines a stage in the constitution of a woman's identity in and through significant moments in her child's development: for instance, weaning from the breast, weaning from the holophrase (learning to speak), weaning from the dyad (periodic separation from the mother), the first questions about sexuality and the collection of cathected objects which represent loss, not only of the child but of the maternal body, and finally the child's entry into the law of the father—learning to write, starting school. (Kelly, 1983: 203)

One reason for the similarity between *Document* and *Fragments* is that both place Lacan in the register of learned discourse, as an inventive resource. Both want to represent the mother-son relationship, from different positions in the dyad obviously, including the themes of mourning rehearsing the castration complex (the adjustment to separation and loss experienced in the formation of identity and individuality), exploited, however, for allegorical purposes. In both texts Lacanian theory, in a parody of the objectivity of science (the object in any case of Lacan's critique) functions as a foil displacing the strong emotional tone of the experience of identity. The excessive tone of strong feeling in both cases arises out of the juxtaposition of the levels of discourse—expert, popular, and personal.

Post-Partum Document is a valuable supplement to Barthes's model for mystory because, for one thing, it demonstrates an overcoming of the impasse of representation produced during the age of the world picture, offering an alternative to the opposition between the paradigms of calculation and conjecture (empiricism and semiotics). Kelly weaves together the methodologies of science with the narratives of conjecture within a frame of personal anecdote, producing a hybrid sample of mystory. Acknowledging that mothering is lived in the particular but understood in the abstract, in general, *Document* subordinates the narrative of the mother-child relationship to a scientific taxonomy, refracted through the presentational devices of the archive appropriate to the institution of the museum as a cultural medium (the apparatus of the arts).

What remained at the level of figure in *Fragments* is foregrounded in *Document*, which is literally a record of the entry into language, of the passage from the Imaginary to the Symbolic. At the same time, Kelly is performing a version of the "Book/Life" assignment, emphasizing the parallels between a theory and lived experience. Another important lesson for mystory, then, concerns the status of narrative in *Document*. Within the documentary taxonomy the narrative exists in the form of anecdotes and brief dramatic scenes buried in the notes of Kelly's commentary. Part of the strategy is to appropriate the concepts of expert discourse—psychoanalysis and ethnography—for telling a story, in order to displace the teleology of narrative, similar to the way Barthes adopted encyclopedic lists.

The nature of the ethnographic or natural history displays, the effect of insistence created by mounting as documents the mother's memorabilia or souvenirs (diapers, casts of the child's hand, scrawls, verbal utterances, gifts to the mother such as insects and shells), reinforced by the supporting commentaries, lend to the text the overtones of allegory. The critical indirection is similar to Barthes's exposure of his image-repertoire, made even stronger by the fact that the displays, photographic in book form, are iconic (the book is itself a documentation of what was originally an exhibit). What is exposed is the "nostalgia" and "melancholy" of mourning, sentiments which in turn are given power as political and social critique by means of juxtaposition with the other levels of discourse at work in the text.

As just one illustration of the mix of modes relating narrative and image to theory consider the way *Document* treats the theme of the "world picture."

The heading linking the documentation to the commentary in Part Five is the question "What am I?" (a man or a woman?)—one of the fundamental questions in psychoanalysis (which Lacan treats especially in relation to the case of Schreber). The question is posed within a Lacanian formula, as the signified over the signifier, and juxtaposed with one of Lacan's diagrams of the psyche. The materials of the section, the specimens, were collected by the child, according to his "spontaneous investigations of things in everyday life" over the course of a year (age two to three). "In so far as they were gifts from the child and more importantly, because they coincided with his questions about sexuality, the specimens constituted a set of discursive events" (Kelly, 113). Each event was documented in three sections: 1) mounted specimens and labels, including flowering plants and insects. Each specimen is labeled scientifically. "However, classification, in this document, is used to construct a metaphorical space in which the mother's body is *named* through the researches of her child"; 2) proportional diagrams and research: morphological grids used to work out the theory of transformations used in the study of evolution. "By juxtaposing the diagrams with the child's research the Method of Co-ordinates is also used to suggest the operations of the unconscious; that place where the eccentricity and extravagance of anatomical transformation is not bounded by logic or by the specular image but by the discourse of the Other" (114); 3) statistical tables and indexes, related to a diagram of a full-term pregnancy, having to do with "infant mortality, foetal growth, intra-uterine temperature, etc. The mother's body is systematically scanned in response to the child's questions." All these informational documents are doubled in their articulation, shimmering with connotations, manifesting the style of allegorical critique (showing rather than telling).

Fragments of conversation between the mother and son are juxtaposed, that is, with the images of the specimens and the diagram of the pregnancy (all the items in the display are referred to as "fragments"). The narrative is confined to this documentary position, then, illustrating developmental concepts. Freud argued, for example, that curiosity, the desire for knowledge, begins with the infant's attempt to understand the mystery of birth. The progress of these early researches determine the child's intellectual future (the suppression or expression of the desire to know). The infant's research is doomed, Freud suggested, because the information needed to solve the problem—knowledge of anatomy, of the functioning of the male and female genitals in sexual relations—is unavailable to the child. In one of her conversations Kelly provides her son with the missing data: "Age 3; 10, July 13, 1977. (8:00pm, coming into the bathroom). K [his first name is "Kelly"]. Do babies come from your bottom? M. No, . . . from vaginas. Girls have three holes; one for poohs, one for wees, and one where babies come out—that's the vagina" (148).

Such scenes, juxtaposed with the scientific format of the exhibition and the theoretical commentaries, produce a critical effect exposing the fetishistic dimension of the search for "truth." The scientific and theoretical materials are "détourned" or remotivated in every case to function figuratively or dramatically. The suppression of the heterogeneity of feminine sexuality by a patriarchal taxonomy of medicine which identifies the female of a species exclusively by reproductive organs is put on display. This formal lesson—mounting together the private journals, the family life, and theoretical discourse—as well as the specific theme of the entry into language, is a powerful model for the three-track genre of mystory.

Mary Kelly found herself in the course of family relations in the position of the Queen in Lacan's exemplary story, seeing herself being seen without the ability to act ("the child's spontaneous scopophilia provokes the mother's sense of 'shame' "—161). One lesson of Poe's story for Lacan has to do with repetition automatism: "it is not only the subject, but the subjects, grasped in their intersubjectivity, who line up, in other words our ostriches, to whom we here return, and who, more docile than sheep, model their very being on the moment of the signifying chain which traverses them" (Lacan, 1972: 60). Even while representation is thus shown to be inevitably complicit with scopophilia, the text itself makes available an understanding of the gendering of knowledge. "In moving away from the visible space of nomenclature towards the invisible space of organic structure experimental science leaves a space of *possibility* for the subversion of biological determinism" (Kelly, 114). A mystory brings this positioning into appearance, making it available to thought, and as material for invention, addressing the question of how these stories of love and death might contribute to learning.

Kelly's display of a feminine fetishism (which is said to be a contradiction in terms) indicates how difficult it is to get out of line (out of the series of glances, each finally not seeing itself being seen, the glances that Peter Wollen identified as forming the hermeneutic code—time of seeing; time of interpreting; time of knowing): "These three times follow a logico-temporal order and each is a couplet: what one character sees may be exactly what another character is blind to; every interpretation may be a misinterpretation; a character may deny all knowledge of what s/he knows" (Wollen, 41). Euretics replaces the temporality of hermeneutics (the detective narrative, the search for truth by puzzling through the enigma of riddles) with the temporality of invention, the constellation of opportunity that flashes through a collection of fragments gathered in ignorance and juxtaposed mechanically, without understanding. Mystory is a genre that thinks from the position of the one who does not (already) know.

Both Barthes and Kelly, then, include a representation of the Imaginary and Symbolic registers together in the same text, juxtaposing the image-repertoire and its emotional register with the disciplinary laws of the institutions. Through the gaps in the taxonomic ordering of the fragments and documents the reader may experience a sense of the real, in the form of the desire to find out in his/her own case how the different registers come together, and in what details, what shape, the mystory will come into representation.

Chapter 4

Memory I:
Place/Roots

1. Mnemonic Autoportrait

I have been reading Barthes and Kelly and all the theorists cited so far as *instructions* for how to make a mystory (giving a euretic rather than a hermeneutic reading), how to make a hybrid text, scriptible in any medium, producing a circulation and exchange across the institutional divisions separating one level of discourse from another. Both Barthes and Kelly use Lacan's theory of the unconscious figuratively, reminding us that in teletheory psychoanalysis represents not an explanatory science but the site of emergence of the subject of a new apparatus. It is a question of intervening in this invention, whose outcome is not determined in advance, recognizing that memory will be the point of inception of this change, as people, interacting with electronic technology, come to experience their conduct differently. Foucault states the issue negatively: "We have to promote new forms of subjectivity through the refusal of this kind of individuality [linked to the state] which has been imposed on us for several centuries" (Foucault, 1984: 424). Foucault's contribution to this process is hermeneutic, providing a critique of institutions and of the "technologies of the self" (Foucault, 1988). The task of euretics, supplementing hermeneutics and critique, is to invent the alternatives to what is being refused, something that cannot be done in the abstract, but which must be grounded in specific practices.

The problem of the apparatus may be unified in terms of memory. What happens to human memory when, in addition to the prosthesis it already possesses (alphabetic writing), it gains the services of electronics (specifically, of video)? Mystory is the genre of video as artificial memory. Everything having to do with the logic of the unconscious, primal thinking, the image-repertoire of the Imaginary embedded in the law of the Symbolic, finds its material support in the tradition of patterning (and its reliance on the mnemonics of the ancient rhetoricians) suppressed by the success of science. Scripting video by means of mystory involves the revival and refunctioning of the techniques of artificial memory once used by orators to recall speeches for oral delivery. These strategies, well-suited to the peculiar combination of the features of spoken and written forms in video, are appropriated in mystory for the scripting of invention. In this context we may see that Giulio Camillo's project (never realized) for a memory palace, an actual building, a theater, representing all knowledge, has something in common with teletheory, to the extent that both programs apply the devices of the arts to the representation of knowledge. In the same way that science kept the alchemist's experimentation and dropped their metaphysics, so too does teletheory borrow the alchemists' memory as practice with applications outside its original Neo-Platonic setting.

The fullest account of mnemotechniques, as Frances Yates explained, is found in the *Rhetorica ad Herennium,* a textbook (relevant to our pedagogical interests) compiled in Rome (86–82 B.C.), which was enormously influential throughout the Medieval and Renaissance periods, until the printed book became available. It contains the stock definition of artificial memory—a procedure for relating the places to images (and, as Umberto Eco reminds us, "anyone familiar with ancient logic knows that, in order to reason, you must choose arguments, and these arguments are called places [*topoi* in Greek; *loci* in Latin)]" (Eco, 1986: 90).

> A *locus* is a place easily grasped by the memory, such as a house, an intercolumnar space, a corner, an arch, or the like. Images are forms, marks or simulacra of what we wish to remember. . . . The art of memory is like an inner writing. Those who know the letters of the alphabet can write down what is dictated to them and read out what they have written. Likewise, those who have learned mnemonics can set in places what they have heard and deliver it from memory. . . . It is essential that the places should form a series and must be remembered in their order, so that we can start from any *locus* in the series and move either backwards or forwards from it. . . . The same set of *loci* can be used again and again for remembering different material. The images which we have placed on them for remembering one set of things fade and are effaced when we make no further use of them. (Yates, 6–7)

The mix of oral and literate memory is explicit in the discussion, a mix that in teletheory will shift to a cooperation among oral, literate, and electronic memory.

The rules for the images to be set in the places are equally explicit and detailed, including instructions for both images of things and images of words. One of the most controversial aspects of the *Ad Herennium* was its recommendation of the use of "active images"—striking images that would make a greater impression on the mind and, hence, last longer than images formed from banal or trivial things. The effective memory image ought to be disfigured (stained with blood or soiled with mud) or comic, grotesque, or ridiculous in order to be easily remembered. It is important to keep in mind that mnemotechniques were used in an inner speech, consumed privately. Television today might be thought of as a public display of "active images" produced in the absence of any specific information, and available for use in reasoning. The equivalent of cable and network entertainment in this context for alphabetic literacy would be something like a mail-order delivery of paper, pens, and books of logic. Not that the general populace uses television programs systematically for reasoning, although they certainly do think by means of television images and themes.

Several other aspects of mnemonics should be kept in mind as well. The activation of the memory, for example, was achieved by an imaginary walk through the places with one image located at each site, spaced at regular intervals along the way. The setting for the places was to be one familiar to the speaker so that the associations (the emotional investments) with the setting (as with the active images) could serve to bind the images in place. In short, one used one's autobiography and/or fantasies as the grounds or medium with which to think. The mnemonist described by A. R. Luria worked in precisely this way:

> He would "distribute" [his images] along some roadway or street he visualized in his mind. Sometimes this was a street in his home town, which would also include the yard attached to the house he had lived in as a child and which he recalled vividly. On the other hand, he might also select a street in Moscow. Frequently he would take a mental walk along that street—Gorky Street in Moscow—beginning at Mayakovsky Square, and slowly make his way down, "distributing" his images at houses, gates, and store windows. At times, without realizing how it had happened, he would suddenly find himself back in his home town (Torzhok), where he would wind up his trip in the house he had lived in as a child. The setting he chose for his "mental walks" approximates that of dreams. (Luria, 32)

The editing of such walks, in other words, has something in common with montage, and the Kuleshov effect, and all the devices in filmic writing used to relate one shot to another.

Memory for words was a more difficult, awkward practice, yet, as Yates notes, combined with memory for things, it served as a hidden generator of much imagery in Medieval and Renaissance works that otherwise (to those unaware of the mnemonic function) seems completely esoteric, secretive. Thinking of the unusual, even surrealistic text (dreamlike, paleological) that such a procedure might generate, Yates remarks, "what scope for the imagination would be offered in memorizing Boethius's *Consolation of Philosophy,* as advised in a fifteenth-century manuscript," whose memorization by word hieroglyphics would produce the Lady Philosophy coming to life and wandering, an animated Prudence, through the palaces of memory. An idea of what such a production might be like may be found in the way Luria's mnemonist memorized the opening stanzas of *The Divine Comedy*, the first line of which—"*Nel mezzo del cammin di nostra vita*"—for example, he fixed in this tableau:

> (*Nel*)—I was paying my membership dues when there, in the corridor, I caught sight of the ballerina Nel'skaya. (*mezzo*)—I myself am a violinist: what I do is to set up an image of a man, together with [*vmeste* in Russian] Nel'skaya, who is playing the violin. (*del*)—There's a pack of Deli Cigarettes near them. (*cammin*)—I set up an image of a fireplace [*kamin*] close by. (*di*)— Then I see a hand pointing toward a door [*dver*]. (*nostra*)—I see a nose [*nos*]; a man has tripped and, in falling, gotten his nose pinched in a doorway [*tra*]. (*vita*)—He lifts his leg over the threshold, for a child is lying there, that is, a sign of life—vitalism. (Luria, 45–46)

When I first used this account of mnemotechnics in *Applied Grammatology* I was concerned with Derrida's argument against any absolute distinction between natural and artificial memory. Since then I have come to realize more fully the implications of mnemonics as a point of departure for teletheory. The feature of this thinking that I find most extraordinary and most relevant for academic discourse in the age of television is that whatever a Medieval student was thinking about, learning—law, virtues and vices, theology, the entire curriculum—it was done by a walk through the childhood home, or along the streets of a hometown, or a great public building, finding in each room or next to each familiar location an image, either some extreme aberration (a grisly murder, a two-headed calf) or again something intimately familiar. The information to be learned was fixed and recalled, stored and retrieved, by association with these places and images, producing a parallel, non-mimetic, text, one recited publicly and the other recalled privately. For more than a thousand years the intellect of Europe was transmitted in this highly emotional form. In mystory, the two registers, the public discourse and the private scene, are written together, juxtaposed and manipulated in a technology that frees the mnemotechniques from memorization and makes them available as an alternative to calculation and conjecture.

As I noted previously, the mnemonic pedagogy was replaced after the coming of print by a memorization based on dialectical order perfected in the tree diagrams of Peter Ramus and retained today in the use of outlining. The revival of interest in a refunctioned mnemonics now is apparent in a study such as Michel Beaujour's *Miroirs d'encre*. Mystory is an attempt to do for academic discourse what Beaujour's definition of the "autoportrait" did for autobiography. The crossing point of the two genres is their shared activation of a mode of scripting based on the hieroglyph, as described (disapprovingly) by Hegel: the symbolic material in Egypt functions twice—that which is "presented once as signification is re-utilized as symbol in a related field" (Beaujour, 143). The Rosetta Stone is an important emblem for mystory, in that teletheory assumes the intertranslatability between the expert discourses and the discourses of everyday life both public and private.

In oral culture, individual memory was the guarantee of collective memory. With the evolution of inscription people confided ever more of their memory to external devices (manuscripts, commonplace books, encyclopedias). The autoportrait, Beaujour says, is an attempt to re-interiorize a collective cultural memory (81–82). His project to reorganize the relations between individual and collective memory expresses exactly the position of the subject of knowledge in mystory, and is a model for the relation of the student to the disciplinary object of study in the pedagogy of teletheory. The autoportrait draws on mnemotechniques—the walk through the places—but it tends to reverse the direction of the association (the interchange of meaning between experience and significance is dialectical).

> As opposed to [Renaissance] humanism, the autoportrait considers itself an individual bricolage using for its own ends bits and pieces borrowed from a vast humanist system in which the subject participates to the extent of being a "cultivated" man. It is not a question anymore of normalizing the individual memory with the goal of conforming to a cultural model, but on the contrary of working the fragments to make with them, in their nonconformity to a stereotype, an idiosyncratic ensemble of metaphors in which the subject comes gradually to rediscover itself and to lose itself. (204)

In the convergence of collective and individual materials, of *inventio* and *memoria*, the distinction between the general and the particular is blurred and refunctioned. An individual memory thus is always overdetermined by the participation of the local event, place, or character in a cultural and rhetorical convention, tradition, or heritage. While it has much in common with psychoanalysis, both drawing on the same metalevel of general culture, the autoportrait is finally an art text, a construction, rather than a reconstruction: "the anamnesis of the autoportrait opposes itself to autobiographical reminiscence, always founded to some degree on a belief in the permanence of an individual self whose interiority is its anteriority" (167).

Mystory shares with the autoportrait an interest in a certain break with linearity and the completeness of continuity, resulting in a *dispositio* or arrangement that draws on the features of both classification and narrative. The autoportrait tends not to be composed as a continuous narrative, that is, but rather the narrative is subordinated to a taxonomic deployment or to a principle of assemblage or bricolage (Beaujour, 7–8). As in *La règle du jeu*, by Michel Leiris, however, the logic is not that of an argument: "the binary dialectical method serves here to air a certain material, to disentangle it and to display it, rather than to put it to work for some persuasive or demonstrative end" (255). The metaphor used to describe this "intransitive" arrangement is "braiding" ("*tressage*")—the image of textuality. This subordination of narrative to taxonomy recalls the generation of narrative in mnemotechniques according to the needs of the abstract materials to be memorized.

Some recent examples of this taxonomic or rhetorical ordering of narrative would include Primo Levi's *The Periodic Table* (autobiographical anecdotes—literate version—arranged and motivated according to associations with the various chemical elements); Julian Barnes's *Flaubert's Parrot,* with the protagonist's narrative (his marital problem) framing the scholarship on Flaubert, which itself is organized by a kind of paleological principle of association; Jonathan Spence's *The Memory Palace of Matteo Ricci,* a history of the work of this Jesuit Priest in China, organized according to the themes associated with a few memory images—two warriors grappling, a tribeswoman from the west, a peasant cutting grain. While instructing the Chinese in the art of building memory palaces, Ricci noted that they could be drawn from reality or fiction, but the best ones were a combination of the two, "as in the case of a building one knew well and through the back wall of which one broke an imaginary door as a shortcut to new spaces, or in the middle of which one created a mental staircase that would lead one up to higher floors that had not existed before," to be reviewed until they were "as if real," never to be erased, there to place the images by which to recall knowledge (Spence, 1–2).

Mystory can learn from the autoportrait, which, like Barthes and Mary Kelly, crosses freely between the Symbolic and Imaginary registers, showing how each is made to serve the ends of the other; it can learn how to bring into representation the "technologies of gender," for example, identified by Teresa de Lauretis. The juxtaposition of autobiographical and theoretical discourses in mystory, that is, in the context of euretics rather than hermeneutics, didactics rather than reference, recognizes that the subject of knowledge is constructed through a process of interpellation, and that critical theory for example as much as popular cinema participates in this interpellation as technologies providing representations of *conduct* that are accepted and interiorized by individuals (identification and recognition). Even as it is constituted in this process, the subject of knowledge (which, like de Lauretis's "subject of feminism," is a concept still to be theorized) has its best chance for coming into power by learning how "to map the terrain between sociality and subjectivity" (de Lauretis, 1987: 19). This subject is positioned in an extensive set of systems with which it is complicit necessarily, including "both ideology in general (classism or bourgeois liberalism, racism, colonialism, imperialism, and, I would also add, with some qualifications, humanism) and the ideology of gender in particular—that is to say, heterosexism"

(10–11). The argument of teletheory is that these constructions, brought into representation in mystory, become something like Einstein's compass—a guide for thought rather than a force of oppression. In euretics, as one learns to draw on the image-repertoire, to think through it, with it, to make it say something else (the way a compass, always pointing north, may be used to go in any direction); to turn it or detourn it in the interests of invention (to blow holes in the back walls of these internalized institutions). Euretics is distinguished from critique precisely by this amnesty given to the positioning that shows up inevitably in the image-repertoire, where, in any case, critique itself holds a considerable place, reproducing as a practice the ideological link between the state and individualization. Invention is not the whole of thought and reason, but it is that dimension that has been most neglected in an education conducted by the book.

2. Rhizomes and Mushrooms

The function of the apparatus, working by transference, is to reproduce the institution and its subject intact from one generation to the next. Thus to begin to think inventively within an institution is easier said than done. The notion of "minor literature" developed by Gilles Deleuze and Félix Guattari suggests one inventive strategy, relevant to the gendered, nationalized subject of knowledge.

> The three characteristics of minor literature are the deterritorialization of language, the connection of the individual to a political immediacy, and the collective assemblage of enunciation. We might as well say that minor no longer designates specific literatures but the revolutionary conditions for every literature within the heart of what is called great (or established) literature. Even he who has the misfortune of being born in the country of a great literature must write in its language, just as a Czech Jew writes in German, or an Ouzbekian writes in Russian. Writing like a dog digging a hole, a rat digging its burrow. And to do that, finding his own point of underdevelopment, his own *patois*, his own third world, his own desert. (Deleuze and Guattari, 1986: 18)

The point of this strategy, in teletheory, is not to usurp the moral advantage of the most marginalized groups, but with their help to open an alternative approach to change (without playing all the stops of guilt, the censorship that must be evaded if invention is to get started). In any case, in creating the Rosetta Stone of mystory, the goal is to become a native speaker of theory, but in the manner of Kafka in Prague.

If the notion of minor literature (or minor science) is to be of any use it must be made more specific as a practice. The feature of minor literature that most recommends it for the euretic aspect of mystory is its commitment to "experimentation" rather than to hermeneutics. "We believe only in one or more Kafka *machines* that are neither structure nor phantasm. We believe only in a Kafka *experimentation* that is without interpretation or significance and rests only on tests of experience" (7). How does one relate to such a machine?

> We will enter by any point whatsoever; none matters more than another, and no entrance is more privileged even if it seems an impasse, a tight passage, a siphon. We will be trying only to discover what other points our entrance connects to, what crossroads and galleries one passes through to link two points, what the map of the rhizome is and how the map is modified if one enters by another point. Only the principle of multiple entrances prevents the introduction of the enemy, the Signifier and those attempts to interpret a work that is actually only open to experimentation. (3)

Deleuze and Guattari most clearly indicate in the image of the rhizome the map of relations between subjectivity and sociality, of the circuitry not just of a given corpus, but of an entire apparatus. They give us, that is, an image of wide scope that helps us to experience the quality of a new memory, ordered in a paleological way, as well as to begin to imagine how to remotivate the tradition of mnemotechnics to the needs of electronic cognition. In considering the rhizome, my purpose is to focus on the *place* of memory as a pedagogical construction and strategy (experimentation rather than interpretation), to intensify and elaborate the notion of *loci* or *topoi* in its practical sense in which the actual settings of our lives are appropriated as the materials with which to script a theory.

To reiterate, the rhizome is offered as an image of memory in contrast to tree diagrams used to organize conceptual structure in the apparatus of print.

> A first type of book is the root-book. The tree is already an image of the world, or rather the root is the image of the tree-world. It is the classic book. . . . .the radicel system, or fasciculated root, is the second figure of the book, from which our modernity gladly draws its inspiration. In this case the principal root has absorbed, or has been destroyed near its extremity and some immediate multiplicity of flourishing secondary roots has come to graft itself onto it [eg. Burroughs, Joyce]. . . .. We are tired of the tree. We must no longer put our faith in trees, roots, or radicels; we have suffered enough from them. The whole arborescent culture is founded on them, from biology to linguistics. On the contrary, only underground stems and aerial roots, the adventitious and the rhizome are truly beautiful, loving, or political. . . .. Many people have a tree planted in their heads, but the brain itself is much more like a grass. . . .. In itself the rhizome has very diverse forms, from its surface extension which ramifies in all directions to its concretions into bulbs and tubers. Or when rats move by sliding over and under one another. There is the best and the worst in

the rhizome: the potato, the weed, crab grass. (Deleuze and Guattari, 1983: 5, 10–11, 33)

What the tree diagram was to the book, the rhizome map is to electronics— a model for a new order of memory, whose principles include "connection" ("any point on a rhizome can be connected with any other, and must be"); "Heterogeneity" ("the semiotic chain is like a tuber gathering up very diverse acts—linguistic, but also perceptual, mimetic, gestural, and cognitive"); "multiplicity" (it has neither subject nor object: "there are no points or positions in a rhizome, as one finds in a structure, tree or root. There are only lines"); "a-signifying rupture" ("A rhizome can be cracked and broken at any point; it starts off again following one or another of its lines. . . . There is neither imitation nor resemblance, but an explosion of two heterogeneous series in a line of flight consisting of a common rhizome that can no longer be attributed nor made subject to any signifier at all") (11, 20).

The relationship of the reader to the text, of the text to the world, is rhizomatic: together they form a rhizome, which is not a relationship of representation, resemblance, reference. We will take our time understanding this figure as a pose for academic discourse, although the image suggests at once how the pedagogy that follows from it is likely to be received. Those who conduct the practices of the apparatus go home in the evening, in many cases, to a house with a lawn, for whose care they may consult the Time-Life Books volume by James Underwood Crockett, *Lawns and Ground Covers,* on what to do about weeds.

Despite its bad name, a weed can be an attractive plant; actually a weed is nothing more than a plant that is out of place. The lawn, of course, is no place for weeds. . . . Grassy weeds—crab grass is the more troublesome—can be stopped even before they are visible by "pre-emergent" killers, which destroy the germinating seed. When such weeds do appear, they can be destroyed by chemicals that poison the growing bulb. Broad-leaved weeds, such as chickweed and dandelion, are killed by chemicals that upset their hormone balance, causing the plants to speed up their processes and literally grow themselves to death.

The rhizome, that is, might be considered to be to academic discourse what crab grass is to a lawn, which suggests something about the emotional dimension of the politics involved. Discovery, however, requires the tolerance of weeds—of things that are "out of place."

The rhizome, then, helps to identify one of the models for mystory, whose existence reflects the changes in reading—the rhizomatic relation of the reader to the text—that have begun to be apparent in a postmodern culture. The new instauration (the reorganization of learning in terms of an electronic episteme), in other words, signals its emergence only in certain details. The history of reading and writing, for example, when reviewed at the level of the three epochs of language technology—oral, alphabetic, and electronic— reveals a pattern marking three crucial inventions. The pattern concerns the conduct of three men of the word, conduct deemed worthy of comment in their respective periods as being unorthodox, exceptional, but which later became commonplace, the norm of lettered conduct.

A. *Socrates.* Eric Havelock established that the first Greeks to learn the alphabet borrowed from the Phoenicians were stonecutters, who used the invention to inscribe verse dedications on ritual offerings in the form of monuments. Scholarly writing in the academy continues in this tradition of monumentalization. It being reported that Socrates' father was a stonemason (and likely to have cut his own stones) and his mother a midwife, we may imagine that when Socrates described himself as a midwife of ideas he was deliberately taking his mother's side and refusing the script with which his father was associated. Still, he may have been the one to teach Plato to read, even if his own choice was to be illiterate. That this illiterate stands at the head, a model, for the tradition of literate instruction, is one of the more thought-provoking paradoxes in the history of pedagogy.

Socrates represents for us the final moment of oral high culture, relying upon living memory at least, if not on a system of dead markers, mnemonics (even if Socrates did mock the use of mnemotechniques by the sophists), at a time when systematic reason was rare and remarkable—the moment of the invention of philosophy. Consider the image of Socrates thinking presented in *The Symposium.*

> Socrates got some notion into his head, and there he stood on one spot from dawn, thinking, and when it did not come out, he would not give in but still stood pondering. It was already midday, and people noticed it, and wondered, and said to one another that Socrates had been standing thinking about something ever since dawn. At last when evening came, some of the Ionians after dinner brought out their pallets and slept near in the cool and watched him from time to time to see if he would stand all night. He did stand until it was dawn and the sun rose. Then he offered a prayer to the sun and walked away. (Plato, 114)

This statement establishes the exemplary status of Socrates as thinker, recording a phenomenon so rare as to count as a spectacle capable of holding the attention of an audience from midday to the following dawn, even if the reasoning itself was invisible. Had Socrates been able to take a note, to work out his thoughts in writing, we would not have had this spectacle. Indeed, writing made it possible for anyone to engage in this process of reasoning.

Had Roland Barthes turned his attention to this image in *Mythologies,* he might have identified it as the cliche "lost in thought," the stereotypical act of ratiocination as manifested, for example, in the conduct of Sherlock Holmes at the moment of an abductive leap:

> Holmes leaned back in the carriage, and the conversation ceased. A few minutes later our driver pulled up at a neat little red-brick villa with overhanging eaves which stood by the road. . . . We all sprang out with the exception of Holmes, who continued to lean back with his eyes fixed upon the sky in front of him, entirely absorbed in his own thoughts. It was only when I touched his arm that he roused himself with a violent start and stepped out of the carriage. . . . There was a gleam in his eyes and a suppressed excitement in his manner which convinced me, used as I was to his ways, that his hand was upon a clue, though I could not imagine where he had found it. (Doyle, 341)

Holmes's gesture derives from, and owes its power to, the image of Socrates thinking. It is the popularized, acculturated version of that image, indicating a process that occurs throughout the history of invention, by which the rare and exclusive becomes the shared commonplace (even if Holmes's abductive ability is represented as being unique).

  B. *Ambrose.* These historical examples of spectacles that later become commonplace prepare us to observe such phenomena in their inception in our own time. Well into the era of literacy, for example, St. Augustine reported the great anomaly of Brother Ambrose's habit of reading silently. All reading in the early Medieval period, even that done in private, was aloud, due to the user-hostile nature of manuscripts (the convenient break between the spelled words not yet having been instituted). "When he was reading his eyes glided over the pages and his heart searched out sense, but his voice and tongue were at rest." Again, the conduct was considered so strange that visitors came to observe this prodigy. Needless to say, silent reading passes unremarked today and is enforced as the norm.

  Such is the pattern I seek in our time. Is there some manner of reading now that seems utterly bizarre, worthy of being treated as a spectacle, but that promises, like the oddities of Socrates and Ambrose, especially in the context of rhizomatic memory, to become the commonplace convention of future literacy? If we could identify such an instance we might have a clue to the future status of text in the age of television.

  C. *Cage.* John Cage, the inventor of electronic music, supplies just such a case, representing in the history of reading the epistemic shift underway in the electronic era. Looking for a non-syntactical, "demilitarized" language (following Thoreau who noted that "to hear a sentence is to hear feet marching"), Cage turned to *Finnegans Wake* for a model. But even Joyce was too conventional (in the terms of minor literature, his memory was not yet rhizomatic), so Cage decided to generate a new text entirely out of the *Wake* using the technique of "mesostics": "not acrostics: row down the middle, not down the edge: first letter of a word or name is on the first line and following it on that line the second letter of the name is not to be found. The second letter is on the second line, etc." (Cage, 1981: 134). Using the name "James Joyce," Cage generated a text of some 115 pages, entitled "First time Through Finnegans Wake" (a mesostic journey he has repeated several more times), a text consisting entirely of Joyce's words, selected for their placement around the letters of the proper name. Cage's relation to the *Wake* as a reservoir for the generation of an unreadable, "concrete" text (a text representing the model of mechanical reproduction in writing) qualifies as the emblem of a new age of letters, reflecting the pattern established in the other examples, being a bizarre manner of reading that attracted an audience. Cage, that is, performed his mesostics as part of his musical lectures, before live audiences. Note, then, his account of how to read mesostically:

> From time to time in the course of this work I've had my doubts about the validity of finding in the *Wake* these mesostics on his name which James Joyce didn't put there. However I just went straight on, A after J, E after M, J after S, Y after O, E after C. I read each passage at least three times and once or twice upside down. (Hazel Dreis, who taught us English binding, used to tell us how she proof-read the *Leaves of Grass:* upside down and backwards). When you don't know what you're doing, you do your work very well. J's can thus be spotted by their dots and by their dipping below the line which I's don't do. (136)

In the light of this symptom, it is not surprising to find that Cage's text provides an excellent demonstration of rhizomatic invention. An image for the relation of a text to its "source" often mentioned in debates between critics and postcritics is that of the relation of parasite to host. J. Hillis Miller, speaking for the deconstructionists in a conference session on "The Limits of Pluralism," offered a rebuttal of assertions by Wayne Booth and M. H. Abrams that the "deconstructionist reading of a given work is plainly and simply parasitical on the obvious or univocal reading" (Miller, 439). Given that Derrida describes grammatology as a "parasitical economy," this term may be more descriptive than wounding, at least if one attempts to understand how it functions as theoretical property. Miller responds to the "charge" by problematizing the meaning of "parasite": "What happens when a critical essay extracts a 'passage' and 'cites' it? Is this different from a citation, echo, or allusion within a poem? Is a citation an alien parasite within the body of its host, the main text, or is it the other way around, the interpretive text the parasite which surrounds and strangles the citation which is its host?" The issue is compounded in the case of mystory which carries citation to its limit—collage.

Miller's rebuttal is meant to undermine the very notion of "univocal" reading by showing the equivocal, paradoxical plurality of the meaning of "host" and "guest," which turn out to share the same etymological root and are interchangeable in their sense. The point of this etymological exercise, he says,

> is an argument for the value of recognizing the great complexity and equivocal richness of apparently obvious or univocal language, even the language of criticism, which is in this respect continuous with the language of literature. This complexity and equivocal richness resides in part in the fact that there is no conceptual expression without figure, and no intertwining of concept and figure without an implied story, narrative, or myth, in this case the story of the alien guest in the home. Deconstruction is an investigation of what is implied by this inherence of figure, concept, and narrative in one another. (Miller, 443)

Miller's definition of "deconstruction" will be recognized as a definition of "allegory," deconstruction being one of those contemporary movements supporting a shift in critical writing from allegoresis to allegory. It also supports the possibility, essential to teletheory, of the mutual translatability between popular and expert discourses, highlighting the embedded *mise en abyme* structuration of mystory.

It happens that Michel Serres provided a full elaboration (allegory) of the very story of deconstruction, of the alien guest in the home, in a paraliterary text entitled *Parasite*. Not only does Serres support Miller's point regarding the equivocality of the host-parasite terminology, he supplements it by noting that in French a third meaning is available which permits the story of the parasite to be explored literally as an allegory of communication theory. In short, he shows that research on this theory may be done by telling stories related to the *root metaphor* of the concept in question. In teletheory, of course, we learn that such metaphors behave not like roots but like rhizomes.

> The parasite is a microbe, an insidious infection that takes without giving and weakens without killing. The parasite is also a guest, who exchanges his talk, praise, and flattery for food. The parasite is noise as well, the static in a system or the interference in a channel. These seemingly dissimilar activities are, according to Michel Serres, not merely coincidentally expressed by the same word (in French). Rather, they are intrinsically related and, in fact, they have the same basic function in a system. Whether it produces a fever or just hot air, the parasite is a thermal exciter. And as such, it is both the atom of a relation and the production of a change in this relation. (Serres, 1982: x)

Taking the luck of this homonym as a clue, Serres researches a selection of literary examples, stories about dinners, hosts, and guests, beginning with the fables of La Fontaine and including the return of Odysseus among the suitors, the *Symposium, Tartuffe,* etc., all examined in terms of *interruption,* interference, the noise that frightens away the mice, the call which took Simonides away from the table just before the roof collapsed (his recollection of which guest was sitting where, for purposes of identifying the bodies, is said to be the origin of mnemotechniques). Serres concludes that parasitism is "negentropic," the motor of change or invention—recalling Walter Benjamin's promotion of collage as the art of interruption—consisting of a new logic with three elements: host, guest, and interrupter (noise is the "random element, transforming one system or one order into another").

In spite of its associated complexities and controversies, Derrida's notion of the "gram" offers the theory of language most adequate to the collage mode of invention by interruption. Grammatology—the science of writing of which teletheory is the electronic representative—is poststructuralist in that it replaces the "sign" (signifier and signified—the basic unit of meaning in structuralist semiotics) with a different unit—the gram.

> It is a question of producing a new concept of writing. This concept can be called *gram* or *differance*. . . . Whether in the order of spoken or written discourse, no element can function as a sign without referring to another element which itself is not simply present. This interweaving results in each "element"—phoneme or grapheme—being constituted on the basis of the trace within it of the other elements of the chain or system. This interweaving, this textile, is the *text* produced only in the transformation of another text. Nothing, neither among the elements nor within the system, is anywhere ever simply present or absent. There are only, everywhere, differences and traces of traces. The gram, then, is the most general concept of semiology—which thus becomes grammatology. (Derrida, 1981: 26)

Collage/montage, in other words, is the manifestation at the level of discourse of the gram principle, as may be seen in a comparison of the following rhetorical definition of the collage effect with a definition of the gram effect.

> Its [collage's] heterogeneity, even if it is reduced by every operation of composition, imposes itself on the reading as stimulation to produce a signification which could be neither univocal nor stable. Each cited element breaks the continuity of the linearity of the discourse and leads necessarily to a double reading: that of the fragment perceived in relation to its text of origin; that of the same fragment as incorporated into a new whole, a different totality. The trick of collage consists also of never entirely suppressing the alterity of these elements reunited in a temporary composition. Thus the art of collage proves to be one of the most effective strategies in the putting into question of all the illusions of representation. (Group *mu*, 1978: 13–14)

This undecidable reading effect, oscillating between presence and absence, is just what Derrida tries to achieve at every level of his "double science," from his paleonymic redefinition (remotivation) of concepts to his publishing of two books under one cover (*Glas*)—in short, the puncept replacing the concept.

The notion of the gram is especially useful for theorizing the fact, much discussed in structuralist psychoanalysis and ideological criticism, that signifieds and signifiers are continually breaking apart and reattaching in new combinations, thus revealing the inadequacy of Saussure's model of the sign, according to which the signifier and the signified relate as if they were two sides of the same sheet of paper. The tendency of Western philosophy throughout its history ("logocentrism") to try to pin down and fix a specific signified to a given signifier suppresses, according to grammatology, part of the power of language, which functions, in any case, not in terms of matched *pairs* (signifier/signified) but of *couples*, couplers, or couplings—"a person or thing that couples or links together." The following description of what Derrida calls "iterability" is also an excellent summary of the collage consequences of the gram:

> And this is the possibility on which I want to insist: the possibility of disengagement and citational graft which belongs to the structure of every mark, spoken or written, and which constitutes every mark in writing before and outside of every horizon of semio-linguistic communication; in writing, which is to say in the possibility of its functioning being cut off, at a certain point, from its "original" desire-to-say-what-one-means and from its participation in a saturable and constraining context. Every sign, linguistic or nonlinguistic, spoken or written (in the current sense of this opposition), in a small or large unit, can be *cited*, put between quotation marks; in so doing it can break with every given context, engendering an infinity of new contexts in a manner which is absolutely illimitable. (Derrida, 1977: 185)

In critical theory as in literature collage takes the form of citation, is the limit-case of citation, with Derrida's grammatology being the theory of scripting as citation, although his insistence on the "graft" indicates a heritage of the tree that must be exceeded by the rhizome.

A mystory will be a collage/montage of quotations, then, and John Cage's writings demonstrate both thematically and formally how texts composed according to such principles function. Part of their value is that Cage is famous as a postmodernist musician. His "prepared piano" and early use of electronic equipment, along with his compositional innovations (graphic scores and aleatory procedures) and performance experiments (scores indeterminate as to performance), revolutionized ("postmodernized") music. Mystory can benefit from the fact that Cage decided to apply his philosophy of composition to language ("I hope to let words exist, as I have tried to let sounds exist" [Cage, 1981: 151]).

It is worth noting in this context that Cage, like Adorno, studied music theory with Schoenberg. Cage adopted a view, similar to Adorno's strategy of the "concrete particular," that music should be a kind of *research,* and exploration of the logic of materials, which in Cage's case became extended to include not just the materials of music but everything in the natural and cultural worlds: "art changes because science changes—changes in science give artists different understandings of how nature works" (Cage, 1961: 194). This attitude leads Cage to his own version (a musical one) of the "theoretical object":

> We know the air is filled with vibrations that we can't hear. In *Variations VII,* I tried to use sounds from that inaudible environment. But we can't consider the environment as an object. We know that it's a process. While in the case of the ashtray, we are indeed dealing with an object. It would be extremely interesting to place it in a little anechoic chamber and to listen to it through a suitable sound system. Object would become process; we would discover, thanks to a procedure borrowed from science, the meaning of nature through the music of objects. (Cage, 1981: 221)

Moreover, this procedure is explicitly identified with the collage/montage principle, identified here as "silence" (the "death of the author" in Barthes's terms)—"*The Gutenberg Galaxy* is made up of borrowings and collages: McLuhan applies what I call silence to all areas of knowledge, that is, he lets them speak. The death of the book is not the end of language: it continues. Just as in my case, silence has invaded everything, and there is still music" (117). Here we encounter again the mood of silence directing the joke as simple form, which Cage shows how to treat productively. Cage acknowledges McLuhan, who has been credited with inventing a kind of "essai concret," and Norman O. Brown (whom Hayden White identified as the author of one of the few experimental historiographies)—as important influences on his work.

Cage postmodernizes the critical essay by bringing to bear on its *inventio* and *dispositio* the same collage and aleatory procedures used in working with tape recorders and other electronic equipment in his musical performances. The selection of texts—Thoreau's Journals and Joyce's *Wake*—is not itself random but is part of the statement (the Journals and the *Wake* are appropriated and signed, in the same way that Barthes signed Arcimboldo's paintings). Cage, exemplifying the program of euretics, does not write *about* Thoreau, but uses the Journals for the generation of other texts, which are in fact musicalized simulacra of the originals. These simulacra are collage constructions in that all the words, letters, phrases in them are derived directly from the Journals, selected according to chance operations. "Mureau" ("music" + "Thoreau"), for example, is "a mix of letters, syllables, words, phrases, and sentences. I wrote it by subjecting all the remarks of Henry David Thoreau about music, silence, and sounds he heard that are indexed in the Dover publications of the Journals to a series of I Ching chance operations. The personal pronoun was varied according to such operations and the typing was likewise determined" (Cage, 1974: 1). When confronting such a text in print, the full import of Barthes's advice about writerly reading becomes apparent, for something like "Mureau" may not be read "conceptually." Rather, by skimming the eye over the page, letting it be arrested momentarily by different typefaces so that the sense of those randomly noted words is allowed to register, a powerful effect emerges—the simulacrum of walking through the woods of Concord with the senses open and the attention floating. Cage explains that Thoreau listened "just as composers using technology nowadays listen; . . .and he explored the neighborhood of Concord with the same appetite with which they explore the possibilities provided by electronics."

Some of Cage's other writings display the tendency (again following Walter Benjamin) of montage compositions to rely upon allegory, illuminating specifically the allegorical implications of the host-parasite scene of theory. "Where Are We Eating? And What Are We Eating?" is one example (an account of Cage's travels with Merce Cunningham's dance troupe, entirely in terms of what they ordered when they stopped to eat—an avant-garde version of the "restaurant script" developed in Artificial Intelligence experiments), marking the parallel between Cage's narrative allegory and Serres's *Parasite,* with the latter alerting us to the "extra" import of the many anecdotes concerned with guests, hosts, and dining found throughout Cage's writings. The extraordinary insight made available through Serres's elaboration of the French meaning of "parasite" ("noise," as well as "guest" and "parasite") is that Cage—who is famous as the composer who opened music to noise ("since the theory of conventional music is a set of laws exclusively concerned with 'musical' sounds, having nothing to say about noises, it had been clear from the beginning that what was needed was a music based on noise, on noise's lawlessness. . . . The next steps were social" [Cage, 1974:v])—when he is writing about dining, is *still* or *also* talking about noise. His anecdotes about eating are discursive equivalents of utilizing noise in his musical scores. They are also a commentary on the "parasitical" invention process of citation, collage, upon which both his music and essays depend.

At the center of this allegory about noise and dining is Cage's passion for mushrooms. Cage, founder of the New York Mycological Society, owned one of the world's largest private collections of books about mushrooms. Again, although anecdotes having to do with mushrooms are disseminated throughout Cage's writing, they are the organizing topic in *Mushroom Book,* whose collage construction may be seen in this prospectus: "To finish for Lois Programmed handwritten mushroom book including mushroom stories, excerpts from (mushroom) books, remarks about (mushroom) hunting, excerpts from Thoreau's *Journal* (fungi), excerpts from Thoreau's *Journal* (entire), remarks about: Life/Art, Art/Life, Life/Life, Art/Art, Zen, Current reading, Cooking (shopping, recipes), Games, Music mss., Maps, Friends, Invention, Projects, + Writing without syntax, Mesostics (on mushroom names)" (133–134).

Why mushrooms? Cage remarks that it is because "mushroom" is next to "music" in most dictionaries. But read as mystory, the mushroom may be understood as a model mounted in a discourse for allegorical purposes. Indeed, the mushroom turns out to be a good emblem for what Derrida calls the "pharmakon"—a potion or medicine that is at once elixir and poison (borrowed from Plato), modeling what Derrida calls (by analogy) "undecidables" (directed against all conceptual, classifying systems). The undecidables are:

> unities of simulacra, "false" verbal properties (nominal or semantic) that can no longer be included within philosophical (binary) opposition, but which, however, inhabit philosophical opposition, resisting and disorganizing it, *without ever* constituting a third term, without ever leaving room for a solution in the form of speculative dialectics (the *pharmakon* is neither remedy nor poison, neither good nor evil, neither the inside nor the outside, neither speech nor writing. (Derrida, 1981: 43)

What the pharmakon is in the pharmaceutical (and the conceptual) realm, the mushroom is in the plant world, which is to say a translation is available for both didactic and theoretical work between mycology and grammatology. Of the mushroom Cage remarks, "the more you know them, the less sure you feel about identifying them. Each one is itself. Each mushroom is what it is—its own center. It's useless to pretend to know mushrooms. They escape your erudition" (Cage, 1981: 188). Cage's fascination with mycology is due in part to this undecidability of classification, as indicated in his anecdotes about experts who have misidentified poison species as edible, or of people who have become ill, even died, from eating a variety that had no effect on other people (different individuals react differently to the same species sometimes). When he suggests, in the context of anecdotes about his own experiences of poisoning by mushrooms, that it is too bad that books are not edible, Cage seems to be making a point similar to the one Barthes made in *S/Z* with respect to the *risk* in reading. Sarrasine, having mistaken the castrato Zambinella for a woman, dies "because of an inaccurate and inconclusive reasoning": "All the cultural codes, taken up from citation to citation, together form an oddly joined miniature version of encyclopedic knowledge, a farrago: this farrago forms the everyday 'reality' in relation to which the subject adapts himself, lives. One defect in this encyclopedia, one hole in this cultural fabric, and death can result. Ignorant of the code of

Papal customs, Sarrasine dies from a gap in knowledge" (Barthes, 1974: 184–185). The mushroom demonstrates a lesson about conduct—the conduct of survival.

Following the montage-allegory principle, Cage's mushroom anecdotes constitute collaged fragments alluding to the entire science of mycology. To assess the larger significance of the mushroom as allegory, then, one should review the "logic" of the material thus paradigmatically evoked (just as the absent terms of a semantic field are implied negatively by the specific term used in a sentence). The connotation relevant to our context has to do with the parasite host relationship as a model for the status of the citation in mystory (whose "my" has something to do with mycology). The lesson taught by the kind of fungi hunted (research activity) and eaten by John Cage in particular—the fleshy, fruity, "higher" fungi, Boletus, Morels, and the like—is *symbiosis*. These fungi are not parasites, but *saprophytes* (any organism that lives on dead organic matter), and exist in a symbiotic, mutually beneficial relationship with their hosts (the green plants and trees which supply the organic "food"). The genus "Cortinarius," for example, as described by C. H. Kauffman (whose study, *The Agaricaceae of Michigan*, Cage lists among the ten books that most influenced him), may be found in "the region of pine and spruce, or in old beech forests, where the shade is dense and the ground is saturated with moisture," growing, of course, on the substratum of decaying matter. The trees benefit from the fungi growing among their roots by absorbing the nutrients made soluble as a result of the decomposing process to which the mushrooms contribute.

This symbiotic ecology (related to the usefulness of the lower fungi, whose fermentations are essential to the production of wine, cheese, and bread) is Cage's version of what Benjamin was talking about when he compared allegory to ruins, for it could be said that the saprophyte, living off the decay of dead organisms in a way that makes life possible for living plants, is to nature what the ruin is to culture, or the allegory to thought. For Adorno and Benjamin, the ruins were signs of the *decay* of the bourgeois era, requiring in philosophy a "logic of disintegration." For Derrida, too, deconstruction is a process of decomposition at work within the very *root* metaphors—the philosophemes—of Western thought. But we may see that this work is symbiotic, similar to the "mycorrhizal formation" in which tree roots and fungi supplement one another, enabling each to "live *on*," *sur*-vive, roots and rhizomes together, critique and invention in the same lawn.

The allegory of the mushroom, sustained not by roots but by a mycelium, and thus affiliated with the rhizome, shows that the relationship between the book (root, tree) and electronics (rhizome), between the two memories, the two logics, is symbiotic, mutually sustaining, a source of life and cultural health, vita and tv/ai.

3. Pre/Signature

Cage's *Mushroom Book,* and his textual allegories in general, provide explicit directions (both literally and figuratively) for making a mystory. By means of the rhizome and mushrooms I want to insist on the place of memory as an actual ground, the earth in its materiality, and as a cultural environment as well, specific to each individual in relation to a community place. The rhizome or mushroom is planted in the place of memory, of one's own public and private past. It is not only that the materials of a mystorical inventio come together rhizomatically, but that in a mystory one thinks using the concrete items of a diegetic world, so that one's conduct—hunting mushrooms for example—becomes eloquent. The nostalgia that so many critics identify as part of an emotional failure in our society may be put to work positively in this context as the *punctum* used to collect and inventory one's image-repertoire. The *nature* of this ground in memory being imagistic, it is best to explore it through the scenes of theoretical diegesis, to make a diegesis, from the elements of our models, such as Cage's "Mushroom Book." "Mushroom Book" contributes to a recipe for mystory the example of the text as proof, two features of which are especially valuable formally.

The first feature to be generalized from this model is the operation of science in it, represented by mycology (the "my" of mystory is associated with the "my" in mycology, as well as with the "my" in "Mike," code name for the first thermonuclear bomb, whose index is a mushroom cloud). In montage-allegory the science functions literally and figuratively, in expository, narrative, and poetic names. Cage suggests that his mushrooms could be read allegorically, even if he himself (being, as he says, the "grasshopper" of the fable) is too lazy to undertake the labor required for the comparison (Cage, 1961: 276). In mystory, however, these implications would be at least partially explicit, not left entirely to inference. The social philosophy that he derives from his theory of music, for example, expresses the symbiotic theme of ecology, of cooperation and an end to competition. For, as Cage warns, referring to the current world situation, to the same global implications of the parasite theme that inform Serres's study, "the party's nearly over. But the guests are going to stay; they have no place else to go. People who weren't invited are beginning to arrive. The house is a mess. We must all get together and without saying a word clean it up" (Cage, 1974: vii). Mycology in "Mushroom Book," then, operates the way Lacanian psychoanalysis operates in Mary Kelly's *Post-Partum Document* and Barthes's *A Lover's Discourse.*

The other feature of special interest in this model is the prominent display of anecdotes in its composition. During a significant period of Cage's career the anecdote served as the basic unit of composition in all his scores, lectures, and essays. He began collecting stories, he noted, any that stuck in his mind (the punctum), in a way that anticipates Barthes's commonplace organization of *Fragments*. "Others I read in books and remembered—those for instance from Sri Ramakrishna and the literature surrounding Zen," Cage says of this collection, that also recalls Freud's collection of Jewish jokes. "Still others have been told me by friends—Merce Cunningham, Virgil Thomson, Betty Isaacs, and many more" (Cage, 1966: 260). The stories could stand alone (an entire lecture consisting of nothing but anecdotes), be combined with other media—dance numbers by Cunningham or piano pieces by David Tudor—or be disseminated through collage texts. "My intention in putting the stories together in an unplanned way was to suggest that all things— stories, incidental sounds from the environment, and, by extension, beings— are related, and that this complexity is more evident when it is not oversimplified by an idea of relationship in one person's mind" (260). The relationship, that is, could be mapped as a rhizome.

> When I mentioned the three factors given by
> Ellul that "could
> change the course of
> history" (general war with
> enormous destruction; upsetting the
> technological world on the part of an increasing
> number of people; intervention
> on the part of a decided God), he
> said, "The third is the most
> likely."

> Looked up invention in telephone book:
> Inventaprises Inc
> Inventive Design Inc
> Inventive Music Ltd
> Invento Prods Corp.

> We remain greedy: we never find
> enough. We keep on
> looking for mushrooms
> until we're obligated (an engagement or the fact
> the light's failing) to stop. Only for
> some such reason do we leave the woods (unless,
> by then, we're lost).

> We imagine that
> spores that never before joined in
> reproduction on occasion in the case of
> related species sometimes do:
> possibility of a
> natural invention

What is that now
ancient and decayed
fungus by the first
mayflowers,—trumpet-shaped with a
very broad mouth, the chief
inner part green, the outer dark brown?
. . . dirty-white fungi in nests. Each one is
burst a little at the
top, and is full of dust
of a yellowish rotten-stone
color, which is perfectly dry.
(Henry David Thoreau).
(Cage, 1974: 128–129)

The anecdotes, as in our other models, are integrated here with a diversity of other items (as listed in his inventory), so that, between a recipe and a citation from Mao or Buckminster Fuller one comes upon something like this:

Went to meet Peggy at the airport./ Found myself in Japanese crowd/ (popular politician arriving in the same plane/ from Europe). Jet with engines going drove near to us./ (Rare opportunity.) Was surprised to see people putting fingers in their ears. (118)

What Cage has been practicing for more than three decades has become a dominant mode of art after modernism, judging by the anthology, *Blasted Allegories*, edited by Brian Wallis, who notes the critical function of such story telling, concerned with the "construction and deconstruction of cultural representations." As such, he adds, they are "inescapably allegorical," as defined by Craig Owens: "the allegorist does not invent images, but confiscates them. He lays claim to the culturally significant, poses as its interpreter. And in his hands the image becomes something other . . .he adds another meaning to the image" (Wallis, 1987: xiv–xv). Art as story telling includes not only anecdotes but many other forms—jokes, interviews, parables, dream narratives and the like, Wallis says, working not by innovation but appropriation, reinscribing existing styles in new contexts in ways that are more digressive than coherent. Against "the more formal presumptions and mandarin tone of high theoretical discourse," didactic and specialized, "excluding the subjective and the irrational, and insisting on the political correctness of a specific moral or ethical agenda," the artists' texts approach real events and experiences from the side of pleasure and the personal, enlarging them to explore their implied ethical, social, and political significance (xv). Such, too, is the program of mystory, in order to reopen and redefine the "institutional and exclusionary models" of academic discourse rejected by these artists. The difference is that mystory is not against criticism, but rather is a hybrid in which the oral-anecdotal and the literate-theoretical articulate a third meaning.

Mushroom Book functions allegorically in teletheory, too, appropriated for further work, to indicate the drive of research, to begin with: "In woods, we're misled/ by leaves or play of sunlight; driving along, we sometimes stop, park, and get/ out, only to discover it's a football or a/ piece of trash. Learning from such/ experiences isn't what we do" (Cage, 1974: 128). I have appropriated Cage's mushroom, to follow it as an argument, in conceiving of a history that puts images over stories. In this context *Mushroom Book* becomes an experiment in the new instauration emerging out of Freud's discourse. The fact is that Freud also had a passion for mushrooms, as reported by his biographer:

> The most characteristic feature of Freud's holiday pursuits was his passion for mushrooms, especially for finding them. He had an uncanny flair for discovering where they were likely to be, and would even point out such spots when riding alone in a train. On an expedition for the purpose they would be sure to hear soon a cry of success from him. He would then creep silently up to it and suddenly pounce to capture the fungus with his hat as if it were a bird or butterfly. (Balmary, 29)

Balmary shows that this capture of the mushroom is related to a series of other objects associated with Freud's death anxiety. Samuel Weber reminds us, at the same time, of Freud's use of the image of the mycelium of the mushroom to represent the dream navel, Freud himself having developed, after all, the discourse in which images communicate with theory.

> For Freud does not simply stop at the designation of the dream-navel as the "place where (the dream) straddles the unknown;" he *describes* that unknown, or rather, what emerges from it: the dream-wish, surging forth "like the mushroom out of its mycelium." The dream-wish, which both emerges from the navel of the dream and also renders its "unknown" aspects knowable, is thus inseparable from something called a "mycelium." What, then, is there to be said about a mycelium? (Weber, 81)

To answer this question Weber turns to the O.E.D. and finds this definition: "The vegetative part of the thallus of fungi, consisting of white filamentous tubes (hyphae); the spawn of mushrooms." A look at "thallus" provides this clarification: "A vegetable structure without vascular tissue, in which there is not differentiation into stem and leaves, and from which true roots are absent." The implication of this image in Freud's *Bildersprache* for Weber is that the thallus and not the phallus is the better representation of what is in question in the unconscious. Weber's study follows this possibility in the same direction taken by teletheory—into the book of jokes. Here, however, I cite him only to emphasize that the rhizome and the mushroom bring into representation the site of memory, the place of the unconscious and of the dream-wish, as the ground of electronic cognition.

This site is also the place of invention, in euretics, of the *loci* of the new academic discourse. Derrida brought to our attention another model similar or rather complementary to Cage's model in certain important respects, having to do with the puncept. That the man who composed "Music of Changes," who says he composes all his productions by means of the "Book of Changes" (*I Ching*) in order to change society, happens to be named *Jo Change* (John Cage, anagram), turns out to be not exactly an accident. Francis Ponge, according to Derrida, has represented, if not systematized, the science of the signature in which a text is written in the key of the author's name. Derrida has devoted considerable effort in a variety of books and articles to show that not only poets but also philosophers sign their texts in this way, establishing a homonymy between the personal and the disciplinary registers of discourse (the puncept inventio). In mystory it is not a question of proving that texts have been authored this way, but that they could be, and will be in the new academic discourse. We can see now, in other words, part of the significance of the symptom of electronic literacy in Cage, whose rewriting of the *Wake* through the mesostics on "James Joyce" anticipated or intuited the signature as invention.

Before reviewing Derrida's theorization of Ponge's practice it is important to consider Ponge's journal, *The Making of the "Pré,"* as a text to be mounted allegorically in the discourse of teletheory, for the prairie or *pré* of which Ponge writes is precisely a place where rhizomes and mushrooms flourish. It also happens to be a meditation on invention in relation to memory of place, and as such constitutes in its own right a model for mystory. It shows, that is, both the poem and its invention, combined as one text, rhizomatically linked and inseparable, the two dimensions of intelligence, discovery and justification.

The journal, in the book published by the University of Missouri Press, is itself desirable, raising the desire to write with its montage of handwriting and typescript, through which is disseminated a series of images: a photograph of the place itself—the meadow and the Lignon river at Chantegrenouille; paintings of such places by the likes of Chagall and Botticelli; a musical score by Bach; botanical prints of grasses; enlarged reproduction of a dictionary entry on *"pré"* and *"nature."* The insistence on the quality of the place produced in the image track is replicated in the verbal material by an accumulative permutation and combination of lines repeating the descriptions of grass, rocks, water, wind.

The journal is not only a sketchbook but a theoretical elaboration of the poetics generating the text: *"Ah what beautiful things one could say about the pré! Such as:* 'I cropped from that *pré* the width of my tongue.' *But I would like to derive something else from it: a quality, a law"* (Ponge, 1979: 65). It is at once the thing and its model, the example and the law, practice and theory. He learns to bring the *pré* into language by *emulation*—a key term in the journal—emulating the grass (a rhizome) in language, finding a linguistic equivalent of growth: "in the field of logic we are on the only level which suits us, that of the original onomatopoeias, of the infrasignifications. I will establish the kinship, at this level, of *pré, près, prêt, prépare"* (195). The homophonic similarity with the key of *pré* serves as the generative principle for what enters the poem, including the etymologies that give, "pressed close to the rock and the rill," "ready for mowing or grazing," "prepared for us by nature preadorned," as well as the prefix, as in "pré-sent," but also the music of Josquin des Prés, and thus the Renaissance as such; the Medieval Pré-aux-Clercs, the former location of the University of Paris, evoking scholars with their long debates, and nobles with their short duels. In short, the linguistic material of the poem is produced in large part from the paradigm of *pré*, unpacked and elaborated through all of its encyclopedic possibilities ("We must find a way to get along with our words, at least with our syllables, our roots. . . .relationships working at the root level, where things and formulations merge. Their varieties, their developments, ramifications, foliations, florifications, fruitions, reseedings") (129).

In the middle of this scholarly, philological research there appears suddenly a place of narrative, an anecdote of invention, explaining the emotional genesis of the text, long withheld as the promise of what he was trying to say "about" the *pré*. Ponge returns to Chambon, the place where he met his wife thirty years earlier, and which had previously inspired several poems; a familiar place.

> We had come by car, Odette and I, via a road that overlooks a spot called Chantegrenouille.
> "And why had we come? I could say only too much about it. We had had a daughter. She had come alone to Chambon and we knew that she would be dancing at Chantegrenouille. We had wanted to see the place."
> We had left our car there and had entered a pine woods below which could be seen the *pré* lying beside the little river, the little torrent tamed by mountains that is called the *Lignon*.
> Was it Sunday? Strollers by groups, groups of friends, families, were moving across the *pré*. This *pré* knew a population (in the active sense). There, that was all. Nothing but that. I can say no more about it. I was, I don't know why, gripped by a sort of secret enthusiasm, calm (tranquil), pure, still. (139)

He also knows at once that the vision was permanent, "intact in my memory," so that he had to communicate it, to perpetuate it by telling it. His text gives us a privileged sense of the place of memory in almost its pure state, as an actual site, a location whose emotion in this case is a feeling of hope. Among the allegorical senses of *The Making of the "Pré"*, then, must be counted this insistence on the *nature* of memory as a specific place. Ponge in fact alludes to the places of rhetoric, saying that he has traded them for his prairie, which happens to serve him better: "Then let us leave such porticos or all colonnades. . . . Let us reach this *pré* that nature prepared for us alongside just such a stream of drowning or perdition. . . .memory persists there at the tip of a thousand needlesful of green thread" (151). The blades of grass are sharp in his mind, source of the punctum.

What is at stake in this scene, then, is the source of mystoriography: "According to I know not which mythology, Philippe S. tells me, we walk on our past. The past, it is what we walk on. It is the ground beneath our feet. It is our foundation. Our past, we walk on it. It is situated beneath our feet" (179). Ponge's investigation into the terms of nature in language turns up the peculiar destiny of an individual, the place prepared in advance and made ready by nature for each one, in the interest of which he produces the dictionary entry on *nature,* which includes "The constitution, the tempera- ment of each individual. He is bilious, sanguine by nature," as well as the more general meaning, "the nature of things in general, the necessity which results form the constitution of things" (123, 125).

Part of the allegory has to do with an alchemical theory of psychology and creation, with the *pré* representing in Ponge's poetics a basic unit, containing the four elements—earth, air, fire, water. The meaning of the prairie for Ponge himself is "hope" in the capacity of life to persist, live on, survive, resurrect after catastrophe, which he reads in the cycle of photosynthesis.

> All the actions of the past, all the characters, the persons and passions (successful formulations, expressions, persons of perpetuation) in their finest expressions, in their most minute granulations, were reduced there; then the water filtered in, impregnated them, so that at the summons (at the powerful invocation of the sun) their transmutation might operate.
>
> Which is, in short, no more than a mode of the evaporation of water (H_2O) via the mineral. *Instead of* evaporating directly and metamorphosing into useless and insignificant vapors,
>
> A part of the water *passes* through the mineral, to evaporate, and this is the occasion of an elemental principle of life: of vegetation. (185)

The cycle of photosynthesis, "the most prevalent energy system on the planet," as one handbook explains, in which green plants use sunlight to produce oxygen, is a demonstration of the cycle of knowledge as well, of decay and renewal. "The first stage of the process is the *transduction* of light into electricity." This term—"transduction"—may be borrowed to name the translation process across the registers of culture in teletheory.

The *pré*, finally, is a limited space, the place where each one returns to the earth, the grave or tomb as the place of memory and nature, as Ponge dramatizes by burying his name in the text, as he imagines his body will be buried in the *pré*:

> Then beneath the line, without the slightest space, couch my name
> In lowercase, quite naturally,
>> Save for the initials, of course,
>> Since they are also those
>> Of Fennel and of Purslane
>> That tomorrow will grow above.
>
> ────────────────────
> Francis Ponge (231)

The Making of the "Pré", then, is also a story of mourning, which may be appropriated in teletheory as a model for a genre, "The Making of the Place of Memory," that each one will invent for myself in order to script in the new academic discourse. There may be a pattern observable by now, of the pleasure of the text as dramatizing a funeral, even if (or especially if) it is one's own, thus thematizing the paradox of the monumentalized subject inherent in the experience of literacy.

4. Otobiography

Ponge's example, like Wittgenstein's earlier, indicates that a text of invention has much to learn from the notebooks, journals, and diaries that have played a large part in the history of discovery. The autobiographical aspect of this mode of writing, however, has to be refunctioned to address the new apparatus. Nietzsche exemplifies the peculiar status of the *auto* in Derrida's deconstruction of auto-affection as self-presence (of an immediate, unmediated intuition of identity). In his discussion of Nietzsche Derrida makes explicit the pun directing his thinking about the new autobiography, the transformation of the auto into *oto* (from the Greek, meaning "ear"), indicating the sense he will use to frame the "world picture."

It is necessary not only to pass through the ear, and by the ear that is engaged in all autobiographical discourse which involves always a hearing oneself speak (I tell my story to myself, as Nietzsche said, there you have the story that I tell myself, that signifies that I hear myself speak). I speak to myself in a certain manner and my ear is immediately connected to my discourse and to my writing. (Derrida, 1982: 70)

With the *oto* Derrida calls attention to the way in which the model of logocentrism has been institutionalized, dictating the structure of the academic scene:

> Dream this umbilicus: it holds you by the ear, but by the ear which dictates to you what you presently write when you write according to that mode called "taking notes." In fact the mother—the bad or false one whom the teacher, in his capacity qua functionary of the State, can only simulate—yes, the mother dictates to you precisely that which, passing through your ear, moves along the cord as far as your stenography. This in turn links you, like a leash in the form of an umbilical cord, to the paternal belly of the State. Your pen is its pen; you hold its teleprinter as you hold those ballpoints in the post office which are attached to chains. (53)

The academic apparatus consists of a mouth speaking—lecturing—an ear listening, in a literal way, a hand writing—the cultural machine of note-taking. Such at least is the apparatus of literacy.

But this apparatus has changed before, and will again:

> In the Republican period of ancient Rome, to dictate meant to speak in the elevated, rhythmic manner of the *ductus; scribere* meant the physical act of writing as well as composing. In the Middle Ages the frontier between the two meanings was located quite differently. *Dictare* referred to the act of creating a text, and *scribere* simply to the work done with writing materials. (Illich and Sanders, 45)

The project now, taking the *ductus* into conduction, is to think another apparatus, in which there is more than one way to listen, more than one way to extend the intellectual senses—hearing and sight, knowledge from a distance—by means of audio-visual technology.

Otobiography mixes the modes of critique and fiction, demonstrating the possibility of applying literary devices to the practices of academic discourse. Derrida explains this approach most explicitly in *Signsponge*, his text on the name "Francis Ponge," in which he treats Ponge's *oeuvre* as if it were generated in the key of "Ponge," in the same way that "The Prairie" is generated in the key of *pré*. The value of Derrida's experiment is that it indicates one way to generalize a rhizomatic relation of the text to the world.

There are, Derrida notes with respect to Ponge's name, three modalities of the signature. The first two are perfectly familiar—the act of signing one's name to indicate ownership, property (an invention of literacy); and "style," "the set of idiomatic marks that a signer might leave by accident or intention in his product." The third modality is of special interest:

here, we may designate as general signature, or signature of the signature, the fold of the placement in abyss where, after the manner of the signature in the current sense, the work of writing designates, describes, and inscribes itself as act (action and archive), signs itself before the end by affording us the opportunity to read: I refer to myself, this is writing, I am a writing, this is writing—which excludes nothing since, when the placement in abyss succeeds, and is thereby decomposed and produces an event, it is the other, the thing as other, that signs. (Derrida, 1984: 52–54)

The structuration of the signature effect, corresponding to the embedding notable in the psychoanalytic interview, is figured here in terms of the "placement in abyss," originally from heraldry, "where it denotes a smaller escutcheon appearing in the center of a larger one," used to "refer to a structure in which the whole is represented in miniature in one of its parts" (Derrida, 1978a: 147). The system of heraldry was invented in order to identify the individuals—specifically in terms of their family heritage—who had become unrecognizable in their coats of armor.

While the three modalities of the signature are structurally distinct, Derrida adds, Ponge "is able to fold all three into a single one, or in any case combine them in the same scene for the same drama and the same orgasm" (Derrida, 1984: 54, 56). When the signature is thus inserted into the body of the text, it is *monumentalized,* erected into a "stony object" (the grave in the *Pré*). "But in doing so, you also lose the identity, the title of ownership over the text: you let it become a moment or a part of the text, as a thing or a common noun. The erection-tomb falls. Step and stop of man." Such is the double bind of the signature and the countersignature, the double movement of rising and falling, stated and emphasized in the pun *tomb* (fall, erected monument). Derrida thus calls attention to the monumentality and mourning inherent in the separation of the speaker from the word in writing.

Ponge is credited with founding the "science" of the signature because he manages to line up all three modalities of the proper name in a single scene. It is worth noting exactly how he accomplishes this condensation, since it gives rise to the event that is the effect Derrida seeks to produce in many of his texts (celebrating what a name *founds,* what may be found in a name). In analyzing Ponge's event, it is important to keep in mind the specific nature of the third modality, or rather, to note the superimposition of the three modalities. For the event to take place there must develop not only the figure of antonomasia, in which, in this case, a writer by the name of Ponge writes about all manner of sponge-like (*éponge* = sponge) things and processes (selected either by homonymy in the name, or by the properties of the thing, including the "prairie" itself, with its property of absorbing and releasing water), but that these sponges in turn (and this is the third modality) function explicitly as the representation of a theory of writing. Derrida summarizes how the qualities of the sponge figure writing:

It loses and as easily recovers its form, which is neither proper nor improper, neither simply a thing, nor simply vegetal, nor simply animal. They call this thing either a zoophyte, an animal plant, or else the substance "deriving from a marine zoophyte" (Littré). Solid or plastic, full of air or water, what does the sponge resemble? An animal swollen with water, it is, in effect, a medusa. . . . Able to hold gases or liquid alternatively, "to fill itself with wind or water," the sponge is, above all else, writing. (70)

This conclusion is not simply asserted, but derives from an allegory developed by Ponge, about which Derrida comments: "the sponge is not named in this passage, but as an analog to the medusa, or to any state intermediate between all states—an analog in this respect to the medium of writing, if it can put itself into every state and serve as an intermediary, intercessor, or witness for all manner of thought—the sponge not only constitutes the term of an analog (or allegory or metaphor), but also constitutes as well the very medium of all figures, metaphoricity itself" (72). The attractiveness of the sponge as an emblem of writing is, for Derrida in particular, that, as a zoophyte, its undecidable status on the border of a classification system nicely conveys the undecidable status of the gram and differance. In this respect it has the same signifying power as the mushroom, with the added benefit in English of a "sponge" as a kind of "parasite."

Glas may be seen in this context as an attempt to demonstrate the operation of the signature in philosophical and academic discourse. As a philosopher himself, Derrida is interested in Ponge's distaste for philosophers in general, and for Hegel in particular, whom he finds unclean, disgusting, improper, for want of knowing how to sign a text. (Having once noted that his entire oeuvre is a tireless critique of Hegel, Derrida enlists the aid of all those authors who have similarly reacted to Hegel with disgust or aversion, which includes the signature linking "Hegel" with "Ekel"—disgust or nausea, in German) (Derrida, 1982: 38). "In order to sign," Derrida remarks with respect to Ponge's criticism of philosophy, "one has to stop one's text, and no philosopher will have signed his text, resolutely and singularly, will have spoken in his own name, accepting all the risks involved in doing so. Every philosopher denies the idiom of his name, of his language, of his circumstances, speaking in concepts and generalities that are necessarily improper" (Derrida, 1984: 32).

To simply affix one's name to the end of a book is not to sign in Derrida's sense. Rather, the proper name, that part of the author that sur-vives, lives on, must undergo that transformation from singular reference to general concept that is the essence of the foundation of a system of knowledge out of the autobiography of a unique individual, according to this process: "The proper name, in its aleatoriness, should have no meaning and should spend itself in immediate reference," or so at least says the theory of the proper name established by the Anglo-American philosophy of language. But Derrida wishes to problematize the debate surrounding the nature of the proper name—whether it is denotative, connotative; whether it fixes its referent causally or intentionally—by carrying the question into the domain of iterability. "But the change or the misery of its arbitrary character (always other in each case), is that its inscription in language always affects it with a potential for meaning, and for no longer being proper once it has a meaning. It becomes meaningful once again, of limited range, once it is reinvested with semantic content. It starts to reenter the framework of a general science that governs the effects of the *alea*" (118, 120).

Everything in the paradigm of Text has to do with this *alea*, Derrida's aleatory science being an alternative to the teleology of logocentric thought couched in all the dialectics that have dominated its history. Derrida finds this *alea* in the wing (*aile*) of "Hegel" semanticized as *aigle* (eagle, or, figuratively, "a clever or brilliant person, a genius"). Ponge singled out Hegel as an example of a philosopher who refused to sign—but in this respect he may stand in for academic writing as well—a charge that Derrida repeats in an interview, identifying it as the issue addressed in *Glas*:

> I said in *Glas* that Hegel seemed not to sign and yesterday I began by saying that Nietzsche is someone who wanted to sign. That is in effect the appearance: Hegel presents himself as a philosopher, or a thinker, someone who says to you constantly that his empirical signature, that of the individual named Hegel etc., is secondary, that it effaces itself with respect to the truth that speaks through his mouth, that produces itself in his text, that constructs the system that he constructs, system that is the teleological completion of the whole of occidental life such that at base the individual Hegel is nothing but an empirical shell that may fall without loss for the truth, the history of meaning, etc. As a philosopher he seems to tell us, that not only is it possible, without loss, that his signature or his name disappear, fall outside the system, but that this is even necessary, in his own system, because that is what will be the proof of the truth and of the autonomy of the system. . . . But in fact Hegel also signs. One could show this, I tried elsewhere [*Glas*] to show it, how difficult it is to do the economy of the name of Hegel in his work, of his inscription, let us say personal, biographical, in his work. (Derrida, 1982: 78–79)

Derrida's strategy in *Glas* is to juxtapose Hegel with Genet, an author who does explicitly sign in the same terms or modalities defined in *Signsponge*. The boldness with which Genet sets up *genêt* (broomflower) as the law of his text brings into relief the more effaced *aigle* in Hegel's writings (Ulmer, 1986).

The case of Nietzsche's signature brings out the complexities of the method Derrida is attempting to develop, and calls attention to the preliminary status of everything that he has written in this vein. "Nietzsche had the greatest difficulty in signing, he wanted to sign but he was obliged to differentiate his signature, to confide it to something like the eternal return, that will not sign just once in posing an identity but which will sign indefinitely, continually, will select and finally will not sign except in the form of and differences of forces and qualities. He will not sign in the form of the patronym" (Derrida, 1982: 78). Derrida might have said that, in the affirmation of the eternal return, Nietzsche signed *against* his signature, against his patronym, a Slavic name meaning "nullity," "negation." "Nietzsche" is a challenge to Derrida's project in that the conventional reading of Nietzsche as "nihilist" would seem to correspond to the negation in his signature. But, as Derrida says of Ponge, "he does not give a damn for the sponge. He no more identifies with the sponge than with his own name, all this in the process of also describing the trajectory of a detachment, or an expression. He expresses his name, and that is all. Across the entire corpus" (Derrida, 1984: 70). Nor does Nietzsche identify with the negations in his text. The signature procedure, in other words, is not the naming of a determinism, but an invention, *inventio*, whose purpose is to produce a text. The value of that material remains open to critique, selection, and further construction (hermeneutics).

The importance of *Signsponge* has to do with this charting of a new course for textual studies, which requires our awareness that Derrida is not so much laying out a method as asking a question: "what could a science of the *alea* be?" In the case of the contingency linking "Ponge" to "sponge," Derrida remarks: "if he had another name, and if by some incredible hypothesis he could still have been the same person, would he have written the same thing? Yes and no. What could the pertinence of this question be, anyway? We are at the threshold of such a science, which itself engages in a rather singular relationship with the very name of science" (Derrida, 1984: 116). The question is not pertinent because causality figures here only conductively: the signature does not "explain" anything, but "causes" the text as an inventio, and makes a theoretical point: "To employ a Russellian term, we could say that [Ponge] has diabolized his signature, and all the language and the speech it contaminates, because he disguises every proper name as a description and every description as a proper name, showing by way of this ruse, that such a possibility, always an open one, was constitutive of writing, to the extent that literature works it over on all sides." A text generated out of a signature, then, is not an explanation but "a fable and another way of making history, of writing a story"—"a strange narrative without event," or, in which the narrative event is replaced by the "event" in Derrida's sense— the convergence of necessity and chance marking the place of the impossible subject (102). The concept becomes accessible through the story (recalling J. Hillis Miller's definition of deconstruction). The signature makes a text; it does not communicate an idea. Yet this repetition of the name as a selection principle does produce new knowledge for the receiver, or for the one reading and writing, and that is the mystery that deserves to be made the subject of a science.

The places of memory in mystory, appropriating the signature, are organized into an alternative way to gather materials into a set—a sweep through the encyclopedia following the rhizome of the proper name as inventio. The signature may be a direct transposition of the proper into a common noun (antonomasia), or it may be indirect, marked by a rhythm, a cadence, a fragmented image, a partial scene, a phrase, that repeats in the discourse, relating words to things and resulting in an intelligible collection. The story resulting from this series of juxtapositions constitutes a writing machine. The things generated in the third modality of the signature, that is, represent the model, the metaphors or vehicles for a poetics of invention, a memory system or mnemonics available for thinking about any matter whatsoever. The signature helps find the images of wide scope that make up the imagination (the image-repertoire) of the subject of knowledge, to be used in further research. The purpose of the mystory is not to solve every problem in a given discipline, but to help the student find and render accessible the personal and popular elements required for invention.

Chapter 5

Memory II:
Tour/Routes

1. A Nomadic Relay

The proper name as the inventio of an otobiography is the most basic strategy of teletheory, since it is a writing machine available to everyone, allowing the amateur or the student to simulate at once an idiomatic text with all the qualities of a style. The relationship of the name to the ideas it generates is arbitrary, just as are the relationships of the places and images of the *topoi* to the conceptual information in a mnemonic system. But the uncanny experience—the materiality of a textualist science—is that, through the bliss-sense or the flash of the constellation produced out of this articulation, the relationships become motivated. A mystory, then creates a conceptual oscillation, a pulsing exchange rendering the motivational status of the discourses undecidable.

As a discourse for the age of television teletheory refunctions mnemotechniques—the walk through a place of disseminated images—in order to organize the memory of electronic cognition. The place of mnemonics, as we saw in the previous chapter, is specific, actual, selected from life experience. Ponge and Derrida demonstrated in the signature a way to transduce a place into language, and even into theory. In this chapter I want to review some examples of works and theories that show how to do the walk, or rather the *tour* through the places—the other feature of the memory machine.

The notion of reasoning as taking a walk through the places of memory is related to the conventions of method in which thinking is represented as a journey, as a *way*. Some recent examples of this use of the image include Ludwig Wittgenstein's preface to his *Philosophical Investigations,* in which he compares his style to an artist's sketchbook (in contrast with the treatise, or a finished painting). Writing for him is a kind of recording expedition.

After several unsuccessful attempts to weld my results together into a whole, I realized that I should never succeed. . . . My thoughts were soon crippled if I

166

tried to force them on in any single direction against their natural inclination.—
And this was, of course, connected with the very nature of the investigation.
For this compels us to travel over a wide field of thought criss-cross in every
direction. —The philosophical remarks in this book are, as it were, a number of
sketches of landscapes which were made in the course of these long and involved
journeyings. The same or almost the same points were being approached afresh
from different directions, and new sketches made. Very many of these were badly
drawn or uncharacteristic, marked by all the defects of a weak draughtsman. And
when they were rejected a number of tolerable ones were left, which now had
to be arranged and sometimes cut down, so that if you looked at them you
could get a picture of the landscape. Thus this book is really only an album.
(Wittgenstein, 1968: ix)

The repetitions recall the effect of Ponge's journal, in which the *making* of
the *pré* is recorded, including a permutation and combination of lines and
images of the prospective poem, along with reflections on method, theory,
biography, and the like—the scene of invention. The other point to note is
that Wittgenstein refers to it as an "album." *Philosophical Investigations,* in
other words, is the disciplinary transduction of the family album that emerges
as the rhizomatic thing/image of Wittgenstein's signature. The fragmented
entries in the *Investigations* are organized in the manner of the family photo
album, grounded on that image, and invested with the emotions of the family
story. In teletheory the family story provides the diegesis within which a
theory may be invented.

Wittgenstein's philosophical sketches (the use of scenes, the creation of
theoretical diegesis) are made during a criss-crossing walk through a field—
the field of philosophy, but the "field" can be embodied in terms of any
discipline. The image of method, in other words, is a literalization of "discourse" as such: "*Dis-cursis,*" Barthes explained at the beginning of *A Lover's
Discourse,* "originally the action of running here and there, comings and
goings, measure taken, 'plots and plans'" (Barthes, 1978b: 3). The movement
of discourse, in other words, may be associated with the ancient topos for
rhetorical invention—the walk through the places. Moreover, this wandering, strolling walk, ever since Montaigne compared his mode of thought to
such promenades, has become a topos for the form of the modern essay
(Haas, 1969: 47). A quantity of instances, not surprisingly, comes to mind
in which the experience of method is compared with traveling. "Thinking is
perhaps, after all," Heidegger suggested, "an unavoidable path, which re-
fuses to be a path of salvation and brings no new wisdom. The path is at most
a field path, a path across fields, which does not just speak of renunciation but
already has renounced, namely, renounced the claim to a binding doctrine
and a valid cultural achievement or a deed of the spirit. Everything depends
on the step back, fraught with error" (Heidegger, 1975: 185).

In *On the Way to Language* Heidegger contrasted thinking as a walk in the country, on a field path, with scientific method; against the directions of science we are to follow language, to let it lead us to say its own nature. To listen to language as itself an event is essential to all the theorists and artists modeling mystory. Lacan for example noted a knot in the conjugations of *suivre* (to follow), and *être* (to be), both conjugated in the first person singular as *suis:* "I follow/I am." This knot becomes entangled in another one, the plurality of *sens*—"sense," "meaning," and "direction." In reading Lacan's version of thought as travel, we can understand why Derrida, in his own allegorical journey (the "Envois" section of *The Post Card*), suggested that to do a history of theory we would first need a history of roads.

> The highway is a particularly apt example of what I mean when I speak of the function of the signifier in as much as it polarizes, catches, groups a bundle of significations. . . . The signifier is polarizing. The signifier creates the field of significations. . . . Take a map of the superhighways of communication, and observe how it is traced from south to north, the route that crosses the country to link one river basin to another, one plain to another, to cross over bridges, organizing itself. You will notice that this map best expresses, in its relation of man to the earth, the role of the signifier. Let us not be like that person who marvelled that the water routes passed precisely through the towns. . . . What happens when we lack a highway, and we are forced, in order to go from one point to another, to put together one to another little byways, a more or less divided mode of clusters of significations. To go from one point to another, we would have a choice among different elements of the network. (Lacan, 1981: 328–329)

Lacan was speaking of the way the signifier organizes the unconscious, in the context of an explanation of the delirium of the schizophrenic Senatsprasi-dent Schreber. Our interest is not, for the moment, in the differences, the different places each of these theorists wanted to go, but that they all spoke of their method in this way, having to do with journeys, paths, maps— especially with journeys off the beaten track or highway. The "field" in question may be a field of knowledge, or of signification itself, having to do with the way a space becomes territorialized, the way a memory organizes itself into places and images, a formatting that makes possible the storage and retrieval of knowledge.

Lacan's observation of the knot joining being and following returns me to the "science" of the rhizome—nomadology. I will read N. Scott Momaday's *The Way to Rainy Mountain* as a double figure: as a figure of the *way* as such, of the way to do a journal as journey, the journey as method; as a specific style of thought, evoked in the figure of the American Indian, and demonstrated in the composition of the text. It is not a question of working out this style of thinking systematically, but of beginning to imagine it as an attitude. By returning to this ancient image of method, perhaps it may be possible to discover an alternative to "methodology" as the directing principle of reason.

In this context I refer again to Deleuze and Guattari who take the nomad invention of the "war machine" as an example of the rhizome (referring to the nomads of the steppes—Genghis Kahn—whereas I will be thinking of the Plains Indians, or ex-Plains Indians). What am I trying to imagine by means of this figure? "The problem is that the exteriority of the war machine in relation to the State apparatus is everywhere apparent, but remains difficult to conceptualize. It is not enough to affirm that the war machine is external to the apparatus. It is necessary to reach the point of conceiving the war machine as itself a pure form of exteriority, where the State apparatus constitutes the form of interiority we habitually take as a model, or according to which we are in the habit of thinking" (Deleuze and Guattari, 1986: 5). Everything having to do with the apparatus of academic discourse, then, may be thought along with this counter-concept of the war machine, which the State (all the ideological apparatuses, which include the technologies of language) continually appropriates, and which in turn takes as its primary object not war as such but the invention of "lines of flight." The challenge for us is to think nomadically from within the State apparatus; to think appropriation, inappropriately; to think, that is, the relation and exchange between the State and the war machine, which is also to think about the proper and the improper—all the property and properties of identity formation.

Deleuze and Guattari support this figurative project by noting that the exteriority of the war machine has an epistemological equivalent in a nomad or "minor" science, whose existence was first identified by Michel Serres in the atomic physics of Democritus. This minor science, however, is at odds with the conventions of science, including its image of method. They distinguish between two types of science—"a general theory of routes and paths, and a global theory of waves."

> One consists in "reproducing," the other in "following." The first has to do with reproduction, iteration and reiteration; the other, having to do with itineration, is the sum of the itinerant, ambulant sciences. . . . Following is not at all the same thing as reproducing, and one never follows in order to reproduce. The ideal of reproduction, deduction or induction is part of royal science. . . . Reproducing implies the permanence of a fixed point of *view* that is external to what is reproduced: watching the flow from the bank. But following is something different from the ideal of reproduction. Not better, just different. One is obliged to follow when one is in search of the "singularities" of a matter, or rather of a material, and not out to discover a form; when one escapes the force of gravity to enter a field of celerity. (36)

This passage touches on several crucial points of teletheory, having to do with this distinction between reproducing and following, suggesting how to think beyond method. Reproducing as a method or way has to do with the power effect of subject positioning in a dominant ideology, as well as with the production of general models and forms. It is "grave" in being serious and slow, and in the establishment of the monuments of a royal science. Deleuze and Guattari propose a "noology" to study the image or images of thought that span all thought (in our terms, the mnemonic place). At this level they observe the State model of science that directs academic discourse, against which they propose the nomadic image as supplement and alternative, but not as replacement. One way to state the issue of teletheory as an academic discourse would be to use the terms of this distinction—as a war between colonists and nomads, transduced into procedures and practices.

> A "method" is the striated space of the *cogitatio universalis,* and traces a path that must be followed from one point to another. But the form of exteriority situates thought in a smooth space that it must occupy without counting, and for which there is no possible method, no conceivable reproduction, but only relays, intermezzos, resurgences. . . . The problem of the war machine is that of relaying, even with modest means, not that of the architectonic model or the monument. (45)

The problem is that nomadic texts such as those authored by Artaud or Kleist themselves end up becoming monuments, "inspiring a model to be copied." This alternative—the relay, organized by speed, rather than the gravity of a monument—will be one of the most difficult and important issues for teletheory: how to bring the particular or singular into relation with the general or global in the manner of the relay rather than the model. Is there a contradiction, then, in trying to invent a genre for teletheory (mystory)? Perhaps not, if we keep in mind that unlike the treatise, or the conventional genres of academic scholarship, the mystory does not repeat, is not reproduced, in that no two are alike. Their recognizability as a kind derives from the relationship among the three levels of invention juxtaposed in the process of conducting research. Mystory itself is more a relay than a model, produced not for its own sake but as the trace of convergence of living and artificial memories.

We have already glimpsed the implications of this speed as a strategy of knowledge. The "war" in the "war machine" should be related to the "war" in "He war" of Joyce and Derrida, concerning the relay through language by means of the homophone—"war" as thing *and* as word. "It *was* written *simultaneously* in both English and German. Two words in one (*war*). . . . *War* is a noun in English, a verb in German, it resembles an adjective (*whar*) in that same language, and the truth of this multiplicity returns, from the attributes (the verb is also an attribute), towards the subject, *he,* who is divided by it right from the origin. In the beginning, difference, that's what happens" (Derrida, 1984a: 155). Joyce's *Wake* is the ground for Derrida's most economical definition of "deconstruction: *plus d'une langue*—both more than a language and no more of a language" (Derrida, 1986a: 15). The pun across languages, the macaronic pun, is the purest embodiment of the gram.

Although only recently venturing to write on Joyce, Derrida reminds us that in his earliest published work he stated the choice confronting modern writers between two paradigms of thought and language. From Plato to the present, most philosophers had chosen to write in the paradigm exemplified by Husserl who "proposes to render language as transparent as possible, univocal, limited to that which, by being transmittable or able to be placed in tradition, thereby constitutes the only condition of a possible historicity" (Derrida, 1984a: 149). But Derrida chose another possibility, the one followed by many artists in all eras but rarely if ever adopted as a model for cognitive, theoretical, even scientific application—the model exemplified in *Finnegans Wake*.

> He repeats and mobilizes and babelizes the (asymptotic) totality of the equivocal, he makes this his theme and his operation, he tries to make outcrop, with the greatest possible synchrony, at great speed, the greatest power of the meanings buried in each syllabic fragment, subjecting each atom of writing to fission in order to overload the unconscious with the whole memory of man: mythologies, religion, philosophies, sciences, psychoanalysis, literatures. This generalized equivocality of writing does not translate one language into another on the basis of common nuclei of meaning; it talks several languages at once, parasiting them as in the example *He war*. (149)

Why does Derrida believe Joyce's paradigm has a better chance of success in formulating the solutions to our problems than has the conventional model of univocal transparency? The answer has to do with the "great speed" of Joyce's text-machine, faster than any computer yet built, and with the framing of this machine as a wake, a ritual of mourning.

> *Ulysses, Finnegans Wake*—beside which the current technology of our computers and our micro-computerified archives and our translating machines remains a *bricolage* of a prehistoric child's toys. And above all its mechanisms are of a slowness incommensurable with the quasi-infinite speed of the movements on Joyce's cables. How could you calculate the speed with which a mark, a marked piece of information, is placed in contact with another in the same word or from one end of the book to the other? (147)

Such is the speed of the joke in general through the encyclopedia of culture.

One of the obstacles to problem-solving in the information age is the knowledge explosion itself. We are buried in data which by its sheer quantity impedes comprehension. Moreover, having tended to concentrate more on data processing than on understanding, we are in need of some new ideas (*moiras*). Speed is essential, but not only the algorithmic speed of calculation. The history of invention suggests that however valuable the analytical model may be for exploiting discoveries, the discovery process itself works with the poetic devices of analogy—with the association of elements previously unrelated (as in the surprise editing of the joke).

At the level of language the pun is precisely the device capable of relating elements with the least motivation, hence with the greatest economy or speed (the pun as linguistic collage). One way to understand Derrida's project is as an extension to the level of discourse of this logic of least motivation. The point to stress for now is that, with his choice of Joyce over Husserl as the model for his linguistics, Derrida transformed the status of aesthetic discourse in the hierarchy of the university apparatus from *object* of study (powerless) to a *subject* of knowledge—to a source of cognition to be applied directly to problem-solving across the divisions of knowledge.

The gram, functioning as puncept, makes available a rhizomatic relay for movement through discourse. Deleuze and Guattari have a similar notion in mind as reflected in their list of the features of nomadic science, drawing on such qualities or features as "assemblage" rather than unity, "event-affects" rather than matter-form models ("It is a question of surrendering to the [material], then of following where it leads by connecting operations to the materiality instead of imposing a form upon a matter") (Deleuze and Guattari, 1983: 98).

The purpose of introducing the images of thought (the State versus the war machine) is not to propose a systematic opposition, but to suggest the possibility of generating an alternative style of thought with a new relationship to the State apparatus. Within the sedentary space of our institution there is a rhizomatic, nomadic possibility, "with its gaps, detours, subterranean passages, stems, openings, traits, holes" (109). We may begin to read our assignments *both* in the tree-like way, then, and in the rhizomatic style, exploring for ourselves the path of the relay, in order to understand the nomadic and State sciences in terms of articulation, not opposition. "In the field of interaction of the two sciences, the ambulent sciences confine themselves to *inventing problems* the solution of which is linked to an entire set of collective, nonscientific activities, but the *scientific solution* of which depends, on the contrary, on royal science and the way it has transformed the problem by introducing it into its theorematic apparatus" (40). The war machine, then, has something to do with the tenses of the verb "to be," with the mood of being, and with the temporality of invention.

Keeping in mind nomadology and its link with minor science, I want to discuss N. Scott Momaday's *The Way to Rainy Mountain* not so much as a model, but as a relay, for mystory. To learn from *Rainy Mountain,* the story of a nomadic people, in a nomadic way, we take it not as a model, but as a relay, or affect-event. What this means in practice is that we traverse the text, taking from it what we need to live on. We do not try to reproduce it. It is sacred not in the way of a monument, but in the way of a buffalo (useful in the Real as well as in the Symbolic). We may use this metaphor of the hunter, reframed as conduction rather than as abduction, to see where it leads. As a relay, *Rainy Mountain* supplies us with a figurative version of one of the principal themes of mystory, as well as with a representational structure that takes up where Derrida's signature left off. Derrida's relay, that is, demonstrated how to move between the particular and the general with the speed of singularity, by means of the proper name. Momaday now shows us how to make a similar movement at the level of history. What we need to learn from this example, and from all the examples in the chapter, is how to tour the places of memory.

One of the things to borrow from Momaday, then, is the tripartition of his materials in the body of the text, consisting of the following elements, arranged in sets of three anecdotal fragments: 1) Kiowa myths and legends; 2) history of the Kiowa in general, or of Momaday's family specifically; 3) autobiographical details of Momaday's reminiscences. These levels may be appreciated on their own terms first, as the dimensions of experience with which we must deal as well. To extrapolate from *Rainy Mountain* to academic discourse requires a translation from the history of a nomadic tribe to the history of an institution at the three levels of legend, history, and autobiography. We might begin to assemble these parts in the way that Momaday demonstrates, with the light, fast touch of poetic association. Each strand is allowed to stand on its own, juxtaposed to the other two, linked only by one trait, such as common theme directly or indirectly stated. In unit III, for example, the three fragments consist of the following: a legend about the time long ago when dogs could talk (enemies are approaching, "But the dog said: 'You know, I have puppies. They are young and weak and they have nothing to eat. If you will take care of my puppies, I will show you how to get away'"); an historical point concerning the principal warrior society of the Kiowas, known as "Real Dogs" ("Tradition has it that the founder of the Ka-itsenko had a dream in which he saw a band of warriors, outfitted after the fashion of the society, being led by a dog. The dog sang the song of the Ka-itsenko, then said to the dreamer: 'You are a dog; make a noise like a dog and sing a dog song'"); the author's recollection of the dogs who lived at his grandmother's house ("Some of them were nameless and lived a life of their own. They belonged there in a sense that the word 'ownership' does not include"). Similarly we might collect the facts of our discipline (its texts) in juxtaposition with stories of its founders (myths of creation, legends of famous men) and of one's responses—emotional, intellectual—to the other two levels.

Momaday frames the tripartite body with a prologue that contains a number of themes with figurative value for teletheory. The text as a whole, to begin with, is motivated by his return to Rainy Mountain to attend the funeral of his grandmother, Aho. The text is an account of mourning, of a journey undertaken as an act of mourning. Beside Aho's grave, looking at her tombstone, Momaday formulates this resolve:

> Once in his life a man ought to concentrate his mind upon the remembered earth, I believe. He ought to give himself up to a particular landscape in his experience, to look at it from as many angles as he can, to wonder about it, to dwell upon it. He ought to imagine that he touches it with his hands at every season and listens to the sounds that are made upon it. (Momaday, 83)

Such, too, is the program of Ponge's "The Prairie," which in this context may be seen also in terms of *discursis*—the people out for a Sunday stroll; *Mushroom Book*, too, shows us Cage out in the woods, running back and forth, mushrooming, the movement of discourse through the places of memory.

The recollection of place is for Momaday a journey, in which he mourns for a whole people, for the Kiowa, through his mourning for Aho, by telling the story, the history and mythology, of the emergence and decline of a civilization. He conducts a pilgrimage, retracing the formation of the Kiowas as they migrated from the headwaters of the Yellowstone, in Montana, eastward into the great plains, the brief golden age lived there, and the decline and cultural death resulting from the conflict with the white man. That Momaday is of mixed blood makes his story all the more emblematic of the nomadic relation with the State apparatus.

Some of the most relevant features of *Rainy Mountain* include the act of mourning, the grave site, and the journey. Momaday notes that his way "is preeminently the history of an idea, man's of himself, and it has old and essential being in language. The verbal tradition by which it has been preserved has suffered a deterioration in time. What remains is fragmentary: mythology, legend, lore, and hearsay" (4). His tripartite structure preserves or represents the interaction between the written and oral traditions of history. He insists upon the value of both traditions, which is another way of attending to the multiple dimensions of thought, for "the journey is made with the whole memory, that experience of the mind which is legendary as well as historical, personal as well as cultural. And the journey is an evocation of three things in particular: a landscape that is incomparable, a time that is gone forever, and the human spirit, which endures. The imaginative experience and the historical express equally the traditions of man's reality" (4). Evocation, that is, is an alternative to analysis, for thinking beyond method.

Momaday's text offers a relay for mystory both in its version of the triptych of fragments covering the levels of the cycle of invention, and in terms of the themes that it evokes—the journey to a place of memory, marked by a monument, a grave. Deleuze and Guattari provided an argument for the authority of a nomadic approach to thought at an abstract level of argument. Momaday offers something more specific—a text about a nomadic people, about a journey, that shows how to bring into appearance, for ourselves, the imaginative register of materials we are likely to need in the process of invention. *Rainy Mountain* evokes history rather than exhausting it in explanations or interpretations. It has the same function in my discourse, evoking a sense of how to go on, even as it tells about the end of a journey. But this is the effect of a relay. As an exemplar, it may also offer a warning, raising the theme of colonization and the fate of the nomads in America.

2. Monu/Mentality

I want to learn how to remember mystorically. The earth artist, Robert Smithson, provides a further relay for understanding the mnemonic tour organizing mystory, especially in his text, "A Tour of the Monuments of Passaic, New Jersey" (collected in *Blasted Allegories*). Smithson's "Tour" takes up in its own way most of the themes of the other relays in this chapter, continuing the association of the "place" with a grave site, as well as demonstrating a version of the form of the fragments.

"Tour" is a narrative, illustrated by photographs, telling of the day, Saturday, September 30, 1967, that Smithson took a bus trip from New York City to Passaic, New Jersey. The piece is brief, and the account is unified as an anecdote, but it includes all the elements—the references—of Barthes's fragment format: "ordinary reading" (Barthes referred to Goethe's *Sorrows of Young Werther*) has to be inferred from Smithson's biography—that he was born in Passaic, and that William Carlos Williams was his pediatrician. "Tour," Smithson noted in an interview, is an appendix to Williams's *Patterson* (Smithson, 187). Williams is at once the "reading" and the "want-to-be" of "Tour," combining the role of *Werther* and Gide in *Fragments*. The scene of reading takes place on the bus, Smithson having taken with him a copy of the *New York Times* and a paperback copy of *Earthworks* by Brian Aldiss. *Earthworks* represents "insistent" reading—related to Smithson's interests as an artist, and the *Times* in his "occasional" reading (popular or general culture), with both levels being filled out by a number of other allusions or citations, including the epigraphs—one from a popular work of science fiction, *Jesting Pilot,* by Henry Kuttner, and the other from Nabokov's *Invitation to a Beheading*. The register of "lived experience," of course, is the trip itself, this tour of his hometown.

The readings prepare us for the peculiar point of view which Smithson takes to this site or place of memory. The contents of the art section of the

Times is reviewed, providing an inventory of art history and contemporary interests, including a "blurry reproduction" of Samuel F. B. Morse's *Allegorical Landscape,* in which "the sky was a subtle newsprint gray, and the clouds resembled sensitive stains of sweat reminiscent of a famous Yugoslav watercolorist whose name I have forgotten" (52). John Canaday, in his column, "referred to the picture as 'standing confidently along with other allegorical representatives of the arts, sciences, and high ideals that universities foster.'" Having invoked this ironic mood, Smithson produces his own version of an "allegorical landscape," viewing the urban industrial sprawl of New Jersey as a concentration of "monuments." He gets off the bus, that is, and walks along the river, stopping to photograph both major and minor locations—"The Bridge Monument," "Monument with Pontoons: The Pumping Derrick," "The Great Pipes Monument," "The Fountain Monument," "The Sand-Box Monument (also called the Desert)."

Marjorie Perloff was right to refer to these as "anti-monuments," marking the shift in attitude toward technology and the urban landscape from the Futurists to the Postmoderns. Smithson has his own allegory in mind, which I want to review, while observing his text at the same time as an allegorical statement of how to relate to the monumental element in the academic apparatus. Smithson considered his work in general to be about the apparatus of the art institution ("I'm not really discontent. I'm just interested in exploring the apparatus I'm being threaded through") (200). "Tour" as relay for mystory, especially when it is read in the context of Smithson's "poetics," may be read as a performance of the problematic informing teletheory. The trip, for example, is made intelligible by being framed in terms of the filmic.

Noon-day sunshine cinema-ized the site, turning the bridge and the river into an over-exposed *picture.* Photographing it with my instamatic 400 was like photographing a photograph. The sun became a monstrous light-bulb that projected a detached series of "stills" through my instamatic into my eye. When I walked on the bridge, it was as though I was walking on an enormous photograph that was made of wood and steel, and underneath the river existed as an enormous movie film that showed nothing but a continuous blank. (53)

Smithson frequently discussed his site selections in terms of how he might make films of them, as settings for films, and he did make a film of *Spiral Jetty,* his own monumental earthwork. His work, that is, may be understood as an enactment of filmic thinking, which involves, as we have seen in the other sections, not simply the features of a technology, but of an apparatus engaging every dimension of life in the era of electronics. Referring to the crystalline structure informing *Spiral Jetty* ("growth in a crystal advances around a dislocation point, in the manner of a screw. The Spiral Jetty could be considered one layer within the spiraling crystal lattice, magnified trillions of times"—112), Smithson alludes to Joyce in a way that brings his project into relation with the theorists of teletheory: "This description echoes and reflects Brancusi's sketch of James Joyce as a 'spiral ear' because it suggests both a visual and an aural scale, in other words it indicates a sense of scale that resonates in the eye and the ear at the same time" (the "ear" in "earth"). "For my film," he adds, "(a film is a spiral made up of frames) I would have myself filmed from a helicopter (from the Greek *helix, helikos* meaning spiral) directly overhead in order to get the scale in terms of erratic steps" (113). The shot, like the scenes in the *Pré*, is motivated by language.

Part of the value of Smithson's earthwork as a relay of mystory is just this attitude Smithson took to sites, which he treated literally as if they were *topoi*, performing the metaphor of rhetoric in which argument requires a tour of the places. What mystory performs as a thought experiment Smithson acted out in his constructions. In Passaic, that is, the place itself, and not only his snapshots, becomes the "album," the family memory book that is one dimension of our genre. This experience of walking on photographs is central to Smithson's *inventio*, as may be seen in comparison with his use of the metaphor of writing in an explanation of his first work explicitly formulated in terms of his "site/non-site" dialectic.

> Initially I went to the Pine Barrens to set up a system of outdoor pavements but in the process I became interested in the abstract aspects of mapping. At the same time I was working with maps and aerial photography for an architectural company. I had great access to them. So I decided to use the Pine Barrens site as a piece of paper and draw a crystalline structure over the landmass rather than on a 20 x 30 sheet of paper. In this way I was applying my conceptual thinking directly to the disruption of the site over an area of several miles. So you might say my non-site was a three-dimensional map of the site. (172)

His thought covers the site like a map, and not just any site. At first the sites (the pun on "cite" alerts us to the area of application) are in New Jersey: "Since I grew up in New Jersey I would say that I was saturated with a consciousness of that place . . . . those landscapes embedded themselves in my consciousness at a very early date, so that in a sense I was beginning to make archaeological trips into the recent past to Bayonne, New Jersey" (155). Once the identification is established, the "signature" quality identified, the site may be selected anywhere—Nevada, Utah, the Yucatan— anyplace that has the quality of being "pulverized," disturbed and cast off, such as quarries, gravel pits, burnt fields, sand banks. As in Ponge's *Pré*, a direct correlation is stated between the mind (memory) and the landscape.

> One's mind and the earth are in a constant state of erosion, mental rivers wear away abstract banks, brain waves undermine cliffs of thought, ideas decompose

into stones of unknowing, and conceptual crystallizations break apart into deposits of gritty reason. . . . This movement seems motionless, yet it crushes the
landscape of logic under glacial reveries. . . . The entire body is pulled into the
cerebral sediment, where particles and fragments make themselves known as
solid consciousness. A bleached and fractured world surrounds the artist. To
organize this mess of corrosion into patterns, grids, and subdivisions is an esthetic
process that has scarcely been touched. (82)

Ponge emphasized the vegetal cycle of growth and decay, whereas Smithson
focuses on the mineral equivalent. In the alchemical terms of the signature,
which Smithson also provides (the *nature* Ponge mentioned), Ponge would
be classified as a "dank brain," that is, any artist or critic who appreciates
"anything that suggests saturation, a kind of watery effect, an overall seepage"
(89), while Smithson might place himself as "desert brained," concerning
the hot and dry, a place "that swallows up boundaries." Smithson manifests,
in other words, the mineral version of the rhizome in his application of
crystalline structures (which later become maps).

The names of minerals and the minerals themselves do not differ from each
other, because at the bottom of both the material and the print is the beginning
of an abysmal number of fissures. Words and rocks contain a language that
follows a syntax of splits and ruptures. Look at any *word* long enough and you
will see it open up into a series of faults, into a terrain of particles each containing
its own void. This discomforting language of fragmentation offers no easy gestalt
solution; the certainties of didactic discourse are hurled into the erosion of the
poetic principle. (87)

As in the signature theory of invention, however, the idiom of the author,
manifested in the identifying thing (in this case of crystalline realm) internalized in consciousness (or rather unconsciousness), may be transduced into
the third modality of poetics, as a model for composition. "I think it had
something to do with the way crystals build up too. I did a series of pieces
called *Stratas*. Virginia Dwan's piece called *Glass Strata* is eight feet long by
a foot wide, and looks life a glass staircase made out of inch-think glass; it's
very green, very dense and kind of layered up. And my writing, I guess,
proceeded that way. I thought of writing more as material to sort of put
together than as a kind of analytic searchlight" (154). The branching fissures
of the crystalline structures or the abstract lines of mappings represent the
speculative medium in which converge the site, the real place, and the non-
site, the art representation mounted in a gallery space. The lines trace the
dis-cursis of discourse: "I guess these sites had something to do with entropy,
that is, one dominant theme that runs through everything. You might say my
early preoccupation with the early civilizations of the West was a kind of a
fascination with the coming and going of things" (153). The "coming and

going" of time is embodied, that is, in the dialectic of reference that braids the raw materials of the site into the artifice of a non-site ("it's a back and forth rhythm that goes between indoors and outdoors"—160).

> The route to the site is very indeterminate. It's important because it's an abyss between the abstraction and the site; a kind of oblivion. You could go there on a highway, but a highway to the site is really an abstraction because you don't really have contact with the earth. A trail is more of a physical thing. There are all variables, indeterminate elements which will attempt to determine the route from the museum to the [Cayuga Salt] mine. I'll designate points on a line and stabilize the chaos between the two points. Like stepping stones. If I take somebody on a tour of the site, I just show them where I removed things. Not didactic, but dialectic. (169)

The significance of Smithson's *dis-cursis* is associated with Freud's *fort/da* rhythm, the model of the grandson playing "gone" with the reel, an act of mourning placed in the abyss of *Beyond the Pleasure Principle,* where Freud defines the death drive. The monuments of Passaic, then, address the theme of mourning in a new way, based on the theory of entropy, which Smithson mounts in his writings the way Mary Kelly mounted Lacan, transducing the emotions of mourning into the abstractions of science (and vice-versa). The monuments embody the allegory of ruins, but no longer with reference to the past. They are "ruins in reverse," "rising into ruins before they are built" (54), a factor of the planned obsolescence of the "slurbs." The Passaic monuments are not positioned in time the same way as the artificial monuments produced by Smithson's peers in the art world: "Instead of causing us to remember the past like the old monuments, the new monuments seem to cause us to forget the future. . . . They are not built for the ages, but rather against the ages. They are involved in a systematic reduction of time down to fractions of seconds, rather than in representing the long spaces of centuries. Past and present are placed into an objective present" (10). The suburbs really are without a past, and have only a future, but it is an "abandoned" or "out of date" future, which allows Passaic to replace Rome as a new manner of "eternal city," designed, a French theorist might say, in the future prefect. The "Sand Box Monument" captures this entropic emotion:

> Under the dead light of the Passaic afternoon the desert [sand box] became a map of infinite disintegration and forgetfulness. This monument of minute particles blazed under a bleakly glowing sun, and suggested the sullen dissolution of entire continents, the drying up of oceans. . . . Every grain of sand was a dead metaphor that equaled timelessness, and to decipher such metaphors would take one through the false mirror of eternity. This sand box somehow doubled as an open grave—a grave that children cheerfully play in. (56)

The places of an artificial memory are a personal cemetery, the way a museum, Smithson says, is a kind of tomb. The signature is related to Lacan's account of the Name-of-the-Father as founding metaphor of language, invented to mark the tomb of the Dead Father.

> Each time we find a skeleton, we call it human if it is in a sepulchre. What reason could there be for putting this debris in a stone wrapping? For that there must have been already established a whole symbolic order, which includes that the fact that a mister had been Mister So-And-So in a social order requires that one indicate this on the stones of a tomb. The fact that he was called So-And-So surpasses in itself his vital existence. That does not imply any belief in the immortality of the soul, but simply that his name has nothing to do with his living existence, surpasses it and perpetuates it beyond. (Lacan, 1981a: 111)

This point, Lacan insisted, is the one Freud established as the basis for psychoanalysis—that the symbolic order "subsists outside the subject, distinct from its existence, and determines it." The dead father and the law of the institutions that fixed the place of fatherhood informs the register of the symbolic as language: "there is in the ego something fundamentally dead, and always doubled by this twin, which is discourse" (165). The challenge of mystory is to learn how to think with this dead, artificial, part of the memory as naturally as one does with the living part. And this thinking has to be done in the middle voice, since it cannot simply be a matter of deciding to reason unconsciously.

Smithson's monuments are related to the sepulchre founding the symbolic. The sentiment underlying Smithson's monuments, and the monumentality of all his site/non-sites, is of considerable importance to understanding the emotion invested in the places of memory, and identification with the site. Ponge talked about life as "a very banked fire," but emphasized the hope that comes of renewal in the vegetal cycle. Smithson, perhaps because he focuses on a much slower process—the mineral cycle of mountain building and erosion—tends to call attention to the destructive side of decay. In both cases, however, the cycle of decay is an allegory of memory. Smithson's place, relaying mystory, then, carries a feeling of catastrophe. The monuments mark the site of a disaster in the temporality of the already-not-yet, on a scale of geological time, with Smithson's sites being micro-models of glaciers writing on the earth. "I like the idea of quiet catastrophes taking place. . . . It's a slow process of destruction. The world is slowly destroying itself. The catastrophe comes suddenly but slowly" (177). In teletheory Smithson's geological catastrophe is transduced into historical time, relative to cultural rather than to mineral ages.

We saw earlier that the monumental has something to do with the particular temporality of invention, figured historically as "catastrophe." It is important to try to clarify the sense of catastrophe that pervades the places, regardless of whether the death figured there is marked as entropic or negentropic, since in either case it carries the mood of history. It is the emotion of mourning, relating to the monument as crypt in psychoanalytic theory. Noting that Freud compared the hysterical symptom to a monument erected in commemoration of an event (such as the death of Anna O's father), Nicholas Abraham and Maria Torok commented:

> A monument, by all means, but a monument which lives on and does not cease acting. A memorial, however, which attests to an event willfully disregarded: the recording of an identity between perception and fantasy, between the centripetal emissary and the centrifugal emissary. The "Mnemic trace" is also a monument raised on the occasion of such an attestation of identity. Fantasy and perception, as memory traces, form an indissoluble unity. It is in this that their structure is similar to that of a symptom and symbol: they derive their being from the unity they effectuate between two opposing demands: Envelope and Kernel. (Abraham and Torok, 1979: 24–25).

What of this mnemic trace as a message passed between the Shell and the Kernel? In the *Ad Herennium* the message effect was unmotivated; in the case of the Wolfman it is motivated. But both examples, ancient and modern, teach us how to invent. Isn't this the back and forth of *dis-cursis,* of which Smithson's maps between site/non-site are one manifestation? To describe the way the material (body, somatic) realm interacts with the mind (conceptual order), Freud proposed the symbol of the "messenger." "The concept of the messenger is a symbol insofar as it makes allusion to the unknowable by means of an unknown, while only the relation of the terms is given. . . . What is the precise content of this symbol of the messenger, of the representative, that we have just been considering? It is called either Instinct or Drive with its cortege of affects, representations, or even fantasies" (21).

The monument related to the messenger becomes active as a crypt hiding a secret and haunted by a ghost. The monument does not communicate, but evokes a confusion or perplexity, typical of allegories, as in Dante's *Divine Comedy* ("Nel mezzo del cammin di nostra vita/mi ritroval per una selva oscura") (Owens, 219). The talking cure is effected in the clinic through transference, in which the analysand works through with the analyst the relationship with the parents or parental figures (mourning). In Abraham's account, transference is precisely mourning—working through the loss of the loved object, the ideal ego, either by introjection or incorporation. The malady of mourning (incorporation) is a failed introjection in which the subject, rather than internalizing the object as symbol in order to give it up in the Real, hangs onto the object by preserving the Real (the outside) in a crypt—a kind of exquisite corpse, the living-dead. The object is preserved secretly in a crypt inside, representing a refusal of change, conserving a state prior to trauma, the catastrophic event commemorated in the monument marking the crypt. The effect of a monument is to gather people into groups.

One of the most intriguing aspects of this secret, according to Abraham and Torok, constituting, they say, one of the chief discoveries of psychoanlysis, is that the secret does not originate with the subject but may be inherited, carried over from the previous generation by means of direct communication of one unconscious to another within a family heritage. A tradition haunts the child, whose speech serves the ghost by means of a kind of ventriloquism, reaching appearance, however, only in fragments, suffering a kind of decay in passing between generations.

In teletheory this problematic of the crypt is applied to the dynamics of the apparatus of education. Abraham himself, in any case, notes the relationship of mourning in transference to the drive of research. All educational acts, he observes, are related to the mother-child relationship—the entry into language being part of mourning in which the loss of the mother is compensated for by the acquisition of speech. The research conducted by educators—the epistemophilia of academic writing—manifests at the level of desire the search for the lost object, to make up for the separation from and loss of the mother. When mourning goes wrong in this context, the drive for research becomes a drive to hide, a cryptophilia. The very act of "coverage," as the pun suggests, may be turned to the interests of occultation in specialized discourse. What has to be hidden? The memory of pleasure, based on the experience of an archaic ego, the oral libido. It keeps secret the guilt of a crime about which there is sadistic ambivalence. Language then is put to the ends of concealment rather than discovery. In terms of teletheory, the oral register of invention is buried. The monument marking this repression hides precisely a representation, an unspeakable word, a monster. The melancholy of the cryptophile results in a particular use of language: demetaphorization (taking words always in their proper, literal sense), and objectification (refusing affect) (261–262). In short, the cryptophile speaks an academic discourse.

There is a way for the cryptonym to rejoin the concept and thus to achieve utterance. The relationship, according to Abraham and Torok, is anasemic, which could be mapped by the rhizomatic or crystalline relays of teletheory. To remember what is in the crypt requires a kind of translation process involving the following elements, as described by Derrida in his introduction to *The Wolf Man's Magic Word:* 1) a story—the anasemic structure in the memory "describes a story or a fable within the concept; the story is described as a path followed backward by the structure in order to reach all the way back beyond the origin, which is nonetheless not in any way a proper, rightful, literal meaning. The concept is re-cited in the course of this journey" (Derrida, 1986b: xxxiv). The anasemic story discovered within the concept will reflect the return of a certain pre-scientific naivete (Abraham and Torok, 1978: 384), a point relevant to the transduction between scientific and popular levels of discourse, and to the displacement of science, its detournment to the ends of other discourses. The "journey" back to the crypt is the *tour* of the places. 2) An angle created within the word: "A change of direction abruptly interrupts the continuity of the process of becoming explicit and imposes on it an anasemic angulation." This angulation occurs by means of homonyms, allosemes, in short, it follows the acoustic dimension relevant to oralysis and to Ponge's "logic of onomatopoeias." 3) A sepulchre: "If the anasemic process inaugurates a mytho-poetic arch-psychoanalytic science that diverts its account toward another event that takes place where it has never been, this is because the loss of the object (for example, in the arch-trauma of tearing away, even before the distinction between mourning and the refusal or sickness of mourning) does not simply play one role among many. It is 'from out of' the possibility of this 'loss' or of the 'death' of the subject, from out of the possibility of a sepulcher, in one form or another, that the entire theoretical space is redistributed" (Derrida, 1986b: xxxiv). This dimension of the "before" in anasemia is figured in the pre-historic temporality of Smithson's "moraines," used as a device for bringing into relationship the different speeds of events, the duration of memory across generations, historical periods, geological epochs.

To open the crypt, to attempt to enunciate a cryptic incorporation, then, involves the violation of a sepulchre—"the very tombstone of the illicit, and marks the spot of an extreme pleasure, a pleasure entirely real though walled up, buried alive in its own prohibition." The angulation, re-cited re-sitings, and fragmented ventriloquisms in which the unsaid may be told, at least if told in the "original," will produce a strange, unheard of narrative indeed. But the transduction may be utterly simple, something at hand, in plain sight, available for designation, by a camera or a cliché. One clue may be Smithson's view of the coalesence of the ages of video and the H-Bomb.

It seems that "the war babies," those born after 1937–38 were "Born Dead"— to use a motto favored by the Hell's Angels. The philosophism of "reality" ended some time after the bombs were dropped on Hiroshima and Nagasaki and the ovens cooled down. Cinematic "appearance" took over completely sometime in the late 50s. "Nature" falls into an *infinite series* of movie "stills"—we get what Marshall McLuhan calls "The Reel World." (Smithson, 74)

Knowledge and narrative come together in Smithson not to make a proposition but to make a figure. His "entropy" evokes the laws of thermodynamics, joining the oblique set that includes Michel Serres's entropics of "parasite" as "noise," the image of thermonuclear war, and the decay (radioactive half-life) in Benjamin's theory of allegory. We learn from him that euretics involves a different relationship to the secret than is found in hermeneutics. The secret is not an object to be exposed either by revelation or interrogation, but a relay, a circuit, powering an invention. His monuments are not interpreted by psychoanalysis, but the two representations of monuments converge in teletheory, marking a place, the ground of an allegory telling how to make a theory.

3. Catastropical Tourists

I want to learn from the relays in this chapter how to organize academic discourse in the age of television, as a practice for electronic cognition. Having adopted the position that this discourse may be understood as a refunctioning of the rhetorical tradition of artificial memory—a walk through familiar places marked by active images—I have taken texts by Cage and Ponge as figurative examples of "place," and by Momaday and Smithson as figurative examples of the tour through the "place." These examples, both in form and theme, provide concrete versions of how to construct a mystory, although there remains the task of a final extrapolation from these relays and the theories in Part One of the features of a specifically "academic" discourse, responsible within the apparatus of schooling for a program of invention, addressing first of all the challenge of joining alphabetic and electronic cognitions.

Thematically the relays have demonstrated the *emotion* of the intellection involved with the tour of one's memory as a process of mourning. The places turn out to be arranged around a monument bearing the signature, if not the family name, related to death and decay. The fact that Smithson died on the site of one of his earth monuments, *Amarillo Ramp* ("On July 20, 1973, while he and a photographer were photographing the staked-out work from the air, the plane they were in crashed on a rocky hillside a few hundred feet from the site of the art") becomes part of this figure. His method of site selection resembles what Barthes described as the *punctum*: "The open limit is a designation that I walk through in a kind of network looking for a site. And then I select the site. There's no criteria; just how the material hits my pysche when I'm scanning it. But it's a kind of low level scanning, almost unconscious" (Smithson, 168). The selection, designated by the click of the camera mediating in the photograph the relation between site and non-site, is the act of memory that is to be tapped in mystory for pedagogical purposes.

The artificial memory constructed in this way, as the non-site hinged rhizomatically with the sites of individual experience and institutional discipline, may be figured, also, as a family album (which, when edited together with the textbooks of a discipline, becomes a machine of invention). A good idea of how this figure works may be found in Michael Lesy's *Time Frames: The Meaning of Family Pictures*. Having become interested in the patterns, the genotypes, he had noticed emerging from his study of thousands of family photos, he contacted people from his home town, more or less of his parents' generation, who had grown up during the Depression and lived through the Second World War, and asked them to give him a "tour" of their family album. This frame is part of the relay for mystory, in that his experience of collecting the stories figures the movement of thought I want to capture in the new genre. His lectures at various universities on the way in which family snapshots were entangled in the collective life of the culture, for example, were treated as a kind of "crabgrass" in the lawn of academic preconceptions, and he could not get a teaching position based on this work. Moreover, the people he interviewed were not strangers, but family friends or relatives or acquaintances with whom his own history was engaged. "There was one woman whose daughter I loved for ten years, but she preferred figure skaters; there was another one whose daughter loved me for just as long, but I never even noticed" (Lesy, xiii). His motives were "monumental"—"I told them I'd be their ghost writer. *Their* words and *their* pictures, on their own terms. So it would not get lost when they died" (xiii). At the same time, Lesy's desire "to know what it all means" is not part of mystory, since it is not a question of what these traces mean, but what can be made by their means. He figures the ghost not only as "ghost writer," but in the function of the album as a communication between the generations of a family, with the images as a spur for questions, and for narratives. The snapshots and anecdotes together constitute a kind of movie evoking all the codes of narrative and archetype, associating the private life with the conventions of representation organizing meaning in the collective life. All the stories, Lesy found, could be classified in terms of what Barthes identified as the Symbolic register of exchanges (love, money, language). The stories were couched in almost every one of the simple, oral forms—myth, legend, joke, and the like. There is however, at least one unifying theme: "All the episodes that follow may be described as variations of the story of Pandora, in which the war is the box, and the principal actors take turns being either Epimetheus or the girl herself" (xiv–xv). "Pandora's Box," it will be remembered, was also the title given to the book investigating the role of the contingent register of everyday life experience in the empirical work of science, with the "war" evoking the mood of the verb "to be."

The tours of the album, then, Lesy explains, could be read as "a fairy tale for adults, complete with morals drawn," the idea being that these monuments, conveying the nearly completed lives of ordinary citizens living through monumentous times should not figure destiny or be the occasion for nostalgia. The album is appropriated in mystory to be constructed not at the end of a life, as a memorial, but much earlier, as a compass. On the one hand, the materials of personal experience turn out to be extraordinarily rich—the fact that most impressed Lesy (his interlocutors were as complex and interesting, he says, as Winston Churchill), as may be observed in Peggy's anecdote:

> I remember—this is very strange—I remember there were these two old ladies. They must have been very old. Sisters. Who had once been schoolteachers. And they used to entertain me *by drawing pictures*. Well, one of them—she used to throw potatoes down and we'd watch them drop on people's heads. [Laughs] That lady—as my sister was being born—she went stark, staring, raving mad. And so her sister called my stepfather—he was a big man. It took *four* men— and they wrapped her in a sheet to hold her down—till they got her in a car to take her to an institution. And I can remember saying, "Can I look at her?" I wanted to see how someone looked when they were mad. And I thought her eyes were very brilliant red. And then everybody was running around; they took her out, down in the car. All these men carrying her. She's screaming. And I heard this other noise. And I said," Something's going wrong." And they said, "Oh, no." And my sister was born. (5).

There is no commentary, and Peggy doesn't elaborate, but as a document this anecdote expresses internally a strong response of sibling rivalry. The anecdotes embedded in Peggy's conversation, as in the psychoanalytic interview, link up in an associational proposition that carries the latent story of Peggy's world view, of her "discourse," whose heading would be taken from one of her evaluative comments: "I thought I dropped from another planet" (4).

Lesy observes the convergence of "four rivers of time" in the tours he collected, joining person, family, nation, and myth. *Time Frames* is useful as an example of the album as snapshot and narrative, but it does not indicate exactly how to articulate these registers of time in one representation, or in one artificial memory. One of the best examples of this sort, demonstrating the necessary relational disparity between private and collective experience, is provided by the work of Alexander Kluge. Kluge is a good relay for mystory because his work is grounded on the catastrophe of that Pandora's Box, the Second World War.

Historiography has long used both the anecdotes about great men, such as Churchill, and about anonymous individuals (as types), such as Peggy (in Lesy's comparison), to represent the meaning of events. Kluge questions this tradition without rejecting narrative entirely, following the modernist insight that the lives of individuals were no longer (if they ever were) integrated with collective occurrences. Brecht was one of the leaders in a trend to refunction the anecdotes found in school textbooks in which they communicated the beliefs of the dominant culture (Schafer, 28–29). Anti-anecdotes, like anti-monuments, would expose the political frame within which the heroics of someone like Julius Caesar could be better evaluated. Part of the importance of this movement for teletheory is that it focused precisely on the anecdotes transmitted by the educational apparatus. The lesson was that there are no "world historical personalities" with pysches capable of mediating the collective social structure. Like the images in the family album, the images communicated between generations by a nation in its schools require a more complex format capable of multiple perspectives.

Kluge develops just such a format, using the conventions of collage/ montage (in both the media of print and film) to represent the relationship or lack of it between individual and collective experience. Kluge, however, does not discredit personal experience, but gives it equal place as one of the levels of a multi-track text. As Andrew Bowie's excellent review of Kluge's method makes clear, Kluge exemplifies the hybrid mode of the electronic era in which the functions of fiction and non-fiction have been redirected and recombined. The mix of fiction, history, and theory in "The Air-Raid on Halberstadt on 8 April 1945," as described by Bowie, is exactly the assembly of levels aimed for in mystory. The key elements of the story are, first, that a particular event in Kluge's childhood—the air-raid on his hometown which he experienced from inside a movie theater, became a compass, a founding anecdotal reference point for his imagination; and second that Kluge does not represent the event as "mémoires," but presents in a collage both the "strategy from below" (the point of view, fictionalized, of a woman caught in the raid; her need for and lack of a means to deal with the catastrophe of an exploding building: "In order to open up a strategic perspective of the kind Gerda Baethe wished for herself on 8 April in her cover . . . seventy thousand determined teachers, all like her, in each of the countries involved in the war would, since 1918, have each had to teach very hard for twenty years" [Bowie, 186]), and the "strategy from above," the abstract level of collective organization, given in historical documents, interviews with pilots and planners, and theories of military strategy. In this hybrid, against the inadequacies of both psychological fiction and conventional historiography, Kluge crosses functions. Leaving the realm of contingent experience, refusing to attempt to dramatize suffering, he replaces metaphorical language with "alienated conceptual language" (188), couching the most emotional issues in the most distanced discourse—theory (as did Barthes and Mary Kelly). At the same time, literature as such is put in a "creditor" position in relationship to the other discourses of knowledge, in that the project as a whole is a fictional *study* of mass events: "the genesis of the process of abstraction is made an object of *literary* investigation" (187).

Then there is also the artificial opposition of documentary and *mise-en-scène*. Mere documentation cuts off relations: nothing exists objectively without the emotions, actions and desires, that is, without the eyes and the senses of the people involved. I have never understood why the depiction of such acts (most of which have to be staged) is called fiction. But it is equally ideological to assume that individuals could determine history. Therefore, no narrative succeeds without a certain proportion of authentic material, i.e. documentation. Such use of documentation establishes a point of reference for the eyes and senses: real conditions clear the view for action. (Kluge, 1984: 206)

The "uncanniness of time" is such that individual experience is at once a real factor in events and exluded from understanding them, as in the case of the disparity registered in the encounter of a modern technology (a bomber formation) and a two-thousand year old city (Mainz). The individual is embedded in an apparatus of prior systems producing events which the individual is powerless to affect. Paradoxically, these systems were invented to realize the fictions formed as dreams and beliefs in the heads of particular individuals. The disparity of individuals and events is a function of the disparity of time, the different speed of those four "rivers of time" Lesy mentioned, leading to the senselessness of the raid on Halberstadt (without military value at that point in the war) or the disaster at Stalingrad (Kluge's other signature event). If one ignores the contribution of fictions such as the thousand-year *Reich* to the conduct of individuals, the march to Stalingrad is a farce.

The next logical step for Kluge, Bowie says, after treating the German disaster at Stalingrad, was to turn to the ultimate issue of total war—the atom bomb—in stories dealing with nuclear strategy. "Individual, sensuous experience in this area of history"—which is, in the face of the atomic threat, everybody's "history"—is further forced into subordination. The threat posed by such technology lies precisely in the way in which it is so inaccessible to human experience" (192). Or at least, Bowie adds, to commonsense notions of experience.

Kluge's artistic investigations of nuclear strategy may have to do with the disparity between technology and sensuous experience, but they demonstrate another capacity, which is the ability of the imagination to appropriate the data of science and technology in a mythical mode of thinking about everyday life. Indeed, one of the principal functions of television has come to be just this kind of working through the information of history and science in this mythical style, interacting with "the film in the spectator's head." "In addition to language, which is public, the public sphere should grant phantasy the status of a communal medium, and this includes the stream of associations and the facility of memory (the two main avenues of phantasy)" (Kluge, 215). Mystory, then, is an attempt to produce in the apparatus of schooling something like the "public sphere" that Kluge aims for in general culture by means of his "counter-history" "The true medium of experience, of desires, of phantasies, and actually of aesthetic appreciation as well, are the real human beings and never the specialists" (Kluge, 208). Counter-history in the schools supports Barthes's call for a revalorization of the "amateur" against the culture of the expert. This position has important consequences for pedagogy, involving an alteration in the direction of explanation away from initiation into a speciality toward a popularization of research. Teletheory shows that this new stance in fact benefits educational apparatus by bringing into appearance and performing the actual cycle of invention operating across the divisions of culture. The postmodernist tendency favoring crossovers between high and popular culture manifests itself in teletheory as the assumption of translatability between the different conceptual systems organizing the various dimensions of life. As Lesy said, justifying his description of family snapshots in terms of myth and theory, "I'd admit that to comprehend a photograph was like opening a set of Chinese boxes, only to discover a message that had to be translated from one language to another. But then I'd recount how, in the Middle Ages, Jewish scholars had translated Aristotle from Arabic into Latin, first for the benefit of the metaphysicians of Paris, and then to the great good fortune of European civilization" (Lesy, xii). Mystory is the genre of "Chinese Boxes," articulating as a kind of personalized Rosetta Stone the embedded levels of discourse, expert, explanatory, common and bliss-sense at once. There remains at least one more important relay showing how this genre might be practiced (to be outlined in the next section).

The ultimate catastrophes of the Second World War—the bombing of Hiroshima and Nagasaki, and the Nazi Concentration Camps—have come to serve a special function in popular culture and everyday life reason which is to constitute the unifying theme, the ground zero, of cultural representations. Indeed, it is possible to say now that the organizing center of culture, bringing into communication the expert systems of theory and the common sense of lived experience, is the scene of the H-Bomb and its associated explanatory systems (physics and politics). This scene replaces in postmodern culture the theoretical and metaphysical narratives that previously organized our discourses, as may be noted even in the language Jean-François Lyotard uses to report the demise of the metanarratives.

Simplifying to the extreme, I define *postmodern* as incredulity toward metanarratives. This incredulity is undoubtedly a product of progress in the sciences: but that progress in turn presupposes it. To the obsolescence of the metanarrative apparatus of legitimation corresponds, most notably, the crisis of metaphysical philosophy and of the university institution which in the past relied on it. The narrative function is losing its functors, its great hero, its great dangers, its great voyages, its great goal. It is being dispersed in clouds of narrative language elements—narrative, but also denotative, prescriptive, descriptive, and so on. Conveyed within each cloud are pragmatic valencies specific to its kind. Each of us lives at the intersection of many of these. However, we do not necessarily establish stable language combinations, and the properties of the ones we do establish are not necessarily communicable. (Lyotard, 1984: xxiv)

The point of greatest instability in experience—the catastrophic possibility of a nuclear war (turning the earth into a generalized Death Camp)—is the point of greatest stability in our cultural representations. The repeated appearance of one version or another of a holocaust image might be a repetition compulsion, of the kind Freud described in terms of the death drive, or as a mental block, a failure of the imagination. Within teletheory, the prevalence of this scene may serve a positive function, holding a place for new expert theories, yet to be invented in the cycle through explanatory and commonsense conceptual systems. It may be that this technology is inaccessible to direct experience, but it *is* intelligible, on the condition that the mediations of the doxa and the episteme are brought into relation, as they are in mystory.

Before reviewing the final relay for the tour of memory, I want to consider the function of the Bomb in imagination, where it represents the principle of unsolved problems of every sort. Cage's mushrooms are about the mushroom cloud, at one level, as are the lines of flight in rhizomatic minor science, indicating how to bring more resources into our thinking. The age of television, after all, is also the age of the Bomb, the same physics having produced both technologies, so that the logo of teletheory is the image of the mushroom cloud shown on a TV screen.

The function of the Bomb as an icon, even as the cliché, of invention in our time may be seen in the tape of Stan VanDerBeek, *Making Art: The Beek Weeks (1984)*, sponsored by Kentucky Educational Television, hosted by Susan Stamberg (aired on PBS). Stan is given access to the full technology and technicians of a television studio for a week. The tape is subtitled "Form out of Chaos" because it represents what happens when an artist's personal vision meets the chaos of studio collaboration (individual/collective encounter). Wanting to "translate" his personal dreams more accurately, Stan prepared for the week by planning a number of possible projects, including everything from a recurring dream about "interiors" to an anti-nuclear political commitment. He favors a world that is self-instructive rather than self-destructive. The time deadline and the distracting curiosity of just seeing what the technology can do, combined with a backlog of three years worth of ideas, produces a crisis of invention that makes this tape instructive for euretics. He can't find a way to bring all the elements together. After the fourth day he had accumulated thirteen hours of raw tape, including much electronic play exploring abstract form and color. Two weeks of editing after the initial week in the studio were needed to produce one finished piece, as a sample of what could be accomplished.

This video, only a few minutes long, entitled "After the Laughter," manifests several of the themes of teletheory, first in its context of *making* a text, and second in its themes of laughter and catastrophe. The abstract circle Stan was shown playing with earlier now appears as the globe of the earth seen from space. A voiceover states, "We won the race of discovery against the Germans." The soundtrack fills with continuous laughter over a montage of Edward Muybridge scenes of everyday life actions. News headlines note such events as war and the race to the moon. Two boxers spar. The sun sets, it is night, the laughter dies down. The H-Bomb explodes. Silence. Formally the video illustrates the capabilities of collage for remotivating individual sounds and images. The point of interest, however, is the fact that the logic and coherence of the piece is provided by the fable of nuclear destruction.

When students are shown this video they recognize at once that it is a cliché; that under the pressures of time and information overload the artist settled for a stereotype to organize his materials and give them "significance." The value of the video in the context of the whole program is that it shows the extent to which the Bomb has become *the* simple form of our discourse, calling to our attention the number of texts that point to this catastrophe like so many compass needles. Using a holocaust as framing device, as metaimage, for oral materials of all kinds, especially anecdotes, generates works of complexity profundity, significance.

Spalding Gray's film monologue *Swimming to Cambodia* is an interesting example of this relationship between anecdotes and catastrophe because, again, it is about the *making* of a text—the film *The Killing Fields* (1984), itself based on a true story related to the genocide in Cambodia. The genocide informs the series of anecdotes about Gray's career as an actor, but lightly; it remains on the periphery of the film, recalled at certain moments in anecdotes about the nuclear threat (Gray's conversation with the sailor whose job it is "to sit in a waterproof chamber, chained one arm to the wall for five hours a day, next to a green button, with earphones on," waiting for the orders to start the Third World War) (Gray, 24). The genocide is there: "It was better to kill an innocent person, the Khmer Rouge said, than to leave an enemy alive. It was nothing like the methodical, scientific German genocide. They were tearing apart little children like fresh bread in front of their mothers, gouging out eyes, cutting open pregnant women. And this went on for four years. Two million people were either killed outright or starved to death" (51). As a counterpoint to these events there is the humor of the anecdotes, as Gray works out his problems with his girlfriend, reflecting his "philosophy": "I don't know what laughter is indicative of, but it has some-thing to do with joy and letting go" (87). The 1987 film adaptation (by Jonathan Demme), if not the theater piece, ends with an allusion to Marilyn and the Bomb, perhaps a reference to Nicholas Roeg's *Insignificance* (1985), another film whose *inventio* is the nuclear fire storm.

What is the function of the anecdotes in such an account? The "Joy" and "Letting Go" says that there are two sides to the catastrophic laugh, to the laugh as trope, associated perhaps with entropy and the laws of thermody-namics, whether what is decaying is mountains or the bourgeois public sphere. It is important to remember how uncanny, how unfamiliar, is the paleologic of electronics, relayed to us in the images of the rhizome and the mycelium. Serres indicates the problematic dimension of the joke in the context of information theory.

> Suddenly, a joker. Can I read it? Certainly. It is enough to recognize the upstream law and the downstream laws. The joker, in the position of bifurcation, makes it possible for the confluence of values that it insures. It is both what has been said and what will be said. It is bi-, tri-, or poly-valent, according to the complexity of the connection. The ramification of the network depends on the number of jokers. But I suspect that there is a limit for this number. Where there are too many, we are lost as if in a labyrinth. What would a series be like where there were only jokers? What could be said of it? Dream logic seems to me to be of this nature. (Serres, 1982: 162)

The gram is a joker.

Another dimension of catastropics (the holocaust as metaimage) as joke may be seen in Claude Lanzmann's *Shoah: An Oral History of the Holocaust* (1985). In *Shoah,* of course, the catastrophe is not peripheral, although formally the documentation is left to "the film in the spectator's head," while only the anecdotes of the survivors are directly presented. If there was any doubt about the capacity of oral forms to mediate work on a monumental scale, this film dispels it. One of its lessons for mystory is its organization as a tour, specifically as an ethnography of a death camp. Lanzmann's interviews are organized principally by his questions about how the camps worked. The tour of the places in mystory then may draw on all the manners of touring available in the culture—ethnography, with its systematic reconstruction of the cognitive map of a specific domain, but also the artist's tour, such as Smithson's visit to the Yucatan to place his mirrors and plant his trees upside down, roots waving in the wind, at selected pulverized locations; and even the tourist's tour, reflected in the use of guidebooks and other examples of the tourist's discourse in works by Smithson, Kluge, Ponge, and others.

There is a "joker" in Lanzmann's film, identifiable at the level of invention. In addition to the narrative series of anecdotes, the film (over nine hours long) coheres around two devices. One is the historical interpretation that comes almost at the center of the film, provided by Raul Hilberg. His interpretation is privileged and highlighted by being the only direct explanation offered for the holocaust, and it comes from him as an "expert." He explains the final solution in terms of invention. In the context of teletheory, Hilberg's insight suggests that euretics may function analytically as well, exposing how something is made, for good or evil. Euretics may itself serve as critique. The elements of invention manifested in the death camps may be measured in the context of historical precedent.

They had to become inventive with the "final solution." That was their great invention, and that is what made this entire process different from all others that had preceded that event. In this respect, what transpired when the "final solution" was adopted—or, to be more precise, bureaucracy moved into it—was a turning point in history. Even here I would suggest a logical progression, one that came to fruition in what might be called closure, because from the earliest days, from the fourth century, the sixth century, the missionaries of Christianity had said in effect to the Jews: "You may not live among us as Jews." The secular rulers who followed them from the late Middle Ages then decided: "You may not live among us," and the Nazis finally decreed: "You may not live." (Lanzmann, 72)

When the order was passed along from headquarters, no explicit directions were provided to the field commanders. Rather, what was meant by "final solution" had to be inferred, but those in the chain of command had no trouble getting the message, sharing as they did the same cultural encyclopedia. There were no jokers in the line.

At the same time, the second organizing device of the film turns out to be the joke structure, representing the practical solution to the logistics, or paleologistics, of genocide. The immediate problem, once the victims were in the camp, was how to enlist their cooperation, which their sheer numbers required. The answer was a massive, grotesque joke—a practical joke— showing that Paulos (the mathematician, not the General at Stalingrad) may have been wrong about the totalitarian lack of a sense of humor. The gas chambers were disguised, as everyone now knows, as "delousing" rooms. The joke was that, in Nazi and anti-Semitic propaganda, reflecting the fictions of the anti-Semitic mind, the Jews were associated with the plague, with (rhizomatic) rats and with the lice they carried (a fact that Art Spiegelman remotivates in favor of the victims in a philosophical comic book, *Maus*). As far as the Nazis were concerned, the holocaust constituted a figurative and literal "delousing" of Europe. This joke figure organizes the memory site of the gas chambers like graffiti scrawled on a synagogue, "writ large," providing an insight at once into the conceptual power of simple forms and the deviousness of a secret hidden in plain sight (the victims didn't get the joke). As Alan Dundes reports, this sense of humor has surfaced again in Germany and elsewhere in the form of "Auschwitz" jokes (Dundes, 19). Bliss-sense, in short, is about love *and* death, and is the source of interruptions and short-circuits destabilizing every level of culture. Teletheory assumes that this dimension of mind needs to be brought into direct accessibility in education.

If the power of the joke as *inventio* rests in its paleological form, bringing together in collage style unrelated domains, its power as a tool of critique rests in its exposure of hostility and aggression both offensively and defensively in the cultural encyclopedia. The joke may be one of the best forms with which to explore for purposes of conduction and transduction the insights of cognitive psychology into "prototype" theory. This theory, the development of which is a symptom that the culture as a whole is shifting to electronic cognition, suggests that category construction in reasoning is not abstract but is a matter of human experience, relying on bodily situation (motor activities, perception), cultural representations, and imagination (metaphor, imagery). The stereotypes in jokes are a particularly salient example of the way prototypical cognition reasons by means of "normal scenarios" made up of bundles of typical features and scripts (Lakoff, 8, 116). One of the most important aspects of this recent turn in cognitive psychology is that its grounding of reasoning in the particulars of cultural and imaginative representations lends further support to the argument of teletheory, that cognition is fully accessible to video technology.

4. Breaking Rout/ines

One more relay for the tour through the places has to be mentioned: Ross McElwee's *Sherman's March: A Meditation on the Possibility of Romantic Love in the South during an Era of Nuclear Weapons Proliferation* (1986). This "documentary" shows how to integrate in a unified narrative the three levels of mystory—personal, popular, and specialized culture. The nuclear theme noted in the title holds the place, as mentioned previously, for the specialized problem-solving of a given discipline. When mystory is practiced at the lower levels of schooling this metaimage may be left in place, or replaced at the more advanced levels with problems from the mystorian's chosen field. The theme of invention is foregrounded in that the making of the film is thematized within the *mise en scène*. Part of the value of the *making* as a pedagogical relay is the simplicity of the means—one person, one camera—raising in others the feeling that it is possible to make a film. It is also a work of "oralysis," in that the reduced camera work and editing frame a series of conversations rich in oral forms. The action develops in the "middle voice," in that "Ross" is from the outset the peripheral focus of the text, including filmed reflections in mirrors and some self-interviews, as well as the voiceovers and the awkwardness of hugging his interlocutors while filming them. Like Smithson, who experienced his hometown as a photograph, McElwee finds his return to his native South to be a filmic experience.

The ostensible motivation for the film is to retrace the route of General Sherman's march through the South during the Civil War, investigating the contemporary remains of that historical event—the first example of total war against a civilian population in a "civilized" nation. This tour turns out to be at one level an exposure of the realities and myths of nuclear power in the region, reflecting the logical development of the philosophy of total war. This political theme is fully integrated with the personal theme, the "marriage broker joke" format in which first his family, then a former teacher, attempt to get him "coupled" (the gram) with a wife. Ross had undertaken the project originally in part to investigate the paradox of Sherman's character—his love for the South, recorded in his memoirs and letters, and his military actions that gave rise to his mythical reputation as the scourge of Southern history. By all accounts the women suffered most from Sherman's invasions, and the romatic developments bring out Ross's ambivalent identification with the General (he attends a costume ball at one point dressed as Sherman) as he in turn cuts a wide, if pointedly unsuccessful, swath through the ranks of Southern womanhood. Each of the women he meets is at once the star of his film and a "date." This confusion of levels is intensified by the fact that several of the women are already aspiring performers—an actress and several musicians. They are historical dates as well, in that their lives engage in one way or another the nuclear theme: one is an activist protesting the nuclear power plant near her home; another is a Mormon who interprets the expected Third World War in terms of "Revelations," and who shows Ross her family's bomb shelter. It is, in short, another "Lover's Discourse," one of whose lessons is that romance is perhaps *the* short-circuit across levels of culture, articulating the private and the public dimensions of existence. As Ross gets to know each of the women, he learns not only about their public concerns, their professional, religious, or political commitments, but also about their love interests—they are all involved in love relationships.

My purpose is not to interpret *Sherman's March,* however, but to inventory its elements, to see how it is made, taking it as a relay for mystory. The following aspects are especially relevant in this context. Indeed, such an inventory amounts to a definition of the genre.

1) *Structure and Interpretation.* The first point to mention is the structuration articulating the three levels of invention—personal, popular, and disciplinary.

a) *Personal:* The trip is a "remake" of his family album, including representations of his parents and sister, a former teacher, "old flames" from high school, in the setting of his home town and native region. The *topoi* come into appearance as one's home ground.

b) *Popular:* The public side of his native experience. In both cases the vehicle for these registers is the predominant and stereotypical *discourse* of the place. As Barthes said, the "love story" is the tribute one pays to be reconciled with the community. When an unmarried child of either sex returns home he or she will have to engage in endless discussions about marriage. Like Robert Smithson, who described his work as "cooperating with entropy," McElwee enters into the marriage broker process, exploiting it to help him find a "star" for his film. The equivalent of this family discourse (headed "why aren't you married yet?") at the popular level (defined as the public side of the personal) is the discourse of the community, the story to which the community is committed, upon which it is founded, and which it quietly enforces unself-consciously. In Ross's hometown of Charlotte,

North Carolina, the state in which was fought the last battle of the Civil War, the popular story is Southern Honor in general, and specifically the legend of General William Tecumseh Sherman as the scourge of the South. "The Confederacy died here in Charlotte," Ross says at the end of his tour.

Ross (as the figure in the film, as distinct from McElwee the filmmaker) is "fascinated" by the story of Sherman, which he first heard as a child in the form of an anecdote about his grandmother's sofa, still bearing the sword holes made by Union troopers looking for hidden valuables, which she refused to repair, as a reminder of the Great Unpleasantness. The story and the legend were so much a part of his native environment that when he matured he found that they were part of his identity, constituting an ego-ideal, vehicle for ambivalence and contradiction; the War between the States made the split subject thinkable for him, at least at the level of image. As a subplot to this process of identification in the popular register is the story of Burt Reynolds, embodiment of the ideal Southern man, "rival" for the affections of his first "date" (Pat) and a professional rival in the film business. While seeking an interview with Burt, Ross meets a Burt Reynolds look-alike whom he mistakes momentarily for the real one. The worshipful response of the crowd waiting near the scene where Burt is making a movie constitutes a commentary on Ross's own identification with Sherman, implying that the star system of the media apparatus is an externalization and institutionalization of identify formation as such. The popularized story of the community (often providing the basis for film and television narratives) makes available the role of the dominant ideology in identity formation. Ross's gendering, for example, is clearly associated with the war legend.

c) *Disciplinary:* At one level the disciplinary discourse in *Sherman's March* concerns McElwee's status as an academic/independent filmmaker, marked by the reflexive element of this film about making a film. This aspect of McElwee's *vita,* however, is subordinated to the theme of nuclear catastrophe. The problem of nuclear war is the metaimage, the universal counter, the joker in contemporary culture, replacing the metanarratives of ideology or metaphysics that until recently provided the rationale for our conduct. In mystory, as an academic discourse, a disciplinary discourse is mapped onto the personal and popular registers in the associational mode of mnemotechniques, not for memorization, but to bring the dimensions of experience, imagination, and phantasy to bear on problem-solving and disciplinary discovery, as recommended in prototype theories of concept formation. McElwee's film indicates how this mapping might be undertaken in his use of the nuclear theme (this is the point of extrapolation from one apparatus to another; from his purposes to mine). The key point is that he shows the role played in thought by legend and myth. Whatever Sherman's March might be in itself, as an historical event, McElwee appropriates it for his own discourse, as a signifier in the new context, to say something about human relationships in the particular circumstances of the present. In fact, like the frontier Indian wars, Sherman's march has been elaborated as an analogy for the Vietnam War, partly because of the tactics involved, but more because of the mythologies that motivate soldiers (Reston).

McElwee appropriates the metaimage of the Bomb as raw material for further thought. It isn't that he "understands" nuclear power, or that he overcomes the problem of the inadequacy of experience to the holocaust noted by Kluge, but that the "unknown" of the Bomb, in relationship to the other levels of his text, *becomes* meaningful. It is "good to think with," as Lévi-Strauss said of the role played by objects in the bricolage of the "savage mind." Thus when things are not going well in his romance and he is depressed he dreams about nuclear missiles firing from their silos, sent into the skies by the thousands. The juxtaposition (editing) of levels produce enough ironic effects to distance the film from Ross's imagery. The identification with Sherman or a nuclear mood coincide with politically more "correct" views on the topics of love, war, and energy. What is at stake is the recognition that he does think as much with the legends and myths of identification as with the ideas of his education. Propagandists and advertisers know that everyone thinks this way and exploit it for the worse, although the same resources of belief and opinion can also be tapped for the better. The goal of mystory is to accept this dimension explicitly into the reasoning process rather than trying to exclude and suppress it; to recognize its positive contribution to invention and at the same time to expose its vulnerability for abuse. In other words, part of the result of juxtaposing discipline formations with the other levels of culture is an exposure of the degree to which such thinking is itself conducted in the styles of myth and legend, and is saturated with ideology, at the same time that its abstractions provide an alternative perspective of intelligibility (as in Kluge's counter-history).

2) *The Scene of Memory.* (The remaining elements in the inventory of *Sherman's March* expand upon one or the other of the above three strands of the text.) One night in a motel room, in a meditative soliloquy spoken to the camera, Ross narrates the ground zero anecdote of the film, similar to Ponge's account, in the middle of his journal, of his visit to the site of the prairie. It is the scene of memory which organizes the places. In this case Ross recalls a vacation with his family when, at some time during his adolescence, they visited Hawaii. One night they wait on the beach to witness the testing of a Hydrogen Bomb, which they have been told will take place eight hundred miles away (it could not have been the top-secret test of "Mike" at Eniwetok in 1952). They listen to the countdown on the radio, and are disappointed when nothing happens at the count of "zero." After a moment, however, the sky suddenly turns bright as noon in a white flash, turning shortly to a lime green, and fading finally from red into black. The scene recalls the end section of J. G. Ballard's *Empire of the Sun* (the filmed

version by Steven Spielberg, 1987), relevant to the catastrophic imagination (the young protagonist transfixed by the light of the Hiroshima blast). Kluge's equivalent scene is the air-raid on Halberstadt, which combines in a single event McElwee's meditations on the past and future destruction of Charlotte (first by Sherman, next by the Bomb?). There will be, in any case, a specific and actual moment that may be recalled as the "ground zero" of the imagination, with the Bomb representing the ultimate punctum, which is already there, already at work, at a primal level, but which may be cultivated in mystory as a point of reference for concept formation.

3) *Tour*. Ross's scene of memory occurs on vacation, calling attention to the importance of tourism in the American experience. Smithson noted that one of the formative events of his imagination was a trip out West with his folks when he was eight years old. In retracing Sherman's route Ross visits a number of tourist attractions related to the war, including a diorama, Fort Sumter, a burned out church, and other sights. The touristic quality of most of these visits is notable as a concrete manifestation at the public and popular level of identity formation at the personal and private level through identification with ego-ideals. Such tours in teletheory, of course, are allegories of artificial memory, manifesting the new condition of memory in electronic cognition. The guided tour, this work suggests, can be a useful relay for making a text of invention and critique at once, in that the alienation of the tourist from the sights, the mediated character of the experience (charted effectively by Dean MacCannell), with the souvenirs constituting an abject discourse, precisely intervenes as a gap between the person and the monuments. "The key figure of the early allegory is the corpse," Walter Benjamin observed. "The key figure of the later allegory is the *'souvenir'*" (Benjamin, 1985: 55). It may be best to tour one's image-repertoire as a tourist rather than as a pilgrim. But there is another part of the experience of this thinking—the meditative dimension of *Sherman's March*—which admits a deeper relationship with the monumental, having to do with the crypt and its secret.

> The monumental makes crowds, gathers tourists, unites a people, but it will send each one away like the suitor who failed the riddle in order to select that single knowing spirit who is willing to unite with it in cultural matrimony and search for its secret, as Mont-Saint-Michel found its Henry Adams and Adams his Chartres. . . . This same sense, this fear of being overwhelmed, invaded, changed (which I mentioned as the magnetism, the magic of the monumental), means that we shall not pick up Proust in an idle afternoon. . . . To those it captures, there is no journey back. Not from the *Elegies*. Not from Nikko. Not from the mountains of Cezanne . . . . no more than from the grave. (Gass, 141)

McElwee manifests the monumental experience in his search for the secret of Sherman and his march. If one is completely immune to this punctum of the monument, even though, as Gass also says, "most monuments lie," then the imagination remains incapable of invention, for it is only through the scene of memory, the places activated by a tour, that this resource becomes productive. The attitude of the tourist in the visit through the place of memory transforms invention into a minor science. The image of tourism also evokes the theme of the parasite, in that it is always a question of hosts and guests with visits away from home.

There is a hybrid condition that needs to be adopted for this allegorical journey, perhaps. Kluge handled the tension between host and guest, to produce the minor emotion of uncanniness (the familiarly unfamiliar) by means of a tourist guide entry, noting both the beauty of the scenery around Halberstadt, and the fact that a concentration camp had been located in the area. Something between Kafka in Prague and the American tourist abroad represents the state of uneasiness that one should feel in relation to this home ground, or ground zero, of place.

The tour of the place of memory, then, may be done in the style of the situationist *dérive*, as an aimless stroll *(dis-cursis)* undertaken in psychogeographical terms in order to restructure, not to celebrate, the environs of memory and culture.

> A rough experimentation toward a new mode of behavior has already been made with what we have termed the *dérive*, which as the practice of a passional journey out of the ordinary through rapid changing of ambiances, as well as a means of study of psychogeography and of situationist psychology. But the application of this will to playful creation must be extended to all known forms of human relationships, so as to influence, for example, the historical evolution of sentiments like friendship and love. Everything leads us to believe that the essential elements of our research lie in our hypothesis of constructions of situations. (Knabb, 24)

Against the nostalgia of monuments, the situationists practiced a "realization" (or "overcoming") of art (Debord), that extended into performance or action the "insubordination of words" ("words embody forces that can upset the most careful calculations") which poets previously were content to confine to literature: "Realizing poetry means nothing less than simultaneously and inseparably creating events and their language. . . . The same judgment leads us to announce the total disappearance of poetry in the old forms in which it was produced and consumed and to announce its return in effective and unexpected forms. Our era no longer has to *write out poetic orders;* it has to carry them out" (Knabb, 115, 116).

The principal device of situationist practice, showing its affinity with textual conduct, is "détournement" (detour of the signifier). Extant art, monuments of the past, in this operation (a version of collage/montage) are refunctioned. "The two fundamental laws of détournement are the loss of importance of each détourned autonomous element—which may go so far as to lose its original sense completely—and at the same time the organization of another meaningful ensemble that confers on each element its new scope and effect. . . . Détournement is thus first of all a negation of the value of the previous organization of expression"ᵢ(Knabb, 55). Of all the examples discussed of "guerrilla tactics" in the mass media, "it is obviously in the realm of the cinema that détournement can attain its greatest efficacity" (12), due to the critical signification generated by the simple juxtapositions created through editing. Griffith's *Birth of a Nation* could be détourned by adding "a soundtrack that made a powerful denunciation of the horrors of imperialist war and of the activities of the Ku Klux Klan." Old historical epics could be reedited, and history rewritten, to "have Robespierre say, before his execution, 'in spite of so many trials, my experience and the grandeur of my task convince me that all is well.'" Or, coversely, "a neorealist sort of sequence, at the counter of a truckstop bar, for example, with one of the truckdrivers saying seriously to the other: Èthics was in the books of the philosophers; we have introduced it into the governing of the nations.'" The rules for the use of détournement are: 1)"the most distant détourned element contributes most sharply to the overall impression, and not the elements that directly determine the nature of the impression"; 2) "the distortions introduced in the détourned elements must be as simplified as possible, since the main force of détournement is directly related to the conscious or vague recollection of the original contexts of the elements"; 3) "Détournement is less effective the more it approaches a rational reply" 4) "Détournement by simple reversal is always the most direct and the least effective" (10–11). Détournement, in short, provides a way to write the tour—the selection and juxtaposition of elements from the three levels of culture that make up a mystory—as joke, whose target is the one who signs.

4) *Monument.* During his tour Ross visits several monuments, including those dedicated to the Confederate War Dead, and especially to Sherman's monument in New York City where he adds a few more anecdotes about Sherman to those he has been telling thoughout the film—about his death from pneumonia in 1891, and the respect paid to him at his grave by his former adversary, General Joseph Johnston, and about his definition of the fate of a "hero": "to be killed in battle and have your name spelled wrong in the paper." For McElwee, taken by Sherman, the monument has a cautionary effect, quite rare according to Gass, reserved for something like the memorial at Auschwitz. The function of the monument as an address, as a discourse, is to "speak to a community, a city, a state; but *monumentally,* as a quality which only a few objects—and some less material works of art—possess, exceeds speech. It moves to make and solidify the society it addresses,

actually drawing toward and even taking *into itself* a public which its significance then shapes" (Gass, 133).

The special, instructive nature of the monuments in *Sherman's March* is
best seen in Ross's visit with his friend Jackie, the anti-nuclear activist, to a
monument for survivors of nuclear war, inscribed in twelve languages with
instructions for how to recontruct civilization. They picnic on the site of this
Rosetta Stone. The term "reconstruction" here calls attention to the linguistic
register of homonymic reasoning that contributes to a mystorical inventio,
representing the gram that hinges the different registers of the triptych (the
tourist trip, the threesome of "Trinity"—code name for the secret of the first
test of an atom bomb). *Reconstruction* hinges the three levels of the narrative,
joining them as predicates of a single subject, moving from Ross's sister's
account of her plastic surgery, "reconstructing" her eyelids and "fanny,"
through the memories of Reconstruction after the Civil War, associated with
Sherman and his attempt to carry out Lincoln's postwar plans for benevo-
lence, to the hope expressed in the monument that there would be survivors
of a nuclear war. The film ends optimistically with Ross listening to Beetho-
ven's Ninth, performed by a symphony orchestra and chorus that includes
in its number his latest romantic interest—an attractive professor of music at
Harvard.

We find again here an example of a monument oriented toward the future,
if not in the same spirit as the planned obsolence of the monuments of
Passaic, New Jersey, suggesting the uncanny temporality which mystory
attempts to bring into academic discourse. Derrida has theorized this temporality in his contribution to "nuclear criticism," which is to say that mystoriography continues Derrida's deconstruction of the apocalyptic tone. Derrida
shows what is at stake in the monumental, indicating that nuclear catastrophe
is the one referent of the literary, in that it is the one event that cannot be
internalized by the Symbolic.

> An individual death, a destruction affecting only a part of society, of tradition,
> or culture may always give rise to a displacement, and so on. In that case there
> is monumentalization, archivization and work on the remainder. Similarly, my
> own death as an individual, so to speak, can always be anticipated phantasmati-
> cally, symbolically too, as a negativity at work—a dialectic of the work, of
> signature, name, heritage, image, grief: all the resources of memory and tradition
> can mute the reality of that death, whose anticipation then is still woven out of
> fictionality, symbolicity, or, if you prefer, literature; and this is so even if I live
> this anticipation in anguish, terror, despair, as a catastrophe that I have no reason
> not to equate with the annihilation of humanity as a whole; this catastrophe
> occurs with every individual death; there is no common measure adequate to
> persuade me that a personal mourning is less serious than a nuclear war. But
> the burden of every death can be assumed symbolically by a culture and a social

memory (that is even their essential function and their justification). Culture and memory limit the "reality" of individual death to this extent, they soften or deaden it in the realm of the "symbolic." The only referent that is absolutely real is thus of the scope or dimension of an absolute nuclear catastrophe that would irreversibly destroy the entire archive and all symbolic capacity, would destroy the "movement of survival," what I call "*survivance*," at the very heart of life. (Derrida, 1984b: 28)

Derrida continues by complicating this account with a paradox that precisely because the nuclear catastrophe was the effacement of all traces, it is itself the one ineffaceable trace. The problematic of our time turns around this paradox, this metaimage of the mushroom cloud, the logo of the mood of silence: "Literature and literary criticism cannot speak of anything else, they have no other ultimate referent," which is why this thought can hold the place for all specific problems in individual disciplines.

The interest of this situation for teletheory is that nuclear catastrophe represents that which resists internalization and therefore escapes mourning. It is not a question of an actual annihilation, but of this image that makes accessible to thought the other of mourning. Derrida elaborates this possibility in his memorial lectures for Paul de Man, *Mémoires,* which consists of three anecdotal recollections of communications with his late friend and colleague, offered as an abject substitute for an account of "deconstruction in America." The turn to the anecdotes is required by the impossibility of accounting for something still being invented. While confessing his own exclusion from narrative ability, Derrida suggests that there is a story to tell.

But is there a proper place, is there a proper story for this thing? I think it consists only of transference, and of a thinking through of transference, in all the senses that this word acquires in more than one language, and first of all that of the transference between languages. If I had to risk a single definition of deconstruction, one as brief, elliptical, and economical as a password, I would say simply and without overstatement: *plus d'une langue*—both more than a language and no more of a language." (Derrida, 1986a: 14–15)

I repeated this definition because it is fundamental to the strategy of mystory as a transduction between the different registers of culture. This password is nonsense, Derrida admits, when thought in terms of alphabetic writing, but, I would add, it describes exactly the simultaneous format of a video text. Derrida's paradigm, that is, originates in the alphabetic mind, but is realizable only in an electronic technology. What is to be translated into what? "Deconstruction and America are two open sets which intersect partially according to an allegorico-metonymic figure. In this fiction of truth, 'America' would be the title of a new novel on the history of deconstruction and the deconstruction of history" (18). "Deconstruction in America" will not even be deconstruction, in fact; it will not be recognizable as European, but will be an invention attempted through the mystorical juxtaposition of poststructuralist theory with the personal and popular discourses of a specifically American culture.

But if transference is involved, how is the story to be told without mourning? We return here to the problematic of the emergence of electronic discourse specifically in the Symbolic register of narrative, organized by the scene of the entry into language and the internalizations associated with mourning. Mystory attempts to work with and through this scene of mourning, to extract form it the wit generated by the transgressive exchanges also operating in this register. Derrida says that remembering Paul de Man led him to understand the possibility of a memory without mourning, which is the name of what he is still inventing. There is a ghost in the story, appearing first in the provoking quality of the past (preparing a place, it would seem, for the subsequent revelations of de Man's youthful collaboration with fascism early in the war). "Ghosts always pass quickly, with the infinite speed of a furtive apparition, in an instant without duration, presence without present of a present which, coming back, only *haunts*. The ghost, *le revenant*, the survivor, appears only by means of a figure or fiction, but its appearance is not nothing, nor is it a mere semblance" (64). The past haunts in this mode because it has never been present and is not mine in the way of past experience. At the same time (and this is what related Derrida to the uncanniness of temporality) the past, even of my self, returns or comes into relation with me only through the other, but an other not interiorized, out of an absolute past which was never present (to me). This paradoxical structure constitutes, Derrida says, an a-logic that now regulates mourning in the strict sense and all relations with the other, including the encounter with the absolute other that motivates all invention: "the sublimity of a mourning without sublimation and without the obsessive triumph of which Freud speaks. Or still again, 'funeral monumentality' without 'paranoid fear'" (38).

What are we being given to think? First, that academic discourse as we know it has been a mourning in the strict sense—funeral monuments *with* paranoid fear, internalizing, incorporating the other in the crypt, the foreclosure of a loss, an arrested mourning. In its place we are offered another possibility, another way to relate to the past. "Allegory speaks (through) the voice of the other, whence the ghost-effect, whence also the a-symbolic disjunction" (80). The ghost-effect refers to the way a text, principally by the figures of allegory and irony, may say something more and other than it says directly, in its signification or semantics. To write deliberately with the ghost-effect is not to repeat the past but to allow it to think in the future, as an artificial memory imbricated with the living one. Plato feared writing because in the absence of the author a written text could only repeat itself, "ringing on like brazen pots, which when struck continue to sound unless someone put his hand on them." The drive of academic writing, however, in its conventional history, has been to do nothing but bang on the monuments like so many pots, wanting them to repeat themselves "in the original," in a kind of "strict constructionism." Instead of that Derrida recommends receiving the past and its texts as gifts, as relays, for future work. There is no monumentalization, because there is no resemblance between the gift and the response. There is instead a causal relationship: the invented text need not reproduce the encyclopedia that causes it (which conducts it).

The encyclopedia is mine to think with, at least within the program of euretics, as much a part of my memory as the stories told me by my grandmother, with an absolute conflation of artificial and living memory. To remember now involves a tour through the archive:

> The immense question of artificial memory and the modern modalities of archivation which today affects, according to a rhythm and with dimensions that have no common measure with those of the past, the totality of our relation to the world: habitat, all languages, writing, "culture," art (beyond picture galleries, film libraries, video libraries, record libraries), literature (beyond libraries), all information or informatization (beyond "memory" banks of givens), techno-sciences, philosophy (beyond university institutions) and everything within the transformation which affects all relations to the future. This prodigious mutation not only heightens the stature, the quantitative economy of so-called artificial memory, but also its qualitative structure—and in so doing it obliges us to rethink what relates this artificial memory to man's so-called psychical and interior memory, to truth, to the simulacrum and simulation of truth. (107–108)

"Deconstruction in America," he adds, cannot be thought apart from this transformation in the apparatus of memory.

If the age of mechanical reproduction was founded on the possibility of exact repetition, the age of electronic reproduction elaborates an invention in which repetition gives exact difference, thus altering the status of the monument in academic discourse. The "death of the author" is the phrase used to recognize this problematic of the monument, which Derrida addresses in the cases of de Man and Nietzsche. "To begin with, he [Nietzsche, or de Man] is dead, *himself*, a trivial fact but at bottom incredible enough and the genius or genie of the name is there to make us forget that" (Derrida, 1982: 18). Nothing, neither for good or evil, can ever return to the bearer of that name, but only to "Nietzsche" or to "de Man," signifiers now detached from that trajectory in which the letter is said to always arrive. And "Nietzsche" *is the homonym of the other one*, Nietzsche—the relation of living or dead persons to their names is that of the pun, which has certian political and moral consequences. The contemporary defense of Nietzsche coming from the left, insisting that Nietzsche never intended any of the things the

Nazi theorists found there, in his texts (or vice-versa with de Man), leaves aside the fundamental issue: "one wonders why and how that which one calls so naively a falsification was possible, why and how the 'same' statements, if they are the same, could serve over again in senses and contexts that one deems different, even incompatible" (39). The same colossal pun that opened Schreber's madness (he started listening to the homophones reverberating in his speech and thought they were addressed to him by God, as an annunciation) allowed Hitler to be the *Führer* Nietzsche spoke of, and put Stalin's Gulag in the words of Lenin and Marx (Ulmer, 1986).

The future of a text, of a monument, is never closed. It includes the temporal possibility of absolute surprise, tomorrow, *demain,* but of what *main,* whose *hand* has been the main thing for Derrida, for example, but Paul de Man?

> *Memoires* speak especially, and often, of the future, that is, of that which cannot be anticipated and which always marks the memory of the past as experience of the promise. I claimed to know what a future should be *in general:* the unforeseeable itself. But without foreseeing as yet, and precisely for that reason, *what* it would be, I named in effect a future that it was absolutely impossible for me to see coming. Add what a future! (Derrida, 1988: 595)

Horrified by his luck, Derrida encounters in the revelation of his friend's youthful collaboration with the fascists further proof of the materiality of his science, producing in the real, for him first of all, the impossible event. It is the same luck manifested in miniature in the incident of the binder on the copy of Ponge's book, that when photocopied, performed in the real the erasing of the name Derrida theorized in *Signsponge* (Derrida, 1984: 150–152).

Is de Man's future, or the future of deconstruction in America, or the problem of the colonization of the life-world, or anything else to be thought within the paradigm of determinism, or of invention? Castoriadis complained that inherited thought from Plato and Aristotle to the present has only been able to think in terms of "the determinacy of being and the idea of being as determinacy which must necessarily be construed as immutability, the inalterability of *eide* as a totality, a system and a hierarchy, closed upon themselves and already given, excluding the possibility of introducing into them *other eide* while leaving intact those that are already found there" (Castoriadis, 197–198). Making, that is, can only be imitation, in the episteme of logocentrism.

Derrida thinks otherwise, however, suggesting that invention is being reinvented just now, precisely through a deconstruction of an opposition between the already-given and the absolutely new. What this new style of invention is cannot yet be defined, but only told, in an allegory, by means of a fable, itself appropriated from Ponge, dedicated to the memory of de Man, narrating the story of its own invention (Derrida, 1987). It is a way of passing through the mirror, the metaphor of subject formation in the Imaginary, of interiorization, transference, identification, imitation, mourning, without reflection or distance. This crossing, like the precession of simulacra described by Baudrillard, produces the event it tells about, inventing the other out of the same, in the difference of repetition. To invent in this way is to "produce iterability," particular and general at once, unique and transmissible, discovered and justified (47), as it must be in a pedagogy of invention.

De Man's memory is not his but ours, our hand, not second-hand. Deconstruction remains to be invented, out of the novelesque of America, even if we are still thinking with his war and that catastrophe. "The most important thing, with respect to the difference of the ear, is that the signature will not be effective, performed, performing, not at the moment when it apparently takes place, but only later, when ears have been able to receive the message. It is on the side of the addressees, or of an addressee who will have an ear sufficiently fine to hear/understand my name, for example, my signature, that with which I sign, that the signature will take place" (Derrida, 1982: 71). And when this exchange takes place, it is in the place of memory, in a transduction from one signature to the next. Derrida repeats himself, then, manifestly the same in your book and in mine. And that is where the institution pretends it would have us stop, as if it were only a question of understanding. As if Derrida never will have arrived at the Little Bighorn in time.

Part 3
Practice

Introduction

Does anyone want to make a mystory? Why not give this assignment to a class, or try it myself as an experiment (since only the genre, but not its exemplars, are transferable).

"Write a mystory bringing into relation your experience with three levels of discourse—personal (autobiography), popular (community stories, oral history or popular culture), expert (disciplines of knowledge). In each case use the *punctum* or sting of memory to locate items significant to you; once located, research the representations of the popular and expert items in the collective archive or encyclopedia (thus mixing living and artificial memories). Select for inclusion in your text fragments of this information most relevant to the items in your oral life story. Arrange the entries to highlight the chance associations that appear among the three levels. Organize the fragments by means of one or the other (or both) of the following formats:

1) *vita minor:* a resume including entries representing the sources of your "images of wide scope" in your personal and community background. The vita minor lists those aspects of your experience that tend to be excluded from the conventional resume presented to prospective employers or granting agencies.

2) *puncepts:* sets of the fragments collected on the basis of a single shared feature.

In both orders the disciplinary discourse may be drawn from your major, or from a discipline in which you have a potential career interest. You may substitute for, or intermix with, this disciplinary discourse fragments on the topic of a major catastrophe (which may or may not be *the* catastrophes of Auschwitz or Hiroshima). If you are making the mystory not simply to represent to yourself the generalization of your signature into an *inventio,* but to discover new points of entry into a specific problem, replace the catastrophic materials with information on that problem. The same format may be used to translate between expert and popular discourses."

This version of "Derrida at the Little Bighorn" is provided as an example of an alphabetic miming of a filmic mode—the compilation film. Like films made from other films, the compilation text is made from other writings, consisting primarily of citations. The "originality" of the piece rests with the actions of selection and combination, treating the archive of extant works as a vocabulary of a higher order discourse. To cite one of Jay Leyda's authorities:

> In this paper I want to consider the film as source material for history in the sense that palimpsest and parchment, hieroglyph and rune, clay tablet and memorial roll are source materials—fragments, sometimes fragments of fragments, often defaced by time, and applied to purposes of historical reconstruction rarely contemplated by the original authors. . . . films can be used, as other historical source material can be used, for various and different historical purposes. (Leyda, 16)

The basic source material for the compilation film, Leyda noted, is the newsreel. Manipulation of the newsreel resulted in a new text—a documentary. This arranged reality could be turned to serve the interests of art, propaganda, instruction, or advertising (10).

It is worth noting that the public mind, or popular culture expressed in the media of everyday life, seems to produce mythology in a similar kind of compilation process, working with historical events the way an editor works with old newsreels.

> Myths are stories, drawn from history, that have acquired through usage over many generations a symbolizing function that is central to the cultural functioning of the society that produces them. Historical experience is preserved in the form of narrative, and through periodic retellings those narratives become traditionalized. These formal qualities and structures are increasingly conventionalized and abstracted, until they are reduced to a set of powerfully evocative and resonant "icons"—like the landing of the Pilgrims, the rally of the Minutemen at Lexington, the Alamo, the Last Stand, in which history becomes a cliché. At the same time that their form is being simplified and abstracted, the range of reference of these stories is being expanded. Each new context in which the story is told adds meaning to it, because the telling implies a metaphoric connection between the storied past and the present. (Slotkin, 16)

In teletheory it is important to learn not only to perform critique, but also to perform mythology. A mystory may be myth and critique at once, functioning for the composer the way Brecht's "learning plays" were intended to educate the actors, and were not meant to be performed for an audience. Hermeneutics may be brought to bear on a mystory at any time, although there is no explicit interpretation of the sample offered here.

One rationale for writing in this manipulative way, selecting and combining a montage text out of the archive of personal, popular, and specialized material, is that in the age of Artificial Intelligence, we are learning the lesson of the integration of artificial and living memory. The technology of print and all its apparatus—the archive of libraries, journalism, the entire great machine of information storage and retrieval—is a prosthesis for the living mind of the student. There are several ways to relate to this apparatus, but the way promoted in teletheory is this operation of taking what is to be found there and using it again in order not to repeat the old work but to make another one that is at least a mystory.

What especially recommends compilation scripting as a practice for academic writing is its simplicity of execution. The historiographical rationale comes from Benjamin: "To write history therefore means to *quote* history. But the concept of quotation implies that any given historical object must be ripped out of its context" (Benjamin, 1983: 24). The research will be guided by the principles of mystory. Once the inventory is brought together, the arrangement follows (writing as selection and combination), including images as well as words. The resulting composition may or may not be of interest to an audience; may be more or less aesthetically or argumentatively coherent. Since mystory is not a text of justification, but of discovery, such judgments are secondary to its primary purpose, which is to help the composer articulate the ground of invention. In this discourse there is a deliberate conflation of the senses of invention, compressing the rhetorical notion of *inventio* together with the scientific sense of original innovation. In the age of mechanical reproduction, in any case, it turns out that exact repetition generates complete difference. The first reader of a mystory—the primary addressee—is the writer. The desired effect is surprise, as if one could tell a joke to oneself for the first time, which is to say that there is no originary time for the mystory. Or its temporality is that of the confluence of the social and psychological imaginaries. One's surprise at the associations produced by the juxtapositions marks the operations of bliss-sense. The third party of this joke, exposing one's image-repertoire, is myself. I am the target of the aggressive wit that replaces the monumental melancholy associated with the pedagogy of specialized high culture.

The following example, then is included to demonstrate one approach to a mystorical compilation. It is valuable only to the extent that it encourages others to turn to their own archives—as a relay and not as a model.

Chapter 6

"Derrida at the Little Bighorn"
—A Fragment

Part One: Vita Minor: "Gregory L. Ulmer"

Languages

French.

CUSTER'S FRENCH
*[Map of "Custer's Hill," site of the Last Stand, showing the deployment of
the Companies that fell with Custer—C (T. Custer), E (Smith), F (Yates), I
(Keogh), L (Calhoun)]*

He wrote on the hillside in French, with the letters of his Companies:
ce fil, *"this yarn."* Fil *gives "thread, wire, yarn, edge, grain,
vein (in stones etc.); (fig.) clue, thread (of a plot etc.); nexus, thread (of an
argument etc.).*
Anything else?
ficel. *We could take this as the root of ficeler, "to bind or tie up
with string? Or as a pun on ficelle (he only had so many Companies to work
with) or he changed its sex: "string; (fig.) dodge; (Theat.) stage-trick; (Mil.
slang) stripe. Montrer la ficelle, to betray the secret motive; connaître les
ficelles, to be up to all the tricks (of the trade), to know the ropes.—a. Il est
ficelle, he's a trickster."*
*He could have read Henry James, you know, the prefaces to the novels,
in which he says, "Half the dramatist's art, as we well know—since if we
don't it's not the fault of the proofs that lie scattered about us—is in the use
of ficelles; by which I mean in a deep dissimulation of his dependence on
them. Waymarsh only to a slighter degree belongs, in the whole business,
less to my subject than to my treatment of it; the interesting proof, in these
connexions, being that one has but to take one's subject for the stuff of drama
to interweave with enthusiasm as many Gostreys as need be" (James).*
No, he couldn't have. You have your dates wrong.

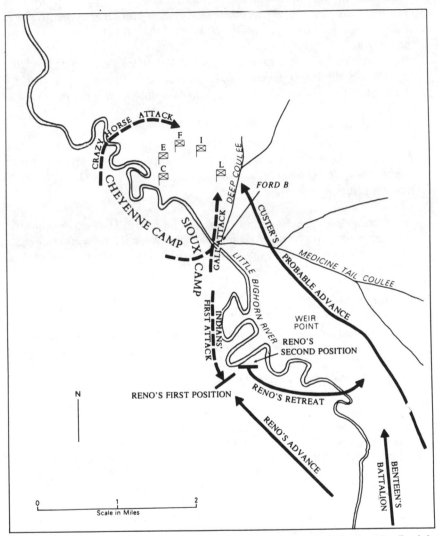

Custer Battlefield map. From CUSTER BATTLEFIELD, a National Park Service Handbook by Robert M. Utley.

213

And le fic?

"Fig"? Could be a macaronic code for "figurative." Or for the insult, "to give someone the fig" (thrusting the thumb between two fingers, or into the mouth) meaning "you aren't worth a fig." But in French they use dalle *(a worthless bit of floor tiling, a small coin) rather than* fic. *The gesture means "I spit on you."*

What about ce fils? *He didn't have an "s," but he was known as the "Boy General," and Whittaker mythologized him as the All-American Boy. Or* fille? *The ambiguity of his gender image is often noted, with the long yellow hair?*

Did Custer speak French?

He found gold on "French Creek" while making an armed reconnaissance of the Black Hills, which led to the treaty violations and the last Sioux war.

Maybe it wasn't Custer who was writing, but Sitting Bull? Didn't he go to France with Buffalo Bill?

> In 1878 the Chicago printing firm of Knight & Leonard published a thirteen-page pamphlet, The Works of Sitting Bull in the Original French and Latin, with Translations Dilligently Compared, to which was appended an eleven-page supplement, The Works of Sitting Bull, Part II. (Connell)

String Stories

> [Two children, playing "Cat's Cradle." The hands, the string. They begin making the loops, and narrating. "There was once/ a little boy/ who slept in a cradle./ But it didn't take long to grow up and when he became a young man he had to go off and serve in the army. Then he slept/ in a soldier's bed . . ." etc.]

Strings can be described as one of the earlier forms of the book. Quite a number of peoples are known to have used strings for record-keeping and historical accounts. The most famous of these string "books" were the quipu of the Incas: long strips of leather knotted and twisted in patterns that told of events in the life of the tribe. In order to tell string stories, one has to study carefully the typical patterns and their names in each culture and then try to re-create the tales imaginatively from the bits and pieces recorded by ethnographers, folklorists, and string figure hobbyists. (Pellowski, The Story Vine)

FORT LINCOLN. FORT KEOGH. FORT DA

This good little boy had an occasional disturbing habit of taking any small objects he could get hold of and throwing them away from him into a corner, under the bed, and so on, so that hunting for his toys and picking them up was often quite a business. As he did this he gave vent to a loud, long-drawn-out "o-o-o-o," accompanied by an expression of interest and satisfaction. His mother and the writer of the present account were agreed in thinking that this was not a mere interjection but represented the German word "fort" ["gone"]. I eventually realized that it was a game and that the only use he made of any of his toys was to play "gone" with them. The child had a wooden reel with a piece of string tied round it. What he did was to hold the reel by the string and very skillfully throw it over the edge of his curtained out, so that it disappeared into it, at the same time uttering his expressive "o-o-o-o." He then pulled the reel out of the cot again by the string and hailed its reappearance with a joyful "da" ["there"]. This, then, was the complete game—disappearance and return. The interpretation of the game then became obvious. It was related to the child's great cultural achievement—the instinctual renunciation which he had made in allowing his mother to go away without protesting. (Freud, Beyond the Pleasure Principle)

"The formation of the I is symbolized in dreams by a fortress, or a stadium." (Lacan, 1977)

Education

CUSTER COUNTY HIGH SCHOOL, MILES CITY, MONTANA, 1962.

[MAP: Custer's route from Fort Abraham Lincoln at Bismarck to the site of the battle. Also showing the convergence on the Little Bighorn from the south (Crook) and west (Gibbon)]

My father grew up in Bismarck, and we lived in Mandan, across the river, until I was five, when we moved to Miles City. There is a symmetry in time and space that I first noticed when I returned home for my father's memorial service. He died on May 17, the same day Custer, in Terry's column, started his march in 1876. The service was delayed (autopsy, cremation, and so forth) until nearly the day of the Last Stand (June 25). In thinking about that coincidence it occurred to me that the movement of our family replicated Custer's route, in that Judy (my sister) after she got married lived in Lodge Grass for about five years (one of the translations of the Indian name for "Little Bighorn," the other being "Greasy Grass"), near the site of the battle. The new Chair of my Department is a Gibbon specialist.

Miles City

Work on the railroad in the Yellowstone Valley in 1872 had to be stopped because of the Sioux and Cheyennes. A surveying party was sent out the next year with a strong military escort, including part of the Seventh Cavalry. "While Custer's men were in the vicinity of Lock Bluff, a few miles above the present location of Miles City, Rain-in-the-Face killed the veterinary surgeon and the regimental sutler, thus beginning an incident which lasted *three years and ended in a myth which has been perpetuated to the present day" (Brown and Felton,* The Frontier Years).

What was the myth?

Custer sent his brother Tom to arrest Rain-in-the-Face for the killings, Rain swore revenge on the Custer brothers for this, and he is said to have been the one who cut out Tom's heart at the Last Stand.

The response to Custer's defeat was a rapid military build-up in the region, fueled by a national passion for revenge. Fort Keogh, named after the owner of the horse that survived the massacre, was established in the fall of 1876, with Nelson Miles in command.

· *Milestown was born in the fall of 1876 when Colonel Miles, becoming tired of having the coffee-doolers loafing at the Tongue River Cantonment, had a stake set about two miles east of the post, and ordered all the hangers-on to move to the other side of the marker. By evening on the day Miles had issued his ultimatum, these civilians had a few tents set up and two saloons and a gambling house in operation. This infant village was a vigorous, lusty, man's town which provided its customers with alcohol, the necessities to support life on the frontier, and women. (Brown and Felton,* The Frontier Years)

When Brown and Felton, the biographers of L.A. Huffman, the "photographer of the plains" whose home and base of operations was Milestown during the frontier years, tried to imagine what Huffman might think about in recalling his own life story, one of their suggestions was, "the Seventh Cavalry on their way to that sagebrush-covered ridge along the Little Bighorn River from which almost half of them never returned."

[Photograph, Huffman collection, "First Monument. Custer Battlefield"]

"Hell with the fires out." (General Sully's description of the badlands).

Like Huffman, my father was a County Commissioner. One of their responsibilities was to keep the roads clear and in good repair. It being Custer County, the County vehicles all had this portrait of Custer on the door, in Romantic style, yellow hair and white hat, red scarf and shoulders of the buckskin jacket. It was the Errol Flynn look. He would drive one of these pickups out to check on the roads.

[Photograph, still, Errol Flynn as Custer.
Still: Ronald Reagan as a young Custer (Santa Fe Trail, 1940).
Painting: "Custer's Last Stand"]

Most Americans know Custer and his Last Stand through the F. Otto Becker depiction than through any other medium. Anheuser-Busch has produced nearly one million copies of Becker's work, a number that rivals the Mona Lisa *or the* Last Supper. *(Rosenberg)*

With the exception of Stuart's Washington, no American picture has been reproduced more often. Millions of school children have gazed up at Washington enduring the discomfort of wooden teeth while millions of fathers have peered drunkenly at the other George battling a cloud of Sioux. (Connell)

B.A., UNIVERSITY OF MONTANA, MISSOULA, 1967. ENGLISH AND HISTORY.

When I arrived in Missoula in 1941, a new Assistant Professor in the English Department at the University of Montana, I was met unexpectedly by the Montana Face. What I had been expecting I do not clearly know; zest, I suppose, naivete, a ruddy and straightforward kind of vigor—perhaps even honest brutality. What I found seemed, at first glance, reticent, sullen, weary—full of self-sufficient stupidity; a little later it appeared simply inarticulate, with all the dumb pathos of what cannot declare itself: a face developed not for sociability or feeling, but for facing into the weather. I felt a kind of innocence behind it, but an innocence difficult to distinguish from simple ignorance. In a way there was something heartening in dealing with people who had never seen, for instance, a Negro or a Jew or a Servant, and were immune to all their bitter meanings; but the same people, I knew, had never seen an art museum or a ballet or even a movie in any language but their own, and the poverty of experience had left the possibilities of the human face in them incompletely realized. (Fiedler, Montana; Or the End of Jean-Jacques Rousseau*)*

I took a humanities class with Leslie Fiedler near the end of his tenure at Montana. We learned about the Western tradition.

Ph.D., BROWN UNIVERSITY, COMPARATIVE LITERATURE, 1972. DISSERTATION: *The Rousseau Tradition.*

Each of us is fashioned by three kinds of teachers. When their lessons are at variance the pupil is badly educated, and is never at peace with himself. Of these three educations the one due to nature is independent of us, and the one from things only depends on us to a limited extent. The education that comes from men is the only one within our control, and even that is doubtful. May I set forth at this point the most important and the most useful rule in all education? It is not to save time but to waste it. It follows from this that the first education should be purely negative. It consists not in teaching virtue and truth, but in preserving the heart from vice and the mind from error. Do the opposite of what is usually done and you will almost always be right. (Rousseau, Emile*)*

First Monument, Custer Battlefield. L. A. Huffman collection. Mr. Frank Rehn, Coffrin Old West Gallery, 1000 Main Street, Miles City, Montana.

I bought a copy of Derrida's De la grammatologie *in 1970, thinking it was a book about Rousseau.*

> "This structuralist thematic of broken immediacy is the saddened, negative, nostalgic, guilty, Rousseauistic side of the thinking of play whose other side would be the Nietzschean affirmation." *(Derrida,* Writing and Difference*)*

> *The first year we collect images and sounds and experiment. Return to zero. (Jean-Luc Godard,* Le Gai Savoir *[1968], a remake of Emile)*

Travel

Vacation: Custer Battlefield National Monument, 1953.

> *[Photograph: "Custer Hill," showing the marble markers or headstones indicating the location where bodies were found after the battle]*

Today marble markers resembling tombstones dot the landscape where Custer and his men died. The stones, set in 1890, stand up in the grasses and sage like soldiers frozen in battle. They more than anything else fix in the imagination of visitors visions of the death struggle. Each says in a bold inscription that a soldier or a civilian fell there on a fateful day in June, 1876. (Scott and Fox, Archeological Insights into The Custer Battle)

Then out of the dust came the soldiers on their big horses. They looked big and strong and tall and they were all shooting. Then another great cry went up out in the dust: "Crazy Horse is coming! Crazy Horse is coming!" Off toward the west and north they were yelling "Hoka Hey!" like a big wind roaring, and making the tremolo; and you could hear eagle bone whistles screaming. The valley went dark with dust and smoke, and there were only shadows and a big noise of many cries and hoofs and guns. There was a soldier on the ground and he was still kicking. A Lakota rode up and said to me: "Boy, get off and scalp him." I got off and started to do it. He had short hair and my knife was not very sharp. He ground his teeth. Then I shot him in the forehead and got his scalp. I thought I would show my mother my scalp, so I rode over toward the hill where there was a crowd of women and children. There were so many of us that I think we did not need guns. Just the hoofs would have been enough. Many of our men were killed and wounded. They shot each other in the dust. I did not see Pahuska, and I think nobody knew which one he was. (Neihardt, Black Elk Speaks)

> There does seem to have been a regimental dog alive on the field after the battle. (Connell)

Research Interests

COMMUNICATIONS STUDIES
1. **Messages**
THE SHELL AND THE COLONEL

This is why psychoanalysis, as a result of the treatment, uses discourses to multiply instances of auto-affection and prises de conscience, providing proofs to the listener that they are dependent upon a beyond that Freud named the Kernel of Being: the Unconscious. (Abraham, "The Shell and the Kernel")

Freud's anasemic procedure creates, thanks to the Somatic-Psychic, the symbol of the messenger and further on we will understand how it serves to reveal the symbolic character of the message itself. By way of its semantic structure, the concept of the message is a symbol insofar as it makes allusion to the unknowable by means of an unknown, while only the relation of the terms is given. What is the precise content of this symbol of the messenger, of the representative, that we have just been considering? It is called either instinct or Drive with its cortege of affects, representations, or even fantasies. Just as drives translate organic demands into the language of the Unconscious, so does the latter utilize the vehicle of the affect or the fantasy in order to move into the Conscious. Thus a passage is enacted each time by appropriate emissaries from a Kernel to its Periphery. Now, would there be messages going in the opposite direction, from the Envelope to the Kernel? This should be the case of memory traces in particular. (Abraham)

Custer's rank at the time of his death was Lieutenant Colonel.

One of the fantasies to emerge from the battle was Custer's alleged call for help. Sergeant Butler, whose body was found well west of the field, was one of the many thought to have been the last man to die, though he is better known as the battalion's messenger sent with a desperate S.O.S. to Reno and Benteen. (Rosenberg, Custer and the Epic of Defeat)

Marker 174 stands near the east boundary fence of the monument, and it is two ravines east of the markers which denote where Captain Keogh and his men fell. A boot nail, three spent .45/55 carbine cartridge cases, a Colt cartridge, a Colt bullet, and a deformed .50/70 bullet were found around the marker. All three carbine cases were fired from the same weapon. These data suggest that the trooper who fell at Marker 174 was trying to escape the melee of the battle. Perhaps he was one of the last survivors, or perhaps he had feigned death among the dead around Keogh and was trying to get away. Perhaps he was a last messenger. As the man dashed across the ravines and up the final side slope, he drew fire from the Indians. He returned fire with his carbine, perhaps his last three rounds, and then fired with his Colt revolver just as he was hit by an Indian bullet. His Colt round struck the ground near where he fell. The bullet that may have struck him was a .50/70 bullet of the type loaded by the army for its Model 1868 and 1870 Springfield rifles. Surplus ammunition did the soldier in. (Scott and Fox)

Thus mutilation of the sexual organs does not entail the elimination of the homologous nucleic function and vice versa, anasemic castration does not imply the excision of the genitals. It is by virtue of this correspondence between the Envelope and the Kernel that Freud localized the source of sexual drives in the somatic zones, meaning thereby the Erogenous Zones, with capitals, that is, originating in the Colonel. (Abraham)

Godfry described his first visit to the Custer battlefield. He seems to have been startled by the colors: "The marble white bodies, the somber brown of the dead horses, tufts of reddish brown grass on the almost ashy white soil." He observed that from a distance the stripped men resembled white boulders. More than two hundred bodies and about seventy animal carcasses had been exposed to the June sun for two or three days when burial parties went to work.
   Mutilations.
   Eyes torn out and laid on the rocks. Noses cut off. Ears cut off. Chins hewn off. Teeth chopped out. Joints of fingers cut off. Brains taken out and placed on rocks, with members of the body. Entrails taken out and exposed. Hands cut off. Feet cut off. Arms taken out from socket. Private parts severed. (Connell)

A tribe signed the bodies of its victims with a wound. A cut throat, for example, was the Sioux signature. (Connell)

Neither The Colonel nor Keogh were mutilated.

Repressed, the trace continues nonetheless to act in relation to the unconscious Colonel, but henceforth obeys its laws exclusively—both to attract into its orbit the other traces that concern it and to erupt into Consciousness as the return of the repressed. (Abraham)

New York Herald, July 23, 1876. "A VOICE FROM THE TOMB" (headline). (Letter written by Custer just before the regiment left on its march up the Rosebud June 22).

My last letter was sent from the mouth of Powder River and described our march from the Little Missouri. I fear it may not have reached its destination, or if it did it was in such a condition as to be illegible owing to a sad accident which befell our mail party. Just as the sergeant with the mail bag on his arm stepped aboard the small boat and was about to push off the boat overturned, throwing all hands into the water. The sergeant at once disappeared below the surface and was never afterward seen. When the sergeant disappeared in the water the mail sack went with him, but fortunately floated between the steamer and the shore, before sinking below the surface. By means of boat hooks the bag and its contents were recovered, but not until they had been under water several minutes. When opened on shore many of the letters were found opened by the influence of the water, and all the stamps displaced . . . . (Custer, in Graham, ed., The Custer Myth)

Who was the one, besides the biographer, Whittaker, who contributed most to the creation of the Custer myth?
It was Bennett, editor of the New York Herald.
You don't mean William Bennett, Secretary of Education under Reagan? Of course not. I mean James Gordon Bennett.

Custer was the perfect hero and spokesman for Bennett's views. The death of such a hero did not suggest forgiveness of enemies; rather it implied the need for revenge. The Herald's own exterminationist rhetoric now escalated and began to ramify and reach out to include social conflicts other than the Indian war. The metaphorical connections thus developed are completely interrelated with each other; and all are recurrently associated with the stories that now centered particularly on the personality and heroic fable of Custer himself. It became the text for yet another sermon on the character of savages and the best means for governing them. Through the familiar devices of language- and image-borrowing and the physical juxtaposition of articles and editorials, the Custer-Sitting Bull material is related to the grandscale war of races and religions then materializing in the Balkans; to the continuing problems of "Red" agitation and violence among the "laboring classes and dangerous classes" of the city; to the proposal to build a Custer monument; and to the issues and personalities of the upcoming presidential canvass. (Slotkin, The Fatal Environment)

2. Jokes
The most popular and enduring subject of Indian humor is, of course, General Custer. There are probably more jokes about Custer and the Indians than there were participants in the battle. All tribes, even those thousands of miles from Montana, feel a sense of accomplishment when thinking of Custer. Custer binds together implacable foes because he represented the Ugly American of the last century and he got what was coming to him. Some years ago we put out a bumper sticker which read "Custer Died for Your Sins." Originally the Custer bumper sticker referred to the Sioux Treaty of 1868 signed at Fort Laramie in which the United States pledged to give free and undisturbed use of the lands claimed by Red Cloud in return for peace. Under the covenants of the Old Testament, breaking a covenant called for a blood sacrifice for atonement. Custer was the blood sacrifice for the United States breaking the Sioux treaty. That, at least originally, was the meaning of the slogan. (Deloria, Jr., Custer Died for Your Sins)

Tom Custer: "I don't think this attack was such a good idea."
George Custer: "So? Sioux me!"

[GRAPH: "CUSP CATASTROPHE"]

As a part of mathematics, catastrophe theory is a theory about singularities. When applied to scientific problems, therefore, it deals with the properties of discontinuities directly, without reference to any specific underlying mechanism. This makes it especially appropriate for the study of systems whose inner workings are not known, and for situations in which the only reliable observations are of the discontinuities. (Saunders, An Introduction to Catastrophe Theory)

Why is Custer's Last Stand so funny?
The essence of humor is defined as expecting "A" and getting "B."

Note that if both rage and fear are high, the behavior exhibited depends on the way the fear and rage were built up. Thus, if at first a little fear was induced and then both rage and fear were increased to certain levels, say x and y, the resulting behavior might be flight. But if a little rage was first induced, and then both rage and fear were increased to the same values x and y, the resulting behavior might well be attack. This property, called divergence, makes the cusp catastrophe particularly useful in the social and biological sciences, where behaviors, responses, attitudes, in addition to being subject to abrupt and discontinuous changes, sometimes vary greatly despite almost identical "causes." (Paulos, Mathematics and Humor)

Custer's greatest fear was that the Indians would flee upon discovering his approach, their general practice being to avoid direct confrontations. His entire strategy was based on preventing the Indians from escaping.

When Custer at last caught sight of the village—extending perhaps four miles— he studied the encampment through DeRudio's field glasses, then waved his hat to the troops and shouted: "Hurrah, boys, we've got them!" This is what the Italian trumpeter told Benteen the general said. If indeed Custer made such a remark after sighting the greatest concentration of militant Indians in the history of North America it sounds like a joke from an old vaudeville routine. (Connell)

Thus the cusp catastrophe combines the cognitive incongruity theory and the various psychological theories of humor with the release theory of laughter—all in one parsimonious model. An incongruity of a pair of possible interpretations is of course necessary. This incongruity must, however, be such that its resolution releases emotional energy (from sexual anxieties, "sudden glory," playfulness, or whatever). Moreover, the model is at least consistent with the derailment theory of humor, since the second (hidden) meaning (x coordinate) often depends critically on the context. (Paulos)

According to the Italian trumpeter Martini, who carried Custer's last message to Benteen ("Come on. Big village. Be quick. Bring packs"), and who admit-

Walt and Hider.

tedly didn't understand English too well, Custer's plan was to sneak into the village unnoticed.

Grants

National Defense Education Act, Title IV, Brown University, 1967–1970.

The Space Age began on 4 October, 1957. On that date the Soviet Union successfully placed Sputnik 1, the world's first artificial satellite, into orbit round the Earth. The 84-kilogram sphere, 58 centimeters in diameter, travelled round the Earth in a period of 96 minutes, its altitude ranging between 229 and 947 kilometres, and all the while its battery-powered radio transmitter emitted the characteristic "bleep, bleep" signal so vividly imprinted on the minds of all who recall the day the Space Age dawned. (Nicolson, Sputnik to Space Shuttle)

The American program to launch a satellite was called "Vanguard."

Teaching Interests
Vanguard theory, arts, pedagogy.

Part Two: TV/AI

(whisper) What is a tv/ai?
It's the same as a vita minor, except it uses punceptual series.

Series "H"

EMPLOYMENT

STANDARD TRANSMISSION

Truck Driver, Miles City Sand & Gravel/Concrete Products. (Walt Ulmer, proprietor)
I was eleven the winter Dad bought the Sand & Gravel from an alcoholic who had let it fall into ruin. But the gravel pit was worth something. On Saturdays I went to the plant to help him. It was bitter cold that winter, skifted snow, the Yellowstone frozen solid, with a wind whistling down the prairie all the way from the arctic. Mostly I stayed in one of the two sheds cleaning truck parts. The shed was about the size of a double garage, two garages deep, with no windows except in the front doors. There was one overhead bare bulb, and a neon light over the tool bench in back. The walls were lined with old Saturday Evening Posts for insulation; the floor was bare concrete heavily stained with grease and oil. The only heat was from a floor heater. I wasted quite a bit of time playing with a truck transmission that I found

there—a floor shift for a dump truck, with the "H"-pattern marking the gear locations still visible on the worn knob. I oiled it up a bit and then shifted through the gears pretending I was driving. The transmission is a mechanism that helps deliver the power of the engine to the wheels.

Pedagogy: the transmission of knowledge from one generation to the next.

THE YELLOW HAT

The summer I graduated from Custer High I was driving trucks for Walt. I was the only kid working that summer, and I was worried about holding my own with the regular drivers. Hoping to blend in with these professionals I developed a costume and style of conduct that I supposed to be very masculine. These consisted of boots, jeans, sleeveless T-shirt, and a short-brim yellow hat, grease-stained, with one side of the brim pinned to the crown by a button that said "Go Naked." Chewing tobacco like the other men was beyond me, since it made me get dizzy and vomit, so I kept the stub of a fat dead cigar clenched between my teeth through which I spit frequently. My speech was peppered with the phrases "summbitch," "horseknobs," and "douchebag."

I had to deliver a yard of sand for a kid's sandbox. When I pulled up in the alley of the address the kid was waiting for me. About six or seven years old I would say, holding a big stick. He watched me maneuver the truck into the designated space, run the box up with a roar of the engine, pulling the trip lever as the box went up. While the box was still up I went around back to give the door a bang. The kid is really taking this all in and I'm thinking he's impressed with how it's going. He says to me, poking his stick in my direction: "Are you a boy, or a man?"

THE LOW HOLE

One day that summer Walt got a call from Baker for a load of pea gravel. The regular drivers were all out on jobs and because the rains had finally let up they needed the gravel at their drill site right away. I loaded ten yards of rock on the International cab-over and headed for the highway. Dad's orders were to ask at the gas stations for directions, and to remember to have somebody sign the ticket accepting the delivery.

The road between Miles City and Baker is hilly, so I had to actually come to a full stop many times because I just couldn't seem to hit the low hole—first gear—while the truck was moving, no matter how I double-clutched. Anyway I did not have a chauffeur's license and I had never made an out of town delivery before. This was my opportunity to show I was up to the job. The first challenge was just to get to Baker and find the drill site before it started raining again.

At the station they told me the place was along the river. Take the gravel road, turn at the third cattle guard. I caught sight of the rig and swung through the next cattle guard without really counting, only to find that the ruts did not lead toward the river but off into a field. I realized at once by the way the engine started to lug down and labor that I was on muddy ground with the land on either side looking even softer than the trail I was on. I knew if the truck stopped I would be stuck. I would have to dump the load there to even have a chance to get the truck out, turning the mission into a failure.

It was do or die for Custer High. I would try to make it into first gear without stopping; if I missed the shift the day was over. I double-clutched, red-lining the tachometer, cranked the transmission lever over-down-back, and hit the low hole clean. Swinging off the trail out into the field I floor-boarded the gas, slowly circling with enough power now to get back onto the road. Feeling tremendously relieved and proud I made it to the drill site without further problems. I backed up toward the rig, guided in the dual mirrors by a man wearing a hard-hat and rain-slicker. He waved me stopped and I did the levers, revved, tripping the back gate as the box went up as I always did. But the guy started screaming. I could hear him over the engine and the rush of the rock. I was out of the cab and around back, thinking maybe I'd buried him somehow. By that time the box was empty. I was amazed to see however this little bit of a heap of rock where there should have been a great pile, twelve tons or so. The guy was fine, just standing there staring at the ground. "Where's the rock?" I asked. When he pointed at the ground I finally realized most of it had gone down the drill hole. I'd forgotten how fast pea-gravel comes out of the box, like water through a sluice, flowing further out onto the ground than you would expect.

The foreman was running toward us. I put the clipboard with the ticket into the guy's hands, who was starting to curse loudly. He signed the ticket automatically and I took off. When I got home I told Dad about the accident. All he did was give me this look, you know. Indescribable. I never got any more out of town assignments.

SPORTS
Letter, Football, 1960–1962, Custer County High School.

POST-GOALS
The goal posts for a football field form a giant "H." There is one of these "H's" at each end of a field. Games are often won by kicking a ball "through the up-rights."

The players on the field are the nuclear core of this macroscopic structure of perhaps 100,000 people. Although the activities of the nuclear core are dominant in determining coherence of the structure as a whole, the energy levels of the players and of the spectators are nevertheless interdependent. One example of this is the home-team advantage: Namely, in general the higher level of excitation *of the fans in the home stadium gives the home team an advantage in competitive sports. The more aggressive the sport, the greater is this advantage. Because the information fed into this nuclear core of players by the activities of the spectators both affects and is effected by the players, this entire stadium—players and fans—constitute a single, highly integrated nucleate social structure. (Brent, Psychological and Social Structures)*

Everyone remarked on Custer's athleticism. Even when he had good evidence that there were far more than the thousand Indians first reported Custer was not concerned. The Seventh Cavalry was the best; number one. It could whip all the Indians in the Northwest put together.

Somehow, within hours, Crook's scouts did learn there had been a fight; of this there can be little doubt, and from their sullen demeanor it is evident that they knew they were on the losing team.

The Custer story is exemplary in two ways: as a model of heroism; as a warning of what happens if one fails to be a team player. (Connell)

THE SPIRIT HAND

The fans of the Florida Gators want to be number one. The President of the University wants it to be number one, and all the programs want to be the best in the country. For example, The Florida Department of English is number one in the country.

Entering the University bookstore the other day I saw as if for the first time a row of Spirit Hands, giant, oversize, pulsing with the orange and blue school colors, index finger extended, inscribed GO GATORS on one side, with the logo of the university on the other. The full meaning of logocentrism became clear to me at that moment. One half of the floor space in the store is devoted to selling books required by the faculty, and the other half is devoted to selling the name and emblem of the school. That side of the store glows with orange and grinning alligators of every description, topped by the row of Spirit Hands.

Every school sells these hands, manufactured out of foam rubber by the Spirit Hand Corporation of America, to permit the student fans to emphasize the gesture meaning "we are number one!" regardless of the ranking of the team. The students, that is, are encouraged to identify with their school—to have school spirit. Later, as alumni, they are expected to support the school with gifts, nor is there any evidence to suggest that graduates of one university would respond to solicitations for gifts from any institution but their own. I know this for a fact because we tried it. We also tried to find a school that applied Brecht's epic approach of distancing and estrangement to alumni relations. Maybe Black Mountain.

THE MAGISTERIAL GESTURE

The Spirit Hand in the classroom—a gestural pun. In The Post Card *Derrida describes a card he had considered including as an illustration in the book along with the one displayed on the cover, depicting Plato dictating to Socrates.*

> The Interest of this other one is that it figures as the inversion of the Sp, its back if you will. It is a photograph of Erich Salomon, entitled The course of Professor W. Khal: seated at his table (rather a desk, slightly oblique), a bearded professor raises his finger (remonstrance, threat, authoritative explication?) while looking toward the back of the class which is out of sight. On the back of this card, a word from [Bernard] Graciet: "He speaks, alone, professorially, barricaded behind the elevated magisterial desk, strangely near, terrible, raising his right index finger toward I don't know what final knell [glas] of the question." (Derrida, The Post Card)

A student may be seen in the photograph as well, neck bent before the judge, silent, taking notes.

What is the relationship between the two gestures—of the fan's Spirit Hand and the magisterial point? Freud once mentioned that he always looked for the sign-painter's hand that could be found in the margin of a dream, indicating a point of concealment, displacement or condensation, indicating the operations of repression. Is it best to look in the direction of the point, following the habits of ostension? Or to look at the hand itself?

> But the words "I see" in our sentence are redundant. I don't wish to tell myself that it is I who see this, nor that I see it. This comes to the same as saying that I can't point out to myself by a visual hand what I am seeing; as this hand does not point to what I see but is part of what I see. (Wittgenstein, The Brown Book)

Derrida raised such questions in a discussion of *Geschlecht, inquiring into the idiomatic usages of this term in Heidegger's texts. Referring in an untranslatable way to matters of sex, race, family, generation, lineage, species, genre,* Geschlecht *is associated with thinking as handiwork, craft, and finally as technology, through the* Schlag *or blow, the imprint of impression, the beat, in which I hear that beating that a team takes when losing. Derrida is studying Heidegger's hands in photographs.*

> The hand's being does not let itself be determined as a bodily organ of gripping. It is not an organic part of the body intended for grasping, taking hold, indeed for scratching, let us add even for catching on, comprehending, conceiving, if one passes from Greif to begreifen and to Begriff. If there is a thought of the hand or a hand of thought, as Heidegger gives us to think, it is not of the order of conceptual grasping. Rather this thought of the hand belongs to the essence of

Chief Gall. L. A. Huffman collection.

the gift, of a giving that would give, if this is possible, without taking hold of anything. (Derrida)

The metaphor of the hand in concept formation—in the German word for concept—is open to further elaboration. The decision to write about the hand was due to its status in Paul de Man's signature (de main), macaronically.

Have you detoured? What is the "H" in Derrida, explicitly?
It has to do with an epilogue from Ponge, the source of Derrida's tutor texts for invention, in which a tree "inscribes on a leaf the common noun that is closest to the proper given name of the author, except for a gender and an aitch, a hatchet. 'Now then, this tree, who is my friend, thought that he had written on his leaves, on each of his leaves (in the language of trees, everyone knows what I mean), that he had written franchise on a leaf.'"

Now the sequel to the epilogue tells how, in brief, the tree becomes an executioner and a victim at one and the same time, signing itself and bleeding to death from the very moment that the woodcutter, after making off with one of its branches, turns it into an aitch, a hatchet with which he then tries to cut down the tree. The eyes of the tree "fasten on the hatchet, the aitch held by the woodsman and it recognizes, in the brand new handle of the hatchet, this aitch, the wood of the branch that was removed in the first place."
What comes back to cut the tree, and then to put it to death, is thus part of the tree, a branch, a son, a handle, a piece detached from the tree which writes, which writes itself on itself, on its leaf, its first leaf, franchise. The tree itself, the signer, cuts itself, and the torn-off piece with which it cuts itself to death is also a hatchet, an aitch, a letter subtracted from the franchise written on the tree, what has to be cut away from this common noun so that the noun can become a proper given name. But the supplementary hatchet, the aitch, by making dead wood, confers a monumental stature on the apologetic tree. (Derrida, Signsponge)

H-BOMB

"Nuclear Criticism," like Kantian criticism, is thought about the limits of experience as a thought of finitude.
Such a criticism forecloses a finitude so radical that it would annul the basis of the opposition and would make it possible to think the very limit of criticism. This limit comes into view in the groundlessness of a remainderless self-destruction of the self, auto-destruction of the autos itself. Whereupon the Colonel, the nucleus of criticism, itself bursts apart. (Derrida, "No Apocalypse, Not Now: (full speed ahead, seven missiles, seven missives")

The idea of the war of extermination is the central theme of the Myth of the Frontier. The catastrophic reading of the Last Stand held that it represented the possible destruction of civilization and progress by an uprising of human savagery from below. The optimistic reading emphasized the sacrificial aspect of the battle, showing that Custer's death struggle wounded the Indians and aroused the slumbering spirit of the American nation, leading in the end to revenge on the Indian and the triumph of a chastened and purified people. (Slotkin)

In his book Custer reproduced a telegram from Sherman to Grant, dated one week after the slaughter [the Fetterman fight], which says in part: "We must act with vindictive earnestness against the Sioux, even to their extermination, men, women, and children. Nothing less will reach the root of the case." If one word of this extraordinary telegram is altered it reads like a message from Eichmann to Hitler. (Connell)

When writing articles for a sportsman's journal, Custer used the pseudonym "Nomad." (Connell)

Then what was Edward Teller's design that, all at once, made the thermonuclear bomb feasible? The core of the device consisted of the thermonuclear fuel itself—in this case liquid deuterium and tritium. These two hydrogen isotopes were surrounded by liquid hydrogen that was the cooling agent to keep the deuterium and tritium in a liquid state. This core of thermonuclear fuel, plus hydrogen coolant, was then surrounded by fissionable material of the kind used in the existing atomic bombs. And, finally, the fissionable material was encased with a conventional explosive.

When the Mike device was detonated, the following sequence of events occurred: The conventional explosive drove the fissionable material inward, compressing it into a critical mass and creating an atomic explosion. This in turn compressed and heated the hydrogen isotopes (deuterium and tritium) to the point where thermonuclear fusion occurred, releasing unprecedented quantities of energy. (Blumberg and Owens, Energy and Conflict: The Life and Times of Edward Teller)

Let us start with a description of what is meant by isotopes: "most chemical elements are a mixture of several components identical in chemical properties but different in atomic weight. They received the name of isotopes, that is, substances occupying the same place in the periodic system of elements." Thus we may conclude that the isotope is one of a group of nucleids which have the same atomic number (2) but differ in both their neutronic number (N) and mass number (A).

Looking now for the linguistic counterpart of isotopes, we find a striking similarity between the latter and some aspects of the linguistic phenomenon called homonymy. Semantically, it is completely irrelevant whether we classify French "louer" [praise, eulogize] from Latin "laudare," and French "louer" [to rent, to book] from Latin "locare" as etymological or semantic homonyms. Both linguistic forms have the same phonetic value and the same spelling, so that the semantic difference may be determined only by a context or a definition. There-

fore for our purposes we shall call homonyms all those linguistic forms which have at the same time an identical spelling and an identical phonetic value, but whose semantic variations can be determined either by a context or by a definition. In other words, our "homonyms" are simultaneously "homographs" and "homophones." (Grava, A Structural Inquiry into the Symbolic Representation of Ideas)

Francis Ponge—d'ici je l'appelle, pour le salut et la louange, je devrais dire la renommée. (Derrida, Signsponge)

Celebration, praising the name, which may be done by "booking" space in the celebrity's text.

Exultantly watching the seismograph register the expected shock waves from Eniwetok, the delighted Teller, "father of the H-bomb," sent off a self-explanatory three-word telegram to Los Alamos—"It's a boy." (Easlea, Fathering the Unthinkable: Masculinity, Scientists, and the Nuclear Arms Race)

SERIES "GALL"

Humor—Gall

This is the humor that is not funny.

A humour is a liquid or fluent part of the body, comprehended in it, for the preservation of it; and is either innate or born with us, or adventitious and acquisite.

Blood is a hot, sweet, temperate, red humour, prepared in the meseraick veins, and made of the most temperate parts of the chylus in the liver, whose office is to nourish the whole body, to give it strength and colour, being dispersed by the veins through every part of it. And from it spirits are first begotten in the heart.

Pituita, or phlegm, is a cold and moist humour, begotten of the colder part of the chylus (or white juice coming out of the meat digested in the stomach) in the liver; his office is to nourish and moisten the members of the body.

Choler is hot and dry, bitter, begotten of the hotter parts of the chylus, and gathered to the gall: it helps the natural heat and senses, and serves to the expelling of excrements.

Melancholy, cold and dry, thick, black, and sour, begotten of the more faeculent part of nourishment, and purged from the spleen, is a bridle to the other two hot humours, blood and choler. These four humours have some analogy with the four elements, and to the four ages in man. (Burton, Anatomy of Melancholy)

The theory of melancholy became crystallized around a number of ancient emblems. One of the properties assembled around Dürer's figure of Melancholy is the dog. The similarity between the condition of the melancholic, and the state of rabies, is not accidental. According to ancient tradition, "the spleen is dominant in the organism of the dog." (Benjamin, The Origin of German Tragic Drama)

Sir William Ramsey, one of the leading experts in the new field of radioactive substances, thought there were no limits to what radium might mean to the world. He wrote that the "philosopher's stone will have been discovered, and it is not beyond the bounds of possibility that it may lead to that other goal of the philosophers of the Dark Age—the elixir vitae." (Hilgartner, Bell, and O'Connor, NUKESPEAK)

After the rise of the explicitly "masculine philosophy" in the seventeenth century and further disparagement and repression of the "feminine," only the manipulative aspect of alchemy remained of what had once been a more holistic endeavor. The role of the true alchemist as man-midwife to "mother nature" had been replaced by the goal of the masculine philosopher to be master and professor of brute (female) matter. In his sympathetic account of alchemical practice, F. Sherwood Taylor, the then Director of the Science Museum in London, has not inappropriately written: "The material aim of the alchemists, the transmutation of metals, has now been realized by science, and the alchemical vessel is the uranium pile. Its success has had precisely the result that the alchemists feared and guarded against." (Easlea)

The ancient Greek scientists thought of the sun as a great big fire in the sky. By the 1930s, it was known that the energy of the sun, and therefore all the other stars, came from atomic reactions, the fusion of very light atoms to release energy. Enrico Fermi made the connection one day early in the year, as he and Teller walked back after lunch to their laboratory at Columbia University, where they were then employed on the bomb project. "Couldn't such an explosion be used to start reactions similar to the reactions of the sun?" (Moss, Men Who Play God)

FIRE is the material associated with choler, along with masculinity and the color yellow. To write the anatomy of choler, now, after Burton's anatomy of melancholy: "to anatomize this humour of [choler], through all his parts and species, as it is an habit, or an ordinary disease, and that philosophically, medicinally, to shew the causes, symptoms, and several cures of it, that it may be the better avoided."

What is the temperament of choler?

Such are bold and impudent, and of a more harebrain disposition, apt to quarrel and think of such things, battles, combats, and their manhood; furious, impatient in discourse, stiff, irrefragable, and prodigious in their tenents; and if they be moved, more violent, outrageous, ready to disgrace, provoke any, to kill them-

selves and others. Cardan holds these men of all others fit to be assassinates, bold, hardy, fierce, and adventurous. (Burton)

WHEN ANGER BECOMES TOO INTENSE, THE PERSON EXPLODES.

When I told him, he just exploded.
She blew up *at me.*
We won't tolerate any more of your outbursts.

WHEN A PERSON EXPLODES, PARTS OF HIM GO UP IN THE AIR.

I blew my stack.
She flipped her lid.
He hit the ceiling.
ANGER IS FIRE. *(Lakoff and Kovecses, "The Cognitive Model of Anger Inherent in American English. In Holland and Quinn)*

Gallbladder: Walt Ulmer, 1916–1983

How did Walt die?
His gallbladder, which they knew was infected, also turned out to be cancerous.
Has his ghost been the problem for you that it was for Hamlet?
What did he want, as a ghost?
Remember what Hamlet said when he saw the ghost of his father?

Oh, answer me! Let me not burst in ignorance, but tell why thy canonized bones, hearsed in death, have burst their cerements, why the sepulcher wherein we saw thee quietly inurned hath oped his ponderous and marble jaws to cast thee up again. What may this mean, that thou, dead corse, again, in complete steel, revisit'st thus the glimpses of the moon, making night hideous.

"What are these rites, really, by which we fulfill our obligation to what is called the memory of the dead—if not the total mass intervention, from the heights of heaven to the depths of hell, of the entire play of the symbolic register." (Lacan, "Desire and the Interpretation of Desire in Hamlet." Yale French Studies *55/56 [1977])*

Walt's Sand and Gravel plant reminded me of "Hamlet's Mill." Hamlet's Mill *is that book by Giorgio de Santillana and Hertha von Dechend on the transmission of knowledge through myth. Amlodhi in Icelandic legend was another melancholic intellectual, forbear of Hamlet. He owned a mill that originally ground out peace and plenty, then, in decaying times, salt, and finally, in the last age, rock and sand, creating a maelstrom at the bottom of*

Miles City Sand and Gravel, 1962.

the sea that opened a way to the land of the dead. One of my first jobs when I worked at the plant was to clean the grids of the screens used to grade the gravel into sizes. Eventually the screens plugged up with stones and I had to knock them loose with a hammer. The pea-gravel screen could be cleaned by running the tip of a large screwdriver along the meshed grids, which produced an almost musical sound. This was the actual "gravel plant." The washer with its three grades of screen, one on top of the other, was fed by a conveyor belt carrying the "pit gravel" from the quarry, and fed in turn three piles of sized rock, with the sand coming out the bottom, to be run through another washer for further grading. The whole contraption made a terrible noise and shook violently.

There was this huge pile, a mountain, of oversize rock that came off the side. Too big for anything, unless we had a crusher, which we couldn't afford. So it just sat there and piled up over the years, always with a few rockhounds climbing over it, looking for agates. You could get a full cubic yard, over a ton of this rock, for two dollars.

One day the hired man, George, came back from lunch with a present for Walt, a birthday present, something he found at the drugstore. Walt opened it and there was this box and inside that was a pet rock. Now there was no difference between this pet rock and the rocks in the oversize pile, except that the pet one had a face painted on it, sort of a frown, as I recall, and it came in a little box. And the pet rock sold for two dollars apiece.

Dad stared at that rock, and this look came over his face.

Anyway, Amlodhi's maelstrom agrees with the anagram of "Ulmer," "le-mur," which, in Roman religion, referred to "the ghosts of the dead of a family." I live now about a mile or two from the "Devil's Millhopper," "a huge sinkhole which formed when a cavern roof collapsed. The bowl-shaped cavity which resulted is 500 feet across and tapers to 100 feet on the bottom. Its depth is 120 feet. The Devil's Millhopper was created through the erosion of underground limestone deposits which formed a cavern and the subsequent collapse of the cavern roof. This natural phenomenon has been visited by the curious since the early 1880s."

Simonides invented mnemonics. He was able to identify the bodies of the party guests killed when a roof collapsed on them by remembering where each had been sitting.

What did the ghost of Hamlet's father want?

Revenge.

If melancholy is tragic, is choler comic?

Walt was cremated in Minnesota, which we all thought was appropriate, considering that his favorite poem was "The Cremation of Sam McGee" by Robert Service. The hospital was shipping the ashes to us, so Judy and I waited for the mail every day, since we didn't want Mom to be the one to get the package. Finally the package came, a heavy metal box wrapped in *brown paper. Judy looked at the registered stamp. $5.95. "If Dad had known how cheap it is to travel this way, he probably would have gotten cremated a lot sooner." (Laughter)*

HANK WORMWOOD

Henry—better known as "Hank"—Wormwood was the first town marshal in Miles City. Hank had one personal peculiarity which set him apart—he wore his sandy-colored hair long, like a dandy who wished to attract attention. One evening the report reached Hank that a swaddy in Strader's saloon and gambling hall was getting "tough drunk" and swearing to his friends that "no red-headed, long-haired son of a so and so could do anything to him. Hank, realizing that his hand was being called, stepped into the saloon and, being careful to keep his hand away from his gun, walked straight up to the soldier in a friendly fashion. All activity stopped immediately and an ominous quiet settled on the room in which there were at least 25 other soldiers. Looking the soldier straight in the eye, Hank said, "What's this I hear? You wouldn't do anything to hurt me, would you?" The soldier, a powerful man but not as tall as Hank, hesitated, and while he hesitated Hank's hands suddenly shot out and his long fingers encircled the man's neck. The marshal quickly lifted him off the floor and held him against the wall with a grip like a hangman's noose. The soldier choked, his tongue popped out of his mouth, and his face went purple. Supporting his victim with one hand, the marshal took the soldier's gun and then set him down. Holding his prisoner at the point of a gun, Hank glanced coolly around the saloon and then addressed those present: "I'm goin' to take this boy back to the fort. I advise you fellows not to interfere." Not a man moved as the marshal walked his man out the door. (Brown and Felton, The Frontier Years)

Wormwood: *"an emblem or type of what is bitter and grievous to the soul."* To be wormwood *or* gall and wormwood: *"to be acutely mortifying or vexing."* Gall: *(fig.) with reference to the bitterness of gall. Bitterness of spirit, rancour (supposed to have its seat in the gall). Spirit to resent injury or insult. (slang) Impudence. (transferred uses) Poison, venom. Name given to the Lesser Centaury, and to other plants. Barren spot in a field, flaw or rotten place in a rock. Part of the carcass that has to be removed as useless and offensive. A painful sore or wound. Something exasperating, galling; a state of mental soreness or irritation. A person or thing that harasses or distresses. A place rubbed bare. A breach, a fault, dike. Filth, impurity, refuse. An excrescence produced on trees by the action of insects. Oak-galls are used in the manufacture of ink and tannin. (O.E.D.)*

HIDER

One day George, the hired man, came out of the root cellar at the plant with his arms full of puppies. The yard dog had hidden her litter down there. A gravel plant is not a very sentimental sort of place, so the ones that nobody wanted were drowned in the Yellowstone. After all the puppies were gone Dad found one more hiding in the cellar. He named it "Hider."

Hider hid himself for a good reason, it turned out, because when he grew up, and he did get very large, he was the ugliest dog anyone could remember seeing. He was pitch black, and his hair (his old man must have been a wire-hair) stuck out like a bed of nails, like you could use him to scrub rust off the plant. He lived under the trucks, and never got used to being big, so he had this streak of grease all along his back, where he rubbed the underside of the trucks. He was very shy. He'd keep off from people a good thousand feet, and if you called to him he would grovel the whole way, wiggling across the yard on his belly, whimpering, until, ashamed of ourselves, we finally gave up calling to him. That was after George threw him in the Yellowstone, to try to clean him up. Then Hider stayed off two thousand feet, and had twice as far to grovel.

One morning we came to work as usual, about six, and we saw Hider laying dead in the road, run over, probably by one of the cattle trucks that went that way. Walt went over to him, to see if he might be alive, and there was this look on his face.

Gall—War

[photograph: Chief Gall, an Unkpapa Sioux, one of the leaders, along with Crazy Horse and Two Moon, in the defeat of Custer]

His name in English is a literal translation of Pizi, given to him by his mother when she came upon him tasting the gall of a dead animal. But he was known also as Red Walker and The Man Who Goes in the Middle.

The Bismarck Tribune had reported that a trader bought from Chief Gall—"the worst Indian living"—an odd little matchbox-compass-whistle device that Custer carried in his pocket. How did this worst of all possible Indians get it? Gall could not have been Custer's angel of death. For one thing he fought with a hatchet and beyond doubt Custer went down with a bullet in the side.

Most Unkpapas considered him a peaceable sort who lost his temper that Sunday after Reno's troops shot two of his wives and three of his children. The act turned his heart bad, as he confided to a journalist many years later, causing him to ride among the soldiers and split their heads with his hatchet. "I killed a great many," he said. (Connell)

What about the compass Gall took from Custer? Connell reads the deployment of the Companies on the hill in a way that suggests the needle of a compass.

From above, as one views the battle field on the museum topographical map, they give the impression of being loosely arranged in the shape of a V—an arrowhead, if one chooses to see it like that—with General Custer at the northern point. Pointing slightly northwest, to be exact.

The needle of a compass never points true north.

The Sioux worshipped the sun. A male proved his manhood by participating in the Sun Dance.

The Sioux arbor usually was about 150 feet across with a twenty-foot pole in the middle from which dangled an array of rawhide or buffalo hair lariats. A medicine man, after having gashed a dancer's chest, would shove sticks beneath the muscles. These sticks would be attached to the dangling lariats and tightened until the brave was forced to stand on tiptoe, which might draw the chest muscles three or four inches out of his body. (Connell)

Gaul—Gallic Philosophy

DERRIDA

At the insistence of his collaborator, Peter Eisenman, in the design of their "folie" in the Parc de la Villette, Derrida provided a drawing for a sculpture based on the metaphor informing the passage in Plato's Timaeus *that he finds most resistant to interpretation—the chora as crible, sieve or sift:*

my verdict is that being and space and generation, these three, existed in their three ways before the heaven, and that the nurse of generation, moistened by water and inflamed by fire, and receiving the forms of earth and air, and experiencing all the affections which accompany these, presented a strange variety of appearances, and being full of powers which were neither similar nor equally balanced, was never in any part in a state of equipoise, but swaying unevenly hither and thither, was shaken by them, and by its motion again shook them, and the elements when moved were separated and carried continually, some one way, some another. As, when grain is shaken and winnowed by fans and other instruments used in the threshing of corn, the close and heavy particles are borne away and settle in one direction, and the loose and light particles in another. (Timaeus)

Derrida comments, describing his design based on this metaphor.

I propose therefore the following "representation," "materialisation," "formation": in one or three exemplars (if there are three, with different scalings), a gilded metallic object . . . will be planted obliquely in the ground. Neither vertical nor horizontal, a most solid frame will resemble at once a mesh, sieve, or grid and a stringed musical instrument. An interpretive and selective filter which will have permitted a reading and sifting of the three sites and the three embeddings (Eisenman-Derrida, Tschumi, La Villette). (Derrida, 1987)

But isn't that a description of the gravel plant, which is a three-layered grid for sizing rock?

Not long after I returned from the memorial service in Montana I received a copy of Feu la cendre from Derrida. He was still at the Ecole Normale at the time, and I noticed really for the first time the return address on the stationery—"45 Rue d'Ulm." He worked on Ulm Street. I felt the same sort of shock when I read that old interview by Godard: "In other countries Cahiers has an enormous influence. People wonder if we're serious. It was bad enough to admit that guys like Ray and Aldrich have genius, but when they see interviews with someone like Ulmer—I am for the Politique des Auteurs, but not just anybody—I find that opening the door to absolutely everyone is a very dangerous thing." Alexander Kluge is associated with the Ulmer Dramaturgien. In the same way, lots of towns and other places are named for Custer.

I read Derrida's text right away, in which he says, "I now have the impression that the best paradigm of the trace is not, as some have believed, the track of a hunt, a marking, a step, and so on, but ashes, that which remains without remaining of the holocaust, of the burn-all." Not senders and receivers, then, in a theory of communication, but cinders. In an idiom referring to the "late," the deceased. A writing without debt that is as good as a burning. No monument, no Phoenix. The "late" is also the "fire" in the idiom, the fire that cannot be effaced in the cinders as trace. It is a word that is in question, that is to be put in place of memory, in the place of memory, to which we are to listen; to take the word into the mouth and ears. Fire. Choler. But it could be any word, any black on white letters. Not icons, but indexes, in this writing. A text will not resemble what it is about, but be caused by it, the way smoke relates to fire.

What did Derrida say to the driver of the charter bus, taking him on a tour of the Custer National Battlefield Monument?

(We commute already with the "bus" that I have just named, in translation and, according to the principles of transmutation, between Übertragung and Übersetzung, metaphorikos still designating today, in what one calls "modern" Greek, that which concerns means of transportation). We are in a certain way— metaphorically of course, and as concerns the mode of habitation—the content and the tenor of this vehicle: passengers, comprehended and displaced by metaphor. (Derrida, "The Retrait of Metaphor").

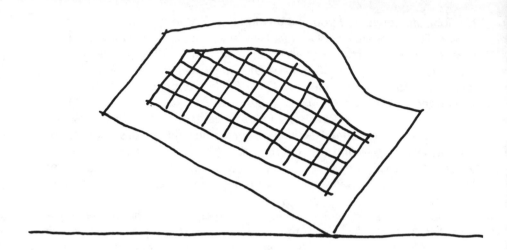

La folie. Jacques Derrida.

242

I came home late from the university one evening. It was dark on the front porch. I was fumbling for my keys when suddenly I felt I wasn't alone. Someone was standing next to me. After a moment I was certain it was an animal: a large one. It hissed or growled in a way that seemed like the beginning of a word or a speech, and then seemed to wait for a reply. I tried frantically to get into the house so I could turn on the light to see what it was. It waited a moment longer, while I dropped my keys on the steps, and then began to stalk away, as if in disgust, at a deliberate pace, with a scraping noise. I finally got inside and turned on the porch light, but the creature had disappeared. We got out flashlights but the thing was gone without a trace. The next day Kathy called me at the office to tell me that the creature had been found about mid-morning by the neighbor's dog, hiding in the bushes by the back fence. The animal control officer identified it. "It was a Bittern, an American Bittern."

"I told the officer on the phone we had a large shorebird in our yard. When she arrived she was carrying several leashes, and asked: 'where's the large shepherd?'"

Works Cited

Abraham, Nicholas (1979) "The Shell and the Kernel." In *Diacritics* 9 (1979).

————, and Maria Torok (1978) *L'Ecorce et le Noyau*. Paris: Flammarion.

Allen, Robert C., Ed. (1987) *Channels of Discourse: Television and Contemporary Criticism*. Chapel Hill: North Carolina.

Altman, Charles F. (1985) "Psychoanalysis and Cinema: The Imaginary Discourse." In Nichols, Ed. *Movies and Methods: Volume II*.

Arieti, Silvano (1976) *Creativity: The Magic Synthesis*. New York: Basic Books.

Armstrong, Nancy, and Leonard Tennenhouse, Eds. (1987) *The Ideology of Conduct: Essays in Literature and the History of Sexuality*. New York: Methuen.

Balmary, Marie (1982) *Psychoanalyzing Psychoanalysis: Freud and the Hidden Fault of the Father*. Trans. Ned Lukacher. Baltimore: Johns Hopkins.

Barthes, Roland (1966) *Critique et vérité*. Paris: Seuil.

———— (1968) "Texte (Théorie du)." In *Encyclopaedie Universalis* XV.

———— (1970) *L'Empire des Signes*. Geneva: Skira.

———— (1970a) "Science versus Literature." In *Introduction to Structuralism*. Ed. Michael Lane. New York: Basic Books.

———— (1970b) *Writing Degree Zero, and Elements of Semiology*. Trans. Annette Lavers and Colin Smith. Boston: Beacon.

———— (1972) "To Write: An Intransitive Verb?" *The Structuralists: From Marx to Lévi-Strauss*. Ed. Richard T. De George and Fernande M. De George. Garden City: Doubleday.

———— (1972a) "Jeunes chercheurs." In *Communications* 19.

———— (1972b) *Mythologies*. New York: Hill and Wang.

———— (1973) *Bernard Réquichot*. Brussels: La Connaissance.

———— (1974) *S/Z: An Essay*. Trans. Richard Miller. New York: Hill and Wang.

———— (1975) *Pleasure of the Text*. Trans. Richard Miller. New York: Hill and Wang.

———— (1975a) "Barthes puissance trois." *La Quinzaine Litteraire*. 205.

———— (1976) *Sade Fourier Loyola*. Trans. Richard Miller. New York: Hill and Wang.

———— (1977) *Image—Music—Text*. Trans. Stephen Heath. New York: Hill and Wang.

———— (1977a) *Roland Barthes*. Trans. Richard Howard. New York: Hill and Wang.

———— (1978) "Arcimboldo." In *Arcimboldo*. Milan: Franco-Maria Ricci.

———— (1978a) *Prétexte: Roland Barthes. Colloque de Cerisy*. Ed. Antoine Compagnon. Paris: Union Générale.

———— (1978b) *A Lover's Discourse: Fragments*. Trans. Richard Howard. New York: Hill and Wang.

_____ (1979) "From Work to Text." In *Textual Strategies: Perspectives in Post-Structuralist Criticism*. Ed. Josué V. Harari. Ithaca: Cornell.

_____ (1980) *La chambre claire: Note sur la photographie*. Paris: Gallimard.

_____ (1981) *Le grain de la voix*. Paris: Seuil.

_____ (1981a) "Theory of the Text." In Robert Young, Ed. *Untying the Text: A Poststructuralist Reader*. Boston: Routledge and Kegan.

_____ (1983) *The Fashion System*. Trans. Matthew Ward and Richard Howard. New York: Hill and Wang.

Baudry, Jean-Louis (1985) "Ideological Effects of the Basic Cinematographic Apparatus." In *Movies and Methods: Volume II*. Ed. Nichols.

Beaujour, Michel (1980) *Miroirs d'encre: rhétorique de l'autoportrait*. Paris: Seuil.

Benjamin, Walter (1969) *Illuminations*. Trans. Harry Zohn. New York: Schocken.

_____ (1977) *The Origin of German Tragic Drama*. Trans. John Osborne. London: New Left Books.

_____ (1983) "N [Theoretics of Knowledge; Theory of Progress]." *The Philosophical Forum* 15.

_____ (1985) "Central Park." *New German Critique* 34.

Berger, John (1972) *Ways of Seeing*. London: British Broadcasting and Penguin.

Biró, Yvette (1982) *Profane Mythology: The Savage Mind of the Cinema*. Trans. Imre Goldstein. Bloomington: Indiana.

Blumberg, Stanley A., and Gwinn Owens (1976) *Energy and Conflict: The Life and Times of Edward Teller*. New York: Putnam.

Bowie, Andrew (1982) "New Histories: Aspects of the Prose of Alexander Kluge." *Journal of European Studies* 12.

Brannigan, Augustine (1981) *The Social Basis of Scientific Discoveries*. Cambridge: Cambridge.

Brent, Sandor B. (1984) *Psychological and Social Structures*. Hillsdale, N.J.: Erlbaum.

Brown, Mark H., and W.R. Felton (1955) *The Frontier Years: L.A. Huffman, Photographer of the Plains*. New York: Bramhall House.

Buchler, Justus (1961) *The Concept of Method*. New York: Columbia.

Buck-Morss, Susan (1981) "Walter Benjamin: Revolutionary Writer (1)." In *New Left Review* No. 125–130.

Burton, Robert (1979) *The Anatomy of Melancholy*. Ed. Joan K. Peters. New York: Ungar.

Cage, John (1966) *Silence*. Cambridge: The M.I.T. Press.

_____ (1974) *M: Writings '67–'72*. Middletown: Wesleyan.

_____ (1981) *For the Birds*. Boston: Boyars.

_____ (1981a) *Empty Words: Writings '73–'78*. Middletown: Wesleyan.

Castoriadis, Cornelius (1987) *The Imaginary Institution of Society*. Trans. Kathleen Blamey. Cambridge: MIT.

Certeau, Michel de (1986) *Heterologies: Discourse on the Other*. Trans. Brian Massumi. Minneapolis: Minnesota.

Cixous, Hélène (1981) "The Laugh of the Medusa." In *New French Feminisms*. Ed. Elaine Marks and Isabelle de Courtivron. New York: Schocken.

Clifton, N. Roy (1983) *The Figure in Film*. Newark: Delaware.

Colie, Rosalie (1967) "Literature and History." In *Relations of Literary Study*. Ed. James Thorpe. New York: Modern Language Association.

Comolli, Jean-Louis (1985) "Machines of the Visible." In *The Cinematic Apparatus*. Ed. Teresa de Lauretis and Stephen Heath. New York: St. Martin's.

Connell, Evan S. (1984) *Son of the Morning Star: Custer and the Little Bighorn*. New York: Harper and Row.

Crombie, David (1986) *The "New" Complete Synthesizer*. New York: Omnibus.

Culler, Jonathan (1982) *On Deconstruction*. Ithaca: Cornell.

Debord, Guy (1970) *Society of the Spectacle*. Detroit: Red and Black.

De Lauretis, Teresa (1984) *Alice Doesn't: Feminism, Semiotics, Cinema*. Bloomington: Indiana.
———— (1987) *Technologies of Gender: Essays on Theory, Film, and Fiction*. Bloomington: Indiana.

Deleuze, Gilles, and Félix Guattari (1983) *On the Line*. Trans. John Johnston. New York: Semiotext(e).
———— (1986) *Kafka: Toward a Minor Literature*. Trans. Dana Polan. Minneapolis: Minnesota.
———— (1986a) *Nomadology: The War Machine*. Trans. Brian Massumi. New York: Semiotext(e).

Deloria, Vine, Jr. (1969) *Custer Died for your Sins: An Indian Manifesto*. London: Macmillan.

Derrida, Jacques (1973) *Speech and Phenomena: And Other Essays on Husserl's Theory of Signs*. Trans. David B. Allison. Evanston: Northwestern.
———— (1976) *Of Grammatology*. Trans. Gayatri Spivak. Baltimore: Johns Hopkins.
———— (1976a) "Entre crochets." *Digraphe*, No. 8.
———— (1977) "Signature Event Context." Trans. Samuel Weber and Jeffrey Mehlman. In *Glyph*, No. 1.
———— (1977a) "Limited Inc, a b c . . ." Trans. Samuel Weber. In *Glyph*, No. 2.
———— (1978) *Edmund Husserl's "Origin of Geometry": An Introduction*. Trans. John P. Leavey, Jr. York Beach, Maine: Nicolas-Hays.
———— (1978a) "Coming into One's Own." Trans. James Hulbert. In *Psychoanalysis and the Question of the Text*. Ed. Geoffrey H. Hartman. Baltimore: Johns Hopkins.
———— (1978b) "The Retrait of Metaphor." *Enclitic* 2:2.
———— (1981) *Positions*. Trans. Alan Bass. Chicago: Chicago.
———— (1982) *L'oreille de l'autre: otobiographies, transferts, traduction*. Ed. Claude Lévesque and Christie V. McDonald. Montreal: VLB.
———— (1984) *Signéponge/Signsponge*. Trans. Richard Rand. New York: Columbia. (Translations slightly modified).
———— (1984a) "Two Words for Joyce." In *Post-Structuralist Joyce: Essays from the French*. Ed. Derek Attridge and Daniel Ferrer. Cambridge: Cambridge.
———— (1984b) "No Apocalypse, Not Now (full speed ahead, seven missles, seven missives)." Trans. Catherine Porter and Philip Lewis. *Diacritics* 14:2.
———— (1986) *Glas*. Trans. John P. Leavey, Jr. Lincoln: Nebraska.
———— (1986a) *Mémoires for Paul de Man*. Trans. Cecile Lindsay, Jonathan Culler, and Eduardo Cadava. New York: Columbia.
———— (1986b) "Fors: The Anglish Words of Nicholas Abraham and Maria Torok." Trans. Barbara Johnson. In Nicholas Abraham and Maria Torok, *The Wolf Man's Magic Word*. Trans. Nicholas Rand. Minneapolis: Minnesota.
———— (1987) *Psyche: Inventions de l'autre*. Paris: Galilee.
———— (1987a) *The Post Card*. Trans. Alan Bass. Chicago: Chicago.
———— (1988) "Like the Sound of the Sea Deep within a Shell: Paul de Man's War." Trans. Peggy Kamuf. *Critical Inquiry* 14.

Donner, Morton, Kenneth E. Eble, and Robert E. Helbling, Eds. (n.d.) *The Intellectual Tradition of the West: Readings in the History of Ideas: Vol. 2.* Glenview, Illinois: Scott, Foresman.

Doyle, Arthur Conan (1950) *The Adventures of Sherlock Holmes.* New York: Heritage.

Dundes, Alan (1987) *Cracking Jokes: Studies of Sick Humor Cycles and Stereotypes.* Berkeley: Ten Speed.

DuPlessis, Rachel Blau (1985) "For the Etruscans." In Elaine Showalter, Ed. *The New Feminist Criticism: Essays on Women, Literature, and Theory.* New York: Pantheon.

Easlea, Brian (1983) *Fathering the Unthinkable: Masculinity, Scientists, and the Nuclear Arms Race.* London: Pluto.

Eco, Umberto (1984) *Semiotics and the Philosophy of Language.* Bloomington: Indiana.
_____ (1986) "Architecture and Memory." *Via* 8.

Eisenstein, Sergei (1957) *"Film Form" and "The Film Sense".* Trans. Jay Leyda. Cleveland: World Publishing.

Feyerabend, Paul (1975) *Against Method.* London: New Left Books.

Fiedler, Leslie (1971) "Montana; or the End of Jean-Jacques Rousseau." In *The Collected Essays of Leslie Fiedler,* Vol. 1. New York: Stein and Day.

Foster, Hal. Ed. (1983) *The Anti-Aesthetic: Essays on Postmodern Culture.* Post Townsend: Bay Press.

Foucault, Michel (1970) *The Order of Things: An Archeaology of the Human Sciences.* New York: Vintage/Random House.
_____ (1980) *Power/Knowledge: Selected Interviews & Other Writings, 1972–1977.* Trans. Colin Gordon, Leo Marshall, John Mepham, and Kate Soper. New York: Pantheon.
_____ (1984) "The Subject of Power." In Wallis, Ed. *Art After Modernism.*
_____ (1988) *Technologies of the Self.* Ed. Luther H. Martin, Huck Gutman, and Patrick H. Hutton. Amherst: Massachusetts.

Freud, Sigmund (1961) *Beyond the Pleasure Principle.* Trans. James Strachey. New York: Norton.
_____ (1963) *A General Introduction to Psychoanalysis.* Trans. Joan Riviere. New York: Simon and Schuster.
_____ (1963a) *Jokes and their Relation to the Unconscious.* Trans. James Strachey. New York: Norton.

Gass, William H. (1982) "Monumentality/Mentality." *Oppositions* 25.

Gilbert, G. Nigel, and Michael Mulkay (1984) *Opening Pandora's Box: A Sociological Analysis of Scientists' Discourse.* Cambridge: Cambridge.

Gilbert, Neal W. (1960) *Renaissance Concepts of Method.* New York: Columbia.

Ginzburg, Carlo (1982) *The Cheese and the Worms: The Cosmos of a Sixteenth-Century Miller.* Trans. John and Anne Tedeschi. New York: Penguin.
_____ (1983) "Morelli, Freud, and Sherlock Holmes: Clues and Scientific Method." In Umberto Eco and Thomas A. Sebeok, Eds. *The Sign of Three.* Bloomington: Indiana.

Goody, Jack (1977) *The Domestication of the Savage Mind.* New York: Cambridge.

Graham, W.A. Ed. (1986) *The Custer Myth: A Source Book of Custeriana.* Lincoln: Nebraska.

Grava, Arnolds (1969) *A Structural Inquiry into the Symbolic Representation of Ideas.* The Hague: Mouton.

Gray, Spalding (1985) *Swimming to Cambodia.* New York: Theatre Communications.

Group *Mu,* Eds. (1978) Collages. Paris: Union Générale.

Gruber, Howard E. (1978) "Darwin's 'Tree of Nature' and other Images of Wide Scope." In *On Aesthetics in Science*. Ed. Judith Wechsler. Cambridge: MIT.

Haas, Gerhard (1969) *Essay*. Stuttgart: Metzlersche.

Havelock, Eric A. (1967) *Preface to Plato*. New York: Grosset and Dunlap.

Heidegger, Martin (1971) *On the Way to Language*. Trans. Peter Hertz. New York: Harper and Row.

——— (1975) *Poetry, Language, Thought*. Trans. Albert Hofstader. New York: Harper and Row.

——— (1977) *The Question Concerning Technology*. Trans. William Lovitt. New York: Harper and Row.

Highwater, Jamake (1981) *The Primal Mind: Vision and Reality in Indian America*. New York: New American Library.

Hirsch, E.D., Jr. (1987) *Cultural Literacy: What Every American Needs to Know*. Boston: Houghton Mifflin.

Holdheim, W. Wolfgang (1984) *The Hermeneutic Mode: Essays on Time in Literature and Literary Theory*. Ithaca: Cornell.

Holland, Dorothy, and Naomi Quinn, Eds. (1987) *Cultural Models in Language and Thought*. Cambridge: Cambridge.

Holton, Gerald (1973) *Thematic Origins of Scientific Thought*. Cambridge: Harvard.

Hubner, Kurt (1983) *Critique of Scientific Reason*. Trans. Paul R. Dixon, Jr., and Hollis M. Dixon. Chicago: Chicago.

Illich, Ivan, and Barry Sanders (1988) *The Alphabetization of the Popular Mind*. San Francisco: North Point.

James, Henry (1964) *The Ambassadors*. Ed. S.P. Rosenbaum. New York: Norton.

Jameson, Fredric (1977) "Imaginary and Symbolic in Lacan: Marxism, Psychoanalytic Criticism, and the Problem of the Subject." *Yale French Studies* 55/56.

——— (1984) "Postmodernism, or the Cultural Logic of Late Captialism." *New Left Review* 146.

——— (1987) "Reading Without Interpretation: Postmodernism and the Video-Text." In Nigel Fabb, et. al., Eds. *The Linguistics of Writing: Arguments Between Language and Literature*. New York: Methuen.

Jennings, Michael W. (1987) *Dialectical Images: Walter Benjamin's Theory of Literary Criticism*. Ithaca: Cornell.

Jolles, Andre (1972) *Formes Simples*. Paris: Seuil.

Keller, Evelyn Fox (1985) *Reflections on Gender and Science*. New Haven: Yale.

Kelly, Mary (1985) *Post-Partum Document*. London: Routledge and Kegan Paul.

Kluge, Alexander (1977) "Der Luftangriff auf Halberstadt am 8 April 1945," *Neue Geschichten*. Frankfort: Suhrkamp.

——— (1984) "On Film and the Public Sphere." *New German Critique* 31.

Knabb, Ken, Ed. (1981) *Situationist International Anthology*. Berkeley: Bureau of Public Secrets.

Kristeva, Julia (1974) *La Révolution du language poétique*. Paris: Seuil.

Labov, William and David Fanshel (1977) *Therapeutic Discourse: Psychotherapy as Conversation*. New York: Academic Press.

Lacan, Jacques (1972) "Seminar on 'The Purloined Letter.'" *Yale French Studies*, 48.

——— (1975) *Le Séminaire, Livre I*. Paris: Seuil.

_____ (1977) *Ecrits: A Selection.* Trans. Alan Sheridan. New York: Norton.

_____ (1978) *The Four Fundamental Concepts of Psycho-Analysis.* Trans. Alan Sheridan. New York: Norton.

_____ (1981) *Speech and Language in Psychoanalysis.* Trans. Anthony Wilden. Baltimore: Johns Hopkins.

_____ (1981a) *Le Séminaire, Livre III: Les Psychoses, 1955–1956.* Paris: Seuil.

Lakoff, George (1987) *Women, Fire, and Dangerous Things: What Categories Reveal about the Mind.* Chicago: Chicago.

Lanzmann, Claude (1985) *Shoah: An Oral History of the Holocaust.* New York: Pantheon.

Laplanche, J., and J.B. Pontalis (1973) *The Language of Psychoanalysis.* New York: Norton.

Leed, Eric (1980) "'Voice' and 'Print': Master Symbols in the History of Communication." In *The Myths of Information: Technology and Postindustrial Culture.* Ed. Kathleen Woodward. Madison: Coda Press.

LeFevre, Karen Burke (1987) *Invention as a Social Act.* Carbondale: Southern Illinois.

Lemaire, Anika (1977) *Jacques Lacan.* Trans. David Macey. London: Routledge.

Lesage, Julia (1985) "*S/Z* and *The Rules of the Game.*" In Nichols, Ed. *Movies and Methods: Volume II.*

Lesy, Michael (1980) *Time Frames: The Meaning of Family Pictures.* New York: Pantheon.

Leyda, Jay (1964) *Films Beget Films.* New York: Hill and Wang.

Lifton, Robert Jay (1987) "The Image of 'The End of the World': A Psychohistorical View." In Valerie Andrews, Robert Bosnak, and Karen Walter Goodwin, Eds. *Facing Apocalypse.* Dallas: Spring.

Linde, Charlotte (1987) "Explanatory systems in oral life stories." In Holland and Quinn, Eds. *Cultural Models in Language and Thought.*

Luria, A.R. (1968) *The Mind of a Mnemonist.* Trans. Lynn Solotaroff. Chicago: Henry Regnery.

Lyotard, Jean-François (1984) *The Postmodern Condition: A Report on Knowledge.* Trans. Geoff Bennington and Brian Massumi. Minneapolis: Minnesota.

_____ and Jean-Loup Thébaud (1985) *Just Gaming.* Trans. Wlad Godzich. Minneapolis: Minnesota.

MacCannell, Dean (1976) *The Tourist: A New Theory of the Leisure Class.* New York: Schocken.

Malcolm, Norman (1958) *Ludwig Wittgenstein: A Memoir.* London: Oxford.

Mander, Jerry (1978) *Four Arguments for the Elimination of Television.* New York: Morrow.

Metz, Christian (1982) *The Imaginary Signifier: Psychoanalysis and the Cinema.* Trans. Celia Britton, et. al. Bloomington: Indiana.

Miller, J. Hillis (1977) "The Critic as Host." *Critical Inquiry* 3.

Momaday, N. Scott (1969) *The Way to Rainy Mountain.* Albuquerque: New Mexico.

Mulvey, Laura (1977) "Visual Pleasure and Narrative Cinema." In *Women and the Cinema: A Critical Anthology.* Ed. Karyn Kay and Gerald Peary. New York: Dutton.

Neihardt, John G. (1972) *Black Elk Speaks: Being the Life Story of a Holy Man of the Oglala Sioux.* New York: Pocket Books/Simon & Schuster.

Nichols, Bill (1981) *Ideology and the Image: Social Representation in the Cinema and Other Media.* Bloomington: Indiana.

_____, Ed. (1985) *Movies and Methods: Volume II.* Berkeley: California.

Nicolson, Iain (1982) *Sputnik to Space Shuttle.* New York: Dodd, Mead.

Nietzsche, Friedrich (1974) *The Gay Science.* Trans. Walter Kaufmann. New York: Vintage/ Random House.

O'Connell, Charles, Ed. (1936) *The Victor Book of the Opera.* Camden: RCA Manufacturing Co., Inc.

Olbrechts-Tyteca, Lucie (1974) *Le Comique du Discours.* Brussels: University de Bruxelles.

Ong, Walter J. (1982) *Orality and Literacy: The Technologizing of the Word.* New York: Methuen.

Owens, Craig (1984) "The Allegorical Impulse: Toward a Theory of Postmodernism." In Wallis, ed. *Art After Modernism.*

Paulos, John Allen (1980) *Mathematics and Humor.* Chicago: Chicago.

Pellowski, Anne (1984) *The Story Vine.* New York: Macmillan.

Perloff, Marjorie (1987) *The Futurist Moment.* Chicago: Chicago.

Peters, F.E. (1967) *Greek Philosophical Terms.* New York: New York University.

Plato (1961) *The Collected Dialogues.* Ed. Edith Hamilton and Huntington Cairns. Princeton: Princeton.

Ponge, Francis (1979) *The Making of the Pré.* Trans. Lee Fahnestock. Columbia: Missouri.

Popular Memory Group (1982) "Popular Memory: Theory, Politics, Method." In *Making Histories: Studies in History-Writing and Politics.* London: Hutchinson.

Pratt, Mary Louise (1977) *Toward a Speech Act Theory of Literary Discourse.* Bloomington: Indiana.

Reiss, Timothy J. (1982) *The Discourse of Modernism.* Ithaca: Cornell.

Reston, James, Jr. (1984) *Sherman's March and Vietnam.* New York: MacMillan.

Rosen, Philip (1986) *Narrative, Apparatus, Ideology: A Film Theory Reader.* New York: Columbia.

Rosenberg, Bruce A. (1974) *Custer and the Epic of Defeat.* University Park: Pennsylvania State.

Roukes, Nicholas (1984) *Art Synectics.* Worcester: Davis Publications.

Santillana, Giorgio de, and Hertha von Dechend (1977) *Hamlet's Mill: An Essay on Myth and the Frame of Time.* Boston: Godine.

Saunders, P.T. (1980) *An Introduction to Catastrophe Theory.* Cambridge: Cambridge.

Schafer, Walter Ernst (1977) *Anekdote—Antianokdote: Zum Wandel einer literarischen Form in der Gegenwart.* Stuttgart: Klett-Cotta.

Scholes, Robert, and Robert Kellogg (1966) *The Nature of Narrative.* New York: Oxford.

Scott, Douglas D., and Richard A. Fox, Jr. (1987) *Archaeological Insights into the Custer Battle.* Norman: Oklahoma.

Sekula, Allan (1987) "Reading an Archive." In Wallis, Ed. *Blasted Allegories.*

Serres, Michel (1974) *Hermes III: La Traduction.* Paris: Minuit.
———— (1982) *The Parasite.* Trans. Lawrence R. Schehr. Baltimore: Johns Hopkins.

Skura, Meredith (1980) "Creativity: Transgressing the Limits of Consciousness." *Daedalus* 109.

Slotkin, Richard (1985) *The Fatal Environment: The Myth of the Frontier in the Age of Industrialization, 1800–1890.* Middletown: Wesleyan.

Smithson, Robert (1979) *The Writings of Robert Smithson.* Ed. Nancy Holt. New York: New York University.

Sontag, Susan (1980) *Under the Sign of Saturn.* New York: Farrar, Straus, Giroux.

Spence, Jonathan D. (1984) *The Memory Palace of Matteo Ricci*. New York: Penguin.

Sperber, Dan (1984) "Anthropology and Psychology: Towards an Epidemiology of Representations." In *Man 20*.

Spiegelman, Art (1986) *Maus: A Survivor's Tale*. New York: Pantheon.

Stewart, Susan (1978) *Nonsense: Aspects of Intertextuality in Folklore and Literature*. Baltimore: Johns Hopkins.

Street, Brian V. (1984) *Literacy in Theory and Practice*. Cambridge: Cambridge.

Timpanaro, Sebastiano (1976) *The Freudian Slip: Psychoanalysis and Textual Criticism*. Trans. Kate Soper. London: NLB.

Tolson, Andrew (1985) "Anecdotal Television." *Screen 26*.

Turkle, Sherry (1978) *Psychoanalytic Politics: Freud's French Revolution*. New York: Basic Books.

Ulmer, Gregory L. (1986) "Sounding the Unconscious." In John P. Leavey, Jr., Ed. *Glassary*. Lincoln: Nebraska.

Vygotsky, L.S. (1978) *Mind in Society: The Development of Higher Psychological Processes*. Ed. M. Cole, V. John-Steiner, S. Scribner, and E. Souberman. Cambridge: Harvard.

Wallis, Brian, Ed. (1984) *Art After Modernism: Rethinking Representation*. New York: New Museum.

_____ Ed. (1987) *Blasted Allegories: An Anthology of Writings by Contemporary Artists*. Cambridge: MIT Press.

Weber, Samuel (1982) *The Legend of Freud*. Minneapolis: Minnesota.

White, Eric Charles (1987) *Kaironomia: On the Will-to-Invent*. Ithaca: Cornell.

White, Hayden (1973) *Metahistory: The Historical Imagination of Nineteenth-Century Europe*. Baltimore: Johns Hopkins.

_____ (1978) *Tropics of Discourse: Essays in Cultural Criticism*. Baltimore: Johns Hopkins.

_____ (1980) "The Value of Narrativity in the Representation of Reality." In *On Narrative*. Ed. W.J.T. Mitchell. Chicago: Chicago.

Winston, Brian (1986) *Misunderstanding Media*. Cambridge: Harvard.

Wittgenstein, Ludwig (1965) *The Blue and Brown Books*. New York: Harper.

_____ (1968) *Philosophical Investigations*. Trans. G.E.M. Anscombe. Oxford: Oxford.

Wollen, Peter (1982) *Readings and Writings: Semiotic Counter-Strategies*. London: Verso.

Yates, Frances A. (1966) *The Art of Memory*. Chicago: Chicago.

Index

abduction, 115
Abraham, Nicolas, 181, 220
Adorno, Theodor, 148
alchemy, 158, 233
aleatory, 162–63
allegoresis, 20
allegory, 14–15, 51, 78, 93, 94–101, 198; and Roland Barthes, 80, 123; and John Cage, 149– 52; and decay, 180; and film, 96; ghost effect, 203; and Francis Ponge, 158; and pun, 75
Altman, Charles, 56
American Bittern, 243
amphibologies, 75–76
analogy, 19, 23, 40, 41, 56–57, 125, 197; and Sigmund Freud, 59
anasemia, 182–83
anecdote, 46, 48, 72, 109, 186, 191, 197; and anti-anecdote, 186; and John Cage, 150, 152–53; and concepts, 103; and family, 74; and theory, 92
Anti-Aesthetic, The, 20
antonomasia, 161
apostrophe, 92
apparatus, 4, 9–17, 68–69, 139, 160; of electronics, 44, 51, 94; of literacy, 1–8, 48, 211; and memory, 133
archive, 14, 204
Arcimboldo, 95
Arieti, Silvano, 41, 55
artificial intelligence, 66, 72, 211
Auerbach, Eric, 26
autobiography, 111; and autoportrait, 136–37; and herstory, 86; and orality 33, 85; and otobiography, 159; and psychoanalysis, 90–91, 121

Bachelard, Gaston, 22
Bacon, Francis, 23
Ballard, J. G., 197
Balmary, Marie, 155
Barnes, Julian, 138
Barthes, Roland, 5, 11, 46; and allegory, 94–101; and codes, 45, 49; intellectual objects, 100; and Marx Brothers, 73–81; and middle voice, 87; and novelesque, 89, 100, 206; and obtuse, 97; and projection, 122; and *punctum*, 11, 73, 96, 110; and third meanings, 24, 95; and writerly, 47–49, 109; *Camera Lucida*, 73; *The Fashion System*, 95; *A Lover's Discourse*, 110, 115–28; *Mythologies*, 101, 142; *The Pleasure of the Text*, 97; *Roland Barthes*, 123; *S/Z*, 45, 79, 116, 150
Baudrillard, Jean, 206
Baudry, Jean-Louis, 50, 108
Beaujour, Michel, 131
Benjamin, Walter, 11, 19, 94, 211, 231; and allegory, 151; and collage, 146; and constellation, 112; and dialectical images, 24; and film, 59; and souvenir, 198; *Theses on the Philosophy of History*, 111
Bennett, James Gordon, 222
Bentham, Jeremy, 88
Berger, John, 11
Biro, Yvette, 60
Black Elk Speaks, 218
Blasted Allegories, 154
bliss-sense, 57, 76, 96, 98, 166, 193, 211
bomb (A and H), 19, 70, 152, 183, 189, 231–232; and *punctum*, 198

Booth, Wayne, 11, 144
Bowie, Andrew, 187
Brannigan, Augustine, 33, 56
Brecht, Bertolt, 186, 210
bricolage, 137, 197
Brown, Norman O., 148
Burton, Robert, 11

Cage, John, 20, 143–51, 190; "Mushroom Book," 149, 152
Carroll, Lewis, 24
Castoriadis, Cornelius, 112, 205
catachresis, 65
catastrophe, 158, and Walter Benjamin, 111; and geology, 180; and mathematics, 53, 222; nuclear, 19, 70; and Pandora, 186; and place, 181; and temporality, 112
catastropics, 184–94
Chapman, Mark, 122
choler, 233
cinema, 26, 47
Cixous, Helene, 76
Clifton, N. Roy, 60
code, 45, 103; cultural, 150; of enigma, 104; hermeneutic, 48, 79, 131; semic, 109; symbolic, 47, 52, 80, 87; syntagmatic and paradigmatic, 48–50
cogito, 4, 21
cognitive psychology, 193
cognitive style, 26, 41–42, 66
Colie, Rosalie, 83
collage, 144, 146, 187; and pun, 172
common sense, 34, 116, 118
Comolli, Jean-Louis, 8
computer, 72, 171
concept, 41, 101, 108; and cryptonym, 182; formation of, 55, 58, 60, 231; and myth, 82
conduction, 44, 62–73, 82, 89, 108, 125, 127, 138, 151, 160, 173
conjecture, 104
Connell, Evan, 214, 217, 221, 223, 239
conversation, 92–93
correspondence, 64
coverage, 13, 182
creativity, 55, 67
crypt, 23, 181; and monument, 182, 198
Culler, Jonathan, 2
Custer, George Armstrong, 213, 215, 221, 228; and Last Stand, 34; and letter, 221

de Antonio, Emile, 57
de Certeau, Michel, 72
deconstruction, 20, 77, 119, 144, 171, 202; and allegory 145; and decomposition, 151
de Lauretis, Teresa, 84, 138
Deleuze, Gilles, 70, 140, 172; and minor literature, 139; and minor science, 169; and nomadology, 168
de Man, Paul, 202–03
Derrida, Jacques, 5, 15, 19, 61, 136, 144, 202; and collage, 147; difference, 24, 63; and envois, 89–94; and Geschlecht, 227; and James Joyce, 170; and middle voice, 86; and otobiography, 159; and pharmakon, 150; and symbolic, 201; and Timaeus, 240–41; "Feu la cendre", 241; Glas, 162; Memoires, 202–05; Signsponge, 160, 205
detournement, 131, 183, 199; and collage, 200
diegesis, 84, 152; in theory, 101–12, 122
discourse, 5, 24, 167, 179, 181; academic, 1–8, 34, 39, 44, 47, 82, 121, 154, 160, 203; analytico-referential, 21, 35, 58, 59; disappearance of, 27; electronic, 44, 46; expert, 34, 128; hybrid, 58; image of, 179; and patterning, 22, 25, 60, 69
discovery, 29–30, 141, 156, 172
dissemination, 29, 54
doxa, 98, 116, 127
Dundes, Alan, 193
DuPlessis, Rachel, 85–86

Eco, Umberto, 54
eidos, 83
Einstein, Albert, 37, 38, 41
Eisenman, Peter, 236
Eisenstein, Sergei, 58–9, 96; and conduct, 65
electronic cognition, 44, 66, 140, 156, 166, 184, 192, 194
empiricism, 35
entropy, 179, 191
enunciation, 31, 51
essay, 4, 5, 45, 103, 148, 167
etymology, 145, 157
euretics, 15–6, 20, 27–8, 35, 71, 139, 183–84; as code, 48; as critique, 192
example, 104
experimentation, 140

explanation, 6, 31
explanatory system, 34, 54, 189
exposition, 102

family, 64, 94; and crypt, 182; and
    photoalbum, 73, 107, 177, 184–88; and
    Wittgenstein, 109–10, 167
Fanshel, David, (see Labov)
feminism, 76, 83, 85
fetishism, 125
Feyerabend, Paul, 26, 28, 31, 47; Against
    Method, 26
ficelle, 213
Fiedler, Leslie, 217
film, compilation, 209
Finnegans Wake, 144, 170
Foucault, Michel, 25, 27, 133; and
    conduct, 65; and Unconscious, 66
Freud, Sigmund, 9, 21–5, 34, 43, 52, 58,
    130; and book, 125; and dream work,
    35; invention, 60; and jokes, 153; and
    mushrooms, 155; and Schreber Case, 68;
    and self-analysis, 86; Beyond the
    Pleasure Principle, 90, 109, 179; The
    Interpretation of Dreams, 43;
    The Psychopathology of Everyday Life,
    30, 35
Frye, Northrop, 19

Gainesville Sun, The, 15
Galileo, 29
Gall (Chief), 233, 239
Gass, William, 198, 201
gender, 84, 138, 196, 226
Genet, Jean, 163
genre, 44, 82; as hybrid, 45, 94, 100, 187;
    and fragment, 116, 128
Gide, Andre, 123
Gilbert, G. Nigel, 31
Ginzburg, Carlo, 39, 87–88
Godard, Jean-Luc, 11, 218, 237
Goethe, Johann Wolfgang von, 121
Goody, Jack, 2, 4, 5, 18, 36, 57, 105;
    Domestication of the Savage Mind, 2
grammatology, 63, 144, 146
Gray, Spalding, 191–92
Griffith, D. W., 46, 200
Group Mu, 146
Gruber, Howard, 37, 39
Guattari, Felix, (see Deleuze)

Hamlet, 235
Hamlet's Mill, 235
Havelock, Eric, 63
Hegel, Georg Wilhelm Friedrich, 162
Heidegger, Martin, 6–7, 18, 19, 106, 167;
    "The Age of the World Picture," 6
heraldry, 161
hermeneutics, 15, 140
herstory, 83–84
Hesiod, 64
Hirsch, E. D., 34
historiography, 6, 18–21, 86, 110, 186; as
    quotation, 211
history, 72, 83, 87, 111, 174, 196; and
    deconstruction, 202; and myth, 210; and
    reading, 142
Holdheim, W. Wolfgang, 106
Holmes, Sherlock, 88, 105
Holton, Gerald, 37, 42
Hopi (Indians), 70
Huffman, L. A., 216
humanism, ii, 4, 10, 40, 137
Husserl, Edmund, 90

ideology, 7, 47, 26, 29, 76, 83, 106–108,
    138; and connotation, 101; and critique,
    85; and emotion, 109–111, 117; of
    individual, 10; of learning, 61; of
    science; of visible, 8
image, 110, 172; active, 134; and
    metaphor, 39; repertoire, 123–24, 126;
    of wide scope, 38, 39, 140; and world
    picture, 130
imaginary, 121–28, 131
inner speech, 135
instauration (new), 21, 23, 27, 44, 66,
    141
interpretant, 41
interview, 93–94; and psychoanalysis, 120,
    161, 186
inventio, 14, 137, 165, 177; and joke,
    193
invention, 6, 22, 31, 42, 70, 116, 119,
    167, 184, 211; and contingency, 37;
    cycle of, 115, 174, 195; and final
    solution, 193; and language, 58; and
    learning, 33; of man, 27; and memory,
    156; and monuments, 199; rhetorical,
    16; and signature, 156; theoretical, 52,
    90

Jakobson, Roman, 79–89, 101
James, Henry, 213
Jameson, Fredric, 5, 6, 10, 11, 12, 119
joke, 50–61, 73; and catastrophe, 54; and
    Custer, 222; and dream work, 53; and
    gag, 74; and holocaust, 193; and
    information theory, 192; and learning,
    56; and speed, 171; and symbolic code,
    46; and theory, 62
joker, 192
Jolles, Andre, 20, 50–51, 53
justification, 30, 55

kaironomia, 112
Kekule, August, 42
Keller, Evelyn Fox, 84
Kellogg, Robert, 45
Kelly, Mary, 20, 128–32, 179, 187; Post-
    Partum Document, 129–30
Kepler, Johann, 22, 23
Kiowas, 174
kitsch, 127
Kluge, Alexander, 186–88, 198, 237
knowledge; conjectural, 87, 104; cycle of,
    54, 57; growth of, 2, 171
Koestler, Arthur, 55
Kristeva, Julia, 120
Kuntzel, Thierry, 93

Labov, William, 48, 92, 120
Lacan, Jacques, 27, 46, 59, 168; and
    double inscription, 121; and entry into
    language, 79; and Hamlet, 232; and
    ignorance, 124; and the imaginary, 107;
    and mirror stage, 124; and pedagogy, 98;
    and Edgar Allan Poe, 80, 88; and subject
    of knowledge, 57, 121; and the
    symbolic, 47, 74, 119
Lanzmann, Claude, 192
laughter, 191
Leed, Eric, 9–10, 13
LeFevre, Karen, 16
Leiris, Michel, 137
Lesage, Julia, 46, 50
Lesy, Michael, 184–88
Levi, Primo, 138
Levi-Strauss, Claude, 22, 197
Leyda, Jay, 210
life story, 34, 43, 76
Lifton, Robert Jay, 70
Linde, Charlotte, 33–34, 54

literacy, 1–8, 34, 44, 45, 57
logic, 23, 63; and the absurd, 146; and
    dream work, 60; and film, 58
logocentrism, 6, 33, 205
Lyotard, Jean-Francois, 88, 189; and middle
    voice, 89

MacCannell, Dean, 198
McElwee, Ross, 194–201; and Roland
    Barthes, 195; and family album, 195; and
    invention, 194; and middle voice, 194;
    Sherman's March, 194–200
McLuhan, Marshall, 4, 148
Mander, Jerry, 9; and analogy, 68
manifesto, 90
Mannheim, Karl, 19
Marx Brothers, 54, 73–81; A Night at the
    Opera, 74–80
Marx, Karl, 54
Meaning of Meaning, The, 78
media, 9–10
melancholy, 12, 129; as humor, 233
memory, 3, 25, 69, 105; artificial, 86, 133,
    134, 180; and place, 152, 170; and
    signature, 165; and tour, 166–69, 175–
    77, 198–99
Menocchio, 40
metacommunication, 54
metanarratives, 86, 119, 189
metaphor, 54, 64, 78–79, 99, 162; and the
    Name-of-the-Father, 180
method, 21, 25; history of, 58; as journey,
    167–68; and nomadology, 170; and
    rhetoric, 84; and science, 26–33; and
    Ludwig Wittgenstein, 105
Metz, Christian, 56, 60
middle voice, 86–87, 89, 180; as pagan,
    88
Miles, Nelson (General), 216
Miles City, 215–16
Miller, J. Hillis, 144, 164
Miranda, Carmen, 62
mnemonics, 3, 133, 137; and landscape,
    177
models, 104, 119, 141; cognitive, 24;
    disciplinary, 39; explanatory, 33, 39;
    folk, 39; and places, 157; and relay, 170;
    and signature, 165
Momaday, N. Scott, 168, 172–74, 184;
    The Way to Rainy Mountain, 172–73;
    and mourning, 174

Monty Python, 72
monumental, 12, 34, 89, 161, 170, 175, 179–80, 192, 198, 200–01
mood, 20, 51, 184
mourning, 1, 28, 74, 126, 128, 129, 171, 174; and death of the author, 127, 204; and psychoanalysis, 180–82
Mulkay, Michael, 31
Mulvey, Laura, 84
mycology, 150, 152
mystoriography, 44, 82, 115, 158, 201
mystory, 2, 20, 33, 43, 45, 82–112, 118, 166, 177, 184; as assignment, 209; and autoportrait, 137; and diegesis, 103; and relay, 170
myth, 9, 82, 197, 210

narrative, 84, 105; and anecdote, 186; and autoportrait, 137; and envois, 89; and mystery, 86; refunctioned, 116
newreels, 210
Nichols, Bill, 56–57, 102–03, 106–07, 109
Nietzsche, Friedrich, 19, 92, 125, 204; and gay science, 62; and otobiography, 154–60, 163–64
nonsense, 54, 57, 124; and invention, 64
nostalgia, 11, 110–11, 152, 185
novel, 45
nuclear criticism, 188–90, 196–97, 201, 228–31

Olbrechts-Tyteca, Lucie, 53, 62
Ong, Walter, 4
oral culture, 26, 33, 72, 134, 137, 142; and Menocchio, 40; and voice, 46
orality, 9; secondary, 9, 41
oralysis, 44, 62, 72, 87, 117, 118; and film, 93
Orwell, George, 54
otobiography, 159–65
Owens, Craig, 96, 154

paleologic, 41, 44, 193
Paracelsus, 21, 22
parasite, 144
Paulos, John Allen, 53
pedagogy, 1, 13, 14, 28–29, 32, 43, 87, 206; and allegory, 96; and amateur, 189; and dissemination, 36; and joke, 54
Pepper, Stephen, 19
periodic table, 19

Perloff, Marjorie, 176
Plato, 7; Phaedrus, 21
politics, 120
Ponge, Francis, 156, 178; The Making of the "Pre", 156–59
popularization, 1
Postman, Neil, 9
postmodernism, 10, 13, 14, 19, 44, 148; and cross-over, 189
poststructuralism, 4, 119
primal thinking, 58, 66
print, 9
program, 65, 71
propaganda, 30, 193, 197
prototype theory, iii
proverb, 46
psychoanalysis, 4, 25, 44, 92; and Barthes, 111; as explanatory system, 34; and film, 57–59
public sphere, 118, 188
pun, 19, 54, 75; and Barthes, 97; conduction, 63, 172; gestural, 227; and gram, 171; and isotopes, 229
puncept, 83, 147, 156, 209

Quintillian, 53

Rabelais, 21
Rainer, Yvonne, 76
Ramus, Peter, 3, 136
Reagan, Ronald, 216
realism, 50
rebus, 35
reconstruction, 201
Reik, Theodor, 121
Reiss, Timothy, 21–23, 27, 59
relay, 166–75
Requichot, Bernard, 76; and collage, 95
Reynolds, Burt, 196
rhetoric, 49, 134; and argument, 49; as choreography, 117; and dispositio, 137; of science, 84; Rhetorica ad herennium, 134, 181
rhizome, 139–42, 144, 172; and mushrooms, 151; and war machine, 169
riddle, 51
right brain, 65–67, 69
Roeg, Nicolas, 191
Rosetta Stone, 137, 139, 201
Rousseau, Jean-Jacques, 217, 219

Safire, William, 15
sampling, 9, 13
schizophrenia, 68
Scholes, Robert, 45
Sekula, Alan, 14
semiotics, 14, 88, 101
Serres, Michel, 61, 145–46, 183
Shoah, 192–93; as tour, 192
signature, 160–61, 178, 206; and
    conduction, 164; and Hegel, 163; and
    history, 164; and Nietzsche, 163–64; and
    relay, 173, 184
silence, 19–20; and modality, 51; and
    mushroom cloud, 202
simple forms, 20, 45, 51, 122, 154, 191
simulacrum, 11
Sitting Bull, 214, 222
situationism, 7, 199–200
Skura, Meredith, 42
Slotkin, Richard, 221, 229
Smithson, Robert, 175–84; and allegory,
    176; and Barthes, 175; and Joyce, 177;
    and relay, 177
Socrates, 70, 142
Sontag, Susan, 11
speech acts, 61
Spence, Jonathan, 138
Sperber, Dan, 36–37
Sputnik, 223
stereotypes, 76, 118, 137, 143; and jokes,
    194
Stewart, Susan, 54, 57
Street, Brian, 5, 36–37
structuralism, 51
subject; fading of, 74; of feminism, 138
surrealism, 58
synectics, 41
Swimming to Cambodia, 191

Tao Te Ching, 125
Tarkovsky, Andrei, 11
Tausk, Victor, 68
technology, 4, 13; and memory, 135–36;
    as prothesis, 71
teletheory, 1–2, 10, 23, 39, 57, 60, 71, 83,
    90, 139, 166, 167
television, 68, 72; effects, 4

Teller, Edward, 231
text, 73–81, 116, 127, 138, 163
theory, 139; and film, 7, 102; as genre, 2,
    90; and Joke, 73
Thom, Rene, 53
Thoreau, Henry David, 148–49
Timpanaro, Sebastiano, 30
Tolson, Andrew, 72
tomb, 23
Torok, Maria, (see Nicolas Abraham)
tourism, 198
transduction, 64, 158, 178
transference, 128, 139; and mourning, 181,
    203
Il Trovatore, 75, 77

Ulmer, Walter, 235
Unconscious, 34; and endocept, 41; logic
    of, 25, 46, 57, 133
utopianism, 40

VanDerBeek, Stan, 190
video, 44, 133, 190–91, 194; and
    deconstruction, 202; and invention, 42,
    56; and logic, 70; and pedagogy, 94; and
    psychoanalysis, 56
videocy, 16
vita, 65, 71
Vobejda, Barbara, 16

Weber, Samuel, 155
White, Eric, 112
White, Hayden, 18–21, 24, 28, 44; and
    narrative, 106; *Metahistory*, 19
Williams, William Carlos, 175
Winston, Brian, 6
Wittgenstein, Ludwig, 102–10; and wit, 62;
    The Brown Book, 103–05; *Philosophical
    Investigations*, 166
Wollen, Peter, 131
Wormwood, Hank, 238
writing, 2–3, 5, 71, 74; as braid, 123; as
    journey, 166; as machine, 165; with
    paradigm, 118–19; and Plato, 204; and
    psychoanalysis, 126; and sponge, 162

Yates, Frances, 134